D0187695

BUD, SWEAT,

SIMON & SCHUSTER
NEW YORK LONDON TORONTO SYDNEY SINGAPORE

AND TEES

Rich Beem's Walk on the Wild Side of the PGA Tour

• ALAN SHIPNUCK •

SIMON & SCHUSTER
Rockefeller Center
1230 Avenue of the Americas
New York, NY 10020

First Simon & Schuster trade paperback edition 2003
SIMON & SCHUSTER and colophon are
registered trademarks of Simon & Schuster, Inc.
For information regarding special discounts for bulk purchases
please contact Simon & Schuster Special Sales:
1-800-456-6798 or business@simonandschuster.com
Designed by Edith Fowler
Manufactured in the United States of America

10 9 8 7 6 5 4 3 2 1

The Library of Congress has cataloged the Simon & Schuster hardcover edition as follows:

Shipnuck, Alan, 1973–
Bud, sweat, and tees : a walk on the wild side of the PGA Tour / Alan Shipnuck.
p. cm.
1. PGA Tour (Association) 2. Golf—Tournaments—United States. 3. Beem, Rich. 4. Duplantis, Steve. I. Title: Walk on the wild side of the PGA Tour. II. Title.

GV969.P75 S55 2001
769.352'092—dc21 *00-047036*
ISBN 0-7432-0070-5
ISBN 0-7432-4900-3 (Pbk)

Praise for *Bud, Sweat, & Tees*

"Alan Shipnuck is fearless—fearless enough to pick out a total unknown on the golf tour to write a book about, then to write a fascinating book about him."

—Dan Jenkins

"This saucy, entertaining tale . . . takes us backstage at golf's rock concert—the PGA Tour—[with] . . . up-and-coming golfer Rich Beem and his out of control caddie, Steve Duplantis."

—*Los Angeles Times*

"An irresistible read. . . . Perhaps the most in-depth look ever at life on the PGA Tour. . . . Shipnuck captures every unforgettable moment in minute detail."

—*The Washington Times*

"Shipnuck paints a rich portrait of Beem and Duplantis, as well as the supporting cast of the PGA Tour, and he manages to make the world of the PGA circuit vivid and dramatic, even for readers who have no particular interest in golf. . . . The author paces his story well as it moves from course to course . . . and he writes with a levity that carries the narrative as though it were told as a locker-room tale."

—*Kirkus Reviews*

"Alan Shipnuck struck gold by picking Beem and his rookie season as subjects to chronicle in *Bud, Sweat, & Tees: Rich Beem's Walk on the Wild Side of the PGA Tour*. To begin with, he found a colorful player with a renegade personality who actually managed to confound the odds and post victory. . . . But there's more. As vivid a character as Beem turns out to be, his caddie Steve Duplantis . . . is a true rogue who makes Beem seem a choirboy by comparison. As fun to read as the greens at Augusta."

—Amazon.com

"*Sports Illustrated* writer Shipnuck's first book affords an earnest and unsentimental portrayal of life on the PGA tour. . . . [The] author clearly knows his subject, and his keen-eyed descriptions of Beem and Duplantis . . . both entertain and enlighten."

—*Publishers Weekly*

"Billed justifiably as a *Ball Four* for golf, the story of former cell phone salesman Rich Beem . . . will be music to the ears of anyone who carries a few beers in his golf bag. An R-rated Cinderella story that will gladden the heart of every golfer who would rather play than practice."

—Booklist

"Shipnuck has a ball exposing the reality of the gentleman's sport through the self-destructive duo in *Bud, Sweat, & Tees*. . . ."

—*The Toronto Star*

"An entertaining book. . . ."

—*USA Today*

"A charming story about life on the PGA Tour . . . entertaining reading."

—*Lancaster New Era*

"Shipnuck's aim is right down the fairway."

—*The Arizona Republic*

"Quickly paced and entertaining. . . ."

—*Chicago Tribune*

"Alan Shipnuck has produced a book many golf fans will find entertaining and informative."

—*The Post and Courier*
(Charleston, South Carolina)

"A good read. . . . Shipnuck has put together a very good look at life on the PGA Tour below the Tiger level."

—*The Richmond Times-Dispatch*

Acknowledgments

In the world of professional golf there is an increasing divide between the participants inside the ropes and those of us who seek to chronicle their exploits. This book could not have happened without the incredible trust and honesty of Rich Beem and Steve Duplantis. Rich and Steve opened up their worlds to me, and were brutally candid on topics from the mundane to the deeply personal. I would like to thank them again for allowing me to tell their stories. I am also indebted to their many friends and family members who were unsparing of their time and insight.

My esteemed colleague Michael Bamberger saw the potential in this story long before I did, and talked me into writing it over a remoulade-intensive dinner at—where else?—the Outback Steakhouse. He was a tireless advocate throughout the process, and his counsel has proved unerring. I am proud to have Michael as a mentor.

I'd also like to recognize Jim Herre, the golf editor at *Sports Illustrated*. The genesis of this book was a pair of assignments that he handed down from on high. I owe much of my development as a reporter and a writer to Jim, who is like the abusive father I never had.

This book was shaped in innumerable ways by Simon & Schuster's Jeff Neuman, an editor whose strong opinions are legendary, and, in my experience, almost always spot on. Jeff, thanks for taking the chance. I would also like to thank my benevolent agent, David Black, who shepherded me through many of the pratfalls of the first-time author.

I am greatly indebted to *Sports Illustrated*'s crackerjack librarians for their help: Joy Birdsong, Angel Morales, Natasha Simon, and, especially, Linda Wachtel.

Last, I would like to thank all the friends and family who sustained me with their encouragement and enthusiasm. Pecking away at a book can be a lonely experience, but I always felt like I had a large and noisy rooting section.

FOR FRANCES,
my love and inspiration

BUD, SWEAT, AND TEES

FOREWORD

"I know what you're thinking," Rich Beem said, by way of hello. "Guy wins one tournament and he thinks he can start dressing like Spicoli."

Turned out in a wrinkled T-shirt, silky purple basketball shorts, and flip-flops, Beem couldn't quite pass for the celebrated stoner from *Fast Times at Ridgemont High,* but tonight he was clearly high on life. Eight days had passed since his stunning victory at the 1999 Kemper Open. Beem had gone into that tournament a clueless twenty-eight-year-old rookie in the throes of a two-month slump, but over four giddy, magical days he summoned the best golf of his life, producing one of the most unlikely victories on the PGA Tour in recent memory. (The headline in *GolfWorld* said it all: "Who in the World is Rich Beem?") Now, bellied up to the bar at an Outback Steakhouse outside Memphis, Beem was still basking in the afterglow. He had just spent the afternoon at the driving range of the Tournament Players Club of Southwind, site of that week's PGA Tour event, the FedEx-St. Jude Classic. Having taken the last week off, for previously scheduled laser surgery to correct his nearsightedness, this was Beem's first day back at work and his new life was beginning to come into focus. His first inkling that things had changed irrevocably in the wake of his victory was when the parking lot attendant at the golf course knew his name, a first. Then he found the front of his locker to be practically invisible, owing to the veneer of hand-scribbled notes that had been taped on. None of this, however, prepared Beem for the scene at the range, where upon his arrival he was treated like the fifth Beatle. His buddy Paul Stankowski dropped to his knees to salaam, and David Sutherland, a ten-year pro, rushed up to say, "I haven't watched golf on TV in years. I hate to watch it on TV. But I watched every minute of the Kemper on Sunday and I was screaming at my TV the whole time." The unctuous manufacturers' reps, who only a week earlier hadn't afforded Beem even the token fawning, now plied him with business cards in the same manner randy patrons at a strip club throw soiled dollar bills at the dancers.

"Some unbelievably cool things have happened to me since the Kemper," Beem said, taking a long swig from his beer, "but nothing compares to seeing that I have the respect of my peers. Nothing. Tell you what, that'll make your head spin."

The first sign of the dizzying hysteria came less than an hour after the final putt had dropped, when Beem checked his cell phone and found seventeen voice messages. (Over the next week he would log some 2,600 minutes on his Motorola, and his phone bill for the month after Kemper would come to nearly $900. "If cell phones do cause cancer," his caddie, Steve Duplantis, said at one point, "then he'll be coming down with a tumor by next week.") When Beem checked his email the morning after the victory there were congratulatory messages from everybody from John Daly to three old friends from Berlin, where Beem, something of a military brat, had spent his high school years. It was serendipity, then, that the laser surgery gave Beem an alibi for skipping the tournament immediately following the Kemper, Jack Nicklaus's exclusive invitational, the Memorial. With his victory Beem had scored an automatic invite, and in his champion's press conference he had made a point of apologizing to "Mr. Nicklaus" for standing him up. (Privately, Beem said, "I think Jack'll get over it.") Beem needed the week off to get a little perspective, so he took refuge with his girlfriend, Amy Onick, in San Diego, where her mother lived. Lying on the beach did wonders for Beem's equilibrium, if not his golf game.

Between the laser surgery and gallivanting around San Diego, Beem spent all of one hour hitting balls in the eight days between the Kemper and his arrival in Memphis. Clearly, his mind was on other things, like, say, what kind of convertible he should buy with the $450,000 winner's check. In the heady moments after his victory Beem had been crowing about purchasing a Porsche Boxster, and the only thing that held him back was that his agents were supposedly burning up the phone line trying to secure an endorsment deal with BMW. "BMer and Beemer," Beem said, invoking his nickname. "How perfect is that?"

Already on his second pint of beer, Beem was properly relaxed, and he laughed at the hardship of having to choose between a Porsche or a BMW. Huddled next to him at the bar was a reminder of his former life, which is to say, his life before Kemper—Todd Pinneo, a former teammate at New Mexico State University. Pinneo had spent the last year and a half on the low-rent Hooters tour, sleeping in fleabag motels and playing for little more than gas money. Like Beem, Pinneo was going to tee it up the following morning at the regional finals of U.S. Open qualifying, hoping to earn a spot in the national championship, which was to be played the following week.

Duplantis was there, too, cradling in his lap a golden little girl in pigtails—his daughter, Sierra, three and a half years old. It was a jarring sight. With his goatee and his Billy Idol sneer, Duplantis, twenty-six, was straight out of central casting for a disaffected Gen-Xer. The kid part didn't add up. Fussing over Sierra was a toothsome young woman who Duplantis introduced as Shannon—no last name, and no nouns attached. Those would come later.

Eventually this motley crew moved to a table for dinner, and the conversation flowed as readily as the Coors Light. Pinneo was having a laugh at his friend's expense, telling of the time that Beem had been drafted into service as a playing coach for the New Mexico State golf team. Before the final round of the tournament Beem had stood in front of his teammates and, voice thick with emotion, said, "Boys, we've got the chance to do something special today. Let's go out there and show them what Aggie golf is all about."

"It was," said a deadpan Pinneo, "one of the most inspirational speeches I have ever heard." This led Beem to fire a crouton across the table at Pinneo.

Before the entrees had even come the golf-centric conversation was bouncing from topic to topic like, well, a stray crouton. For a minute the subject was professional golfers' favorite beer (consensus: Coors Light), which led to the question of how much water a player should drink during a round in Memphis in the summer (eight bottles), which led to a discussion of whether Tour caddies should be able to wear shorts (Answer: No. Why? Two words: Fluff's legs), which led to a dissertation on Nick Faldo's former caddie, Fanny Sunesson (cool girl, with a mouth like a truck driver), which led, inevitably, to an analysis of Faldo's intriguing domestic situation. "This is what I don't get," said Duplantis. "Faldo pays like twenty million dollars to get rid of his wife, and then he goes straight to Brenna [Cepelak, famously a college coed when the romance began]. I'm sorry, but that girl's got a big ol' butt. For twenty million dollars, a guy like Faldo oughtta be getting a better return on his investment."

At this point Beem piped up. "I knew Brenna before Faldo did." There was something lascivious in his tone, and it set the table atwitter.

"What do you mean, you *knew* her?"

"In the biblical sense?"

"All I'm saying," said Beem, "is that I knew her before Nicky did." His Cheshire cat smile said enough.

Noticeably detached from all the jocularity was Shannon, who had kept herself busy throughout the evening by tending to Sierra. Of course, she didn't have to say much to still make an impression. Shannon was curvier than 17 Mile Drive, a fact that was highlighted by a pair of shorts that were little more than a rumor and a clingy, low-cut top. She had a blinding smile, eyes of the bluest sky, and her auburn tresses were done up in a fashionable bob, falling across her forehead just so. Shortly after the Faldo repartee she sashayed to the powder room, and every guy at the table followed her progress with their eyes, including Beem. Noting this, Duplantis said, "Don't hurt yourself, Beemer."

"I just wanted to see where the rest rooms are, in case I have to go later," was Beem's coy response. This brought a smirk from Duplantis. The easy camaraderie was a good sign. Improbably, the Kemper had been their first tournament working together. Two months ealier Duplantis had been fired by Jim Furyk, after four and a half blockbuster years that established Furyk as one of the top players in the world. Out of desperation Duplantis had, the week before the Kemper, rung up Beem to plead for a job. Beem was delighted at the prospect, because he was having such a sorry year that no established caddie would so much as give him the time of day. The player-caddie dynamic is always delicate, to the point that it is often discussed in the nomenclature of courtship. For Beem and Duplantis, then, winning their first tournament together was like sleeping together on a first date—fun, to be sure, but complicated. If Beem and Duplantis were going to have a meaningful long-term relationship they would need a few more nights like this, getting to know each other better.

By the time Shannon returned to the table, the talk had moved to the upcoming British Open (which Faldo had won three times). Hearing this, she perked up visibly.

"Stevie has some interesting stories about the British Open," she said, shooting Duplantis an icy glare.

"Now, now, I don't think we really want to talk about this here."

"Oh, so *now* you're having second thoughts."

"Shannon, c'mon."

Beem spoke for the rest of the table when he asked, "Is there something you two would like to share?"

"No, there's really nothing left to say on the topic," Shannon said archly. The rest of the evening dissolved into thick steaks and hearty laughs. Over dessert, Beem, for the first time, grew a bit pensive. "I kinda feel like tomorrow is the start of the rest of my career," he said. "My whole life I've been clawing to get out here, and now I'm here. I know I've got a job for the next two years [winning a tournament brings a two-year exemption onto the PGA Tour], and I've never had that kind of security. But you know what, winning a tournament dun't mean shit if you disappear afterwards. What I need to do is build from here."

Good-byes were said, and then it was off to bed. Tomorrow would be an eventful day.

U.S. Open qualifying is the purest form of sport. In 1999 a record 7,889 players—both amateur and professional—took a swing and a prayer into the three-layered qualifying. When the dust settled, the ninety-two who had shot the lowest scores earned tee times at the Open. Beem was playing at Memphis National Golf Club, one of thirteen sectional qualifying sites dotted around the country, and, due to the high concentration of Tour regulars, certainly the most cutthroat. One hundred and sixteen players beat the sun to Memphis National to walk thirty-six holes in the brutal summer heat, and only twenty-four would leave happy.

By the end of the morning round Beem looked like a good bet to be one of them. He went out on the tougher South course and shot a 68 that easily could have been a 64 had his putter not overslept. Only nineteen players opened with lower rounds, but with so many gunning for so few spots, Beem knew the afternoon would be a shootout. "It's go low or go home," Beem said. "Pedal to the metal, fire at every flag, and don't stop making birdies until you get to the parking lot." This kind of golf suited Beem just fine. He is an explosive, albeit unpredictable, player. After striking a few practice putts during the lunch break he was confident he still had a low round in him. He stepped to the North course, where he would start on the back nine, and crushed a drive to open his afternoon round. The march to the U.S. Open had begun.

Playing with Beem was a young man named Steve Bell, an assistant pro at Memphis National whose legs were so skinny and white they could have doubled as out-of-bounds stakes. Bell had a nice-looking swing but was clearly rattled by the magnitude of the event and the caliber of player he was competing against. His sideways shots were not the only reason why there wasn't quite the same tension as Sunday at the Kemper. At one point during the round Duplantis relieved himself in a ditch not ten paces from a tee box. By his 25th hole Beem's concentration was visibly fizzling. As he was idling on the tee of number 16, a reachable par-5, he and Bell were distracted by the Spanish of some men working on the roof of a house adjacent to the course. This led Bell to wonder out loud if his playing partner was bilingual, being from the Southwest and all.

"Put it this way," said Beem, "I speak enough Spanish to get you a blow job in Juárez, Mexico, for five bucks."

"That'll be my swing thought," said Bell, as he settled over his ball. He proceeded to uncork a screaming hook, which settled only a few paces short of O.B. After the ball had come to rest there was a pregnant pause, then both Beem and Bell cracked up.

U.S. Open qualifying is not a laughing matter, however, and on the very next hole, a short, straightforward par-4, Beem's insouciance caught up with him. He made a lazy swing with his driver and dumped his ball into a fairway bunker, where it snuggled under the lip, leaving him an impossible lie. He was forced to blast back out to the fairway, and from there he tried to get too cute with a sand wedge, spinning it into a fried-egg lie in a deep bunker fronting the green. He gouged that out to fifteen feet, a putt he missed, resulting in an exceedingly sloppy double bogey. Walking off the green Beem angrily gave the finger to the hole. A stout birdie on the 18th brought him back to even par on his opening nine, and four under overall, but strolling toward the first tee he got a glimpse of the other scores, and the news wasn't encouraging. It looked like it would take 8 or 9 under par to sneak into the Open, which meant Beem needed no worse than a 32 on the final nine to have a shot. Go low or go home, indeed.

At this point Beem and Duplantis got their respective game faces on, but up until then there had been plenty of loose talk. Duplantis was more than happy to circle back to his barbed exchange with Shannon from the previous evening. "Okay, here's the whole story," he said, and over the span of a couple of holes he unspooled a doozy.

It turns out that he had asked Shannon—who did in fact have a last name, Pennington—to marry him less than a year earlier. Duplantis proposed at the Orlando airport just before jetting off for the British Open at Royal Birkdale in Southport, England. It was all very romantic. Two days later Duplantis had a fling with an English lass he met in a bar. "Hey, shit happens," he says. The indiscretion might have remained a secret had Pennington not decided to thoughtfully do her fiancé's laundry upon his return. Stuffed into a pants pocket was a cocktail napkin with some exceedingly incriminating information scribbled on it. "Shannon was pissed, of course," says Duplantis, "but I was pretty much able to put out the fire. I told her it was a meaningless one-time mistake, and that I'd never hear from that chick again. I even gave her a bunch of money to go shopping so she could cheer herself up. Unfortunately, she took my cell phone, too."

That was how Pennington wound up in an animated discussion with Duplantis's English concubine, who had called to reminisce. Pennington immediately packed her bags and went home to Dallas, and they had no contact for ten months. And then in mid-May, two weeks before the fateful Kemper Open, Duplantis traveled to the Byron Nelson Classic in Dallas. He was in desperate need of a loop and had gone to the Nelson to try to drum up some interest. Six weeks had passed since his firing and he hadn't had so much as a nibble from any other players, no doubt because of a reputation for chronic tardiness. As always, Duplantis had his excuses. Since September of 1997 he had had full custody of Sierra, and unlike the coddled millionaires they pack for, Tour caddies have no organized day care while on the road. He was also entangled in some messy divorce proceedings with Sierra's mother, Vicki—a stripper from the Philippines by way of Fort Worth, Texas. When Duplantis had been given his pink slip Furyk told him that he was doing it partly out of benevolence; Furyk wanted him to take some time off to get his life in order. Furyk—who off the course is straighter than six o'clock—also made it clear that he disapproved of Duplantis's lifestyle. Duplantis was well known as a serial skirt-chaser, and for maintaining Keith Richards hours. So, by the time Duplantis bumped into Pennington at a bar in Dallas he was a man trying to mend his ways, or at least give off appearances.

Duplantis told Pennington that he was thinking about calling a struggling rookie named Rich Beem, but he wasn't sure he wanted to head back out on tour again without some help caring for his daughter. In the ten months since the marriage proposal Pennington had often wondered about Sierra. Pennington adored her, and while she was dating Duplantis she had become like a surrogate mom. With little going on in her life back in Dallas she took the bait and agreed to travel with Duplantis as a paid nanny. Pennington made it clear the relationship would be strictly platonic.

"We'll see how long that lasts," Duplantis said from Memphis National, with a wolfish grin.

Back on the front nine Beem was showing some teeth, too,

as he made a twisty thirty-footer for birdie on the second hole. He was now -5, with seven holes to play. Just after Beem had struck his drive on the 3rd hole Pennington showed up at the course, pushing Sierra in a stroller along the cart path. She was a vision in tight denim shorts, and it didn't take long for her to pick up the narrative.

"You know what the most unbelievable thing was?" she said in her Texas twang. "That napkin I found, it didn't just have that girl's home phone number. It had her email address, her business number, her cell phone, you name it. Gawd, I was so stupid. At least I had an excuse. I was only nineteen then."

Pennington eventually had her revenge, at least to some degree. "The engagement ring Stevie gave me was amazing, and of course he wanted it back. Well, I had bills to pay. I had given up my life for him, and when I got back to Dallas I was in debt. So you know what I did? I had a cubic zirconia made. I can only imagine how much he paid for the diamond, because it cost me five hundred dollars to have the zirconia done. Anyway, I pawned the ring and paid off all my bills, and then I gave him the fake one. By the way, I've never told him. I still don't think he knows."

Seeing Pennington talking a blue streak must have made Duplantis a tad uncomfortable, because he kept stealing glances in her direction. Beem, however, was demanding plenty of attention in his own right, as he made a little rally. He gave himself good birdie chances on the third and fourth holes, which he just missed, and after getting into trouble on the short, tricky par-4 5th hole, he holed a thirty-five-foot snake for par to keep hope alive. Meanwhile, Pennington continued to dish.

"You know, I think I'll always be friends with Stevie, because we've shared a lot, but I could never respect him enough to go out with him again," she said. "If he thinks I'm out here for him he's got another thing coming. I mean, if it wasn't for me he wouldn't have even been able to go to the Kemper Open, and who knows where he'd be. But like I said, I'm not out here for him, I'm out here for Sierra. I worry about what kind of life she is going to have. Stevie tries, but he's just a young guy who wants to have fun. I realize now that's why he asked me to marry him. He just wanted someone to take care of Sierra so he could go out and party. That hasn't changed, but at least now we have a business arrangement. I mean, this is how he thinks: he actually took Sierra's mother with him to a party this year, and they're supposedly in the middle of a divorce!"

That was at the season-opening Mercedes Championships, on the island of Maui. Prior to 1999 the Kapalua Invitational had been a small unofficial tournament played every fall, a cherished working vacation at the end of a long year. The players and their families were pampered in every way imaginable, and one of the highlights of the week was always a private rock concert with big name acts imported for the occasion. (An epic evening in 1996 featured Hootie & the Blowfish, at the apex of their popularity, as well as a dozen or so sodden Tour players who joined the group on stage to mangle one of their hits). In 1999 the low-key charm of the Invitational became a casualty in the big-money restructuring of the PGA Tour. Mercedes was brought in as the title sponsor, the field was restricted to winners from the previous season, and, with $2.6 million up for grabs, the players were compelled to act in a far more sober manner. Still, the Wednesday night concert endured, and in 1999 the featured group was the hip neo-swing band the Brian Setzer Orchestra. As good as their raucous two-hour set was, Duplantis stole the show. He spent the evening strolling the grounds of the Kapalua Ritz-Carlton with an impish grin and a darkly exotic beauty on his arm. She was wearing a minidress that appeared to have been painted on, accentuating a gravity-defying figure that called to mind Jessica Rabbit.

"I could tell you some stories about her," said Pennington. "Then again, we all make mistakes. How else can I explain Stevie?" Here she grew reflective. "I think what I need to do is find a nice rich golf pro to take care of me," Pennington said with a sigh. "Someone like Rich. He's a cutie."

At that moment Beem was indeed looking pretty good. After lipping out a fifteen-foot birdie putt on 6 he ran in a shocking fifty-footer for bird on the next hole, bringing him to six under par with two holes to play. Number 8 on Memphis National's North Course was an eminently birdie-able par-5. With the wind picking up in the afternoon, presumably sending scores soaring, Beem was well aware that another birdie might just get him into the U.S. Open. He pounded his drive down the middle of the eighth fairway and stalked after it. Pennington kept pace.

"You know," she said, "I met Rich's girlfriend, Amy somebody, at the Kemper. We all went out to dinner. I didn't like her very much. Typical schoolteacher." Meaning? "She's real quiet, kinda mousy even. And not very attractive. With all that's going on in Rich's life I don't see them lasting through the end of the year. I get the feeling Rich wants a taste of the life Steve's been living."

Beem laid up perfectly at the eighth and then stuck a wedge to five feet. As he was lining up the birdie putt Duplantis actually turned around and put a finger to his lips, trying to get Pennington to lower her voice. Beem didn't appear to have been distracted by her chattering, but after a series of brilliant putts something clearly affected him on this one, because he pulled it badly and never scared the hole. He pantomimed snapping his unfaithful putter over his knee before tapping in for a crushing par. But if Beem has anything, it's *juevos.* He played two textbook shots to the 9th green and then rolled in a frighteningly fast, downhill, right-to-left breaking birdie putt for a round of 69. He was seven under par overall, and there was still a glimmer.

Beem strode to the scoring area shaking his head, both anguished by the missed opportunities and exhilarated by his gutsy play over the final nine holes. There were still so many players on the course that it was impossible to say what the magic number would be, but one volunteer told Beem that -7 should be good enough for a playoff. He retreated to the air-conditioned clubhouse to cool off with a Pepsi, but it wasn't the caffeine that made him so jumpy. "I'll go out there in a playoff and birdie the first four holes if I have to," he said. "They're not gonna keep me out of this sonofabitch."

Not long after Beem sat down his buddy Pinneo strolled into the clubhouse, beaming. "Gimme a number," Beem said.

"Six." That was how many strokes under par Pinneo had finished.

"Well, then, what the hell are you smiling for?"

"Hey," said Pinneo, "not all of us are PGA Tour bigshots. I hung up a couple of good rounds [69-69], and for my first time through qualifying, I'll take it. You better go check the board because they just posted a bunch of scores."

At the moment Beem reached the scoring area there were twenty-three players posted at -8 or better, with five twosomes still unaccounted for. If just one of those ten players came in with a score better than -7, Beem was out of the U.S. Open.

"I may as well bend over and grab my ankles," he said.

By now a hundred players and those who loved them were crowded around the scoring area, and the mood was like an Irish wake—a weird mix of the somber and the euphoric. All attention was trained on two harried volunteers, who, equipped with walkie-talkies and felt tip pens, were feverishly trying to chronicle the action. Suddenly a walkie-talkie crackled, and one of the volunteers—an expressive older woman—put it to her ear. After another burst of noise she said softly, "Oh my." Over to board she scurried, and next to the name of David Toms, an explosive Tour veteran, she scribbled the harsh truth: 64-63, 17 under par. "You have got to be fuckin' shittin' me," Beem said. He ripped off his hat and slapped his knee hard, then began ambling toward the parking lot alone. The United States Open—the biggest tournament of the year—would be played next week and Beem was going to have to watch it on TV, as always.

Apparently life as a PGA Tour champion was not going to be as easy as he imagined.

CHAPTER

• 1 •

THERE WERE NO BARS on the windows at Magnolia Hi-Fi, though it certainly felt that way to Rich Beem. This was where, beginning in September of 1995, he did eight months of hard time in the straight world, a prisoner to a time clock and the whims of the buying public. Tucked into the plush Seattle burb of Bellevue, in the shadow of the Microsoft campus, Magnolia is a high-end playground for wired stock-option millionaires and overprivileged teenagers, and though these weren't exactly Beem's people, he made a clear connection with them. Beem sold cell phones. Lots of them. Not that Beem knew that much about selling phones. He had wandered into Magnolia one day on a lark, seduced by the promise that he could make up to $25,000 a year, at seven dollars an hour plus commission. "That was the most money I'd ever heard of," he says. "I walked into my interview and said, 'Hey, I can barely dial a phone let alone explain one, but I promise you I can sell anything to anyone.' "

Beem had drifted into Seattle along with his fiancée, Tanya Thie, who had transferred to Western Washington University to finish her undergraduate studies. "I always told Tanya I would follow her anywhere," says Beem, and so he did. Thie was a firecracker, a knockout brunette with a sharp tongue and salty sense of humor, her excess of spunk owing to having grown up with nine brothers. Beem loved her tragically, but his move to Seattle was about a lot more than Thie. Beem was running away—from his frustrations on the golf course, from his father, Larry, a brooding presence whose legend had lorded over his life, and from too many drunken nights spent pissing away a life's potential. Come to think of it, Beem had been running for most of his life.

When Beem was eleven the family had moved to Panama,

part of a string of far-flung jobs that Larry took running the golf courses at various military installations. In two and a half years Rich never made any friends in Panama, but he did join the track team, running everything from the eight hundred meters to the ten kilometers. "It was the one thing I could do by myself," he says. Golf is a favorite sport of loners, too, but Beem resisted. "That was my dad's deal," he says. On the rare occasions when Larry Beem was able to drag his son to the course, Rich's potential was eye-popping. "Because of Larry I grew up around golf, and I've seen more than my share of golfers," says Rich's mother, Diana Pompeo. "I've never seen anyone pick up the game as easily as Rich."

After Panama the Beems—Rich, his parents, and two older sisters—landed in Berlin, while the Wall was still standing. Having grown out of what he calls his "dork" phase, Rich began running with the cool crowd at Berlin American High School. The drinking age in Berlin was only sixteen, and though Rich was still a few years shy of it, he and his buddies partied like rock stars. Rich also started hanging around Berlin Golf and Country Club, where his father was head pro, not to visit with the old man but to score pocket money. Larry would cover all of his son's bets, and the soldiers playing hooky from the nearby base were easy marks. Beem was talked into playing for the Berlin American High golf team as a freshman and sophomore, and both years he breezed to victory at the countrywide championship of Defense Department high schools. But Beem was booted off the golf team following the first tournament of his junior year, after getting caught pounding beers on a train ride home. This practically left him doing jumping jacks. Not being able to play meant not being judged by his father's withering standards.

Ah, but if only it were so easy to escape one's DNA. Larry Beem's son simply had too much natural talent to give up on golf, or have the game give up on him. For Rich's senior year in high school the family moved back to Las Cruces, New Mexico, the town where he had been born. (Larry was now running the golf course at White Sands Missile Base.) After the old man made a few phone calls Rich wound up with a scholarship to play for New Mexico State in Las Cruces. There was no hiding from his dad there, for Larry had been NMSU's first golf All-American in

1964, and was memorialized in an oversized poster that hung in the school's on-campus Hall of Fame.

There were times on the golf course, occasionally, when Rich lived up to his father's expectations. At the 1993 New Mexico State Amateur Championship he shot a final round 68, in forty-mile-per-hour winds, to win by six strokes. "If the tournament had gone another nine holes he would have won by twelve, and if it had gone another fifty-four he would have won by one hundred," says Larry. "It was blowing a hurricane but he was just relentless, fearless, aggressive. That was the first time Rich ever showed me he could play."

Rich, of course, found a way of running from those kinds of expectations. Juárez, Mexico, was but a quick car ride from Las Cruces. A border town teeming with vice and mice, in Juárez you only had to be eighteen to drink, which Beem often did. He never won a collegiate tournament at New Mexico State, never even really threatened to, but Beem did collect plenty of stories, like the time when he got his ear pierced on one of Juárez's grungy sidewalks. His sister Tina's then-husband simply snatched an earring from his bride, sterilized it with tequila, and slammed it into Beem's ear. "It was hilarious," says Tina.

Following college, in April of 1994, Beem lit out of Las Cruces for Sioux Falls, South Dakota, where, thanks to the connections of a college girlfriend, he had lined up a job as an assistant pro at Westward Ho Country Club. "All I knew about Sioux Falls was that it was somewhere else," he says. "I wanted to get the hell out of Las Cruces, New Mexico. I didn't care where I was going." After thirty years Larry and Diana's marriage was falling apart. As always, it was easiest for Rich just to run away.

Tanya Thie worked in the grillroom at Westward Ho. Their first date was at a pseudo-French restaurant, and they were engaged less than a year later. Beem only occasionally teed it with the boys from the Westward Ho pro shop, but when he did he made a lasting impression. Says Jeff Brecht, the club's head pro, "There is a lot of professional golf up in this part of the world—maybe not the PGA Tour, but there are a lot of fine players, and they all pass through Westward Ho. I can tell you Rich had the most God-given talent of any player I've ever seen. The game just came so easy for him, or so it seemed. Everytime we'd play

I'd tell Rich, 'You don't belong here. You need to go test yourself against some real competition.' "

Beem eventually took the advice. Following his first summer at Westward Ho, in 1994, he blazed out of Sioux Falls to roll the dice on the Silver State Tour, a micro-minitour that snakes across Nevada. Beem won his very first tournament, in Henderson, Nevada. After opening with a 73 he had gone out in 35 the next day when a monsoon hit. With half of the fifty-four holes complete, the tournament was called and Beem earned a cheap victory, not to mention $1,650. Things went steadily downhill from there, as Beem struggled with his game and his emotions. Two thirds of the way through the season, in February of 1995, Beem and Thie were engaged, and a wedding date was set for the following September. It was a bipolar existence, the hardships of playing golf for a living contrasted with the comforts of being at home with Thie. "I was a mess," says Beem. "I didn't want to be on the road. Half of it was I wasn't playing well, the other half was that being with her made me so much happier. I was young and immature about a lot of things. It was hard to focus on golf." In the summer of 1995 Beem felt compelled to give golf one more chance. He allowed himself a half dozen tournaments on the Dakotas Tour, but his heart wasn't in it.

After two years of studying psychology at the University of Nebraska, Thie, too, was looking for a change of scenery. "Rich and I both grew up landlocked," she says. "We thought it would be nice to be near the water." For Beem this qualified as a cogent plan. At Thie's insistence, he vowed to give up competitive golf and they moved to Seattle, settling into a small apartment at 30th and Avalon. "It had a great view of Puget Sound," says Beem.

FROM THE TIME BEEM ARRIVED in Seattle he refused to allow himself to play a single round of golf, and he rarely let on about his past in the sport. A notable exception came during Magnolia Hi-Fi orientation, when Beem participated in a getting-to-know-you game where he had to tell two truths and a lie, and his coworkers tried to discern which was which. Beem said: 1) I lived overseas for seven years; 2) I have a six-year-old son named

Jacob; and 3) I used to be a professional golfer. Taking stock of Beem—five foot eight and an assless 150 pounds—not one among the forty or so people in attendance believed Beem had ever been a professional golfer.

Maybe Beem didn't believe anymore, either. He had plunged into the domestic life with a vengeance. Beem would set up shop in the kitchen of his apartment and whip up the Mexican dishes that were (and are) the cornerstone of his diet—enchiladas, tacos, a killer bean dip. Tanya's nephew Corey Thie had come to Seattle to live with the betrothed, taping up a sheet to close off the den to make a tiny living space, and he soon picked up a job bartending at a trendy nightclub, 2218. Rich and Tanya frequently came by to drink on the house, and together they explored Seattle's vibrant music scene. Occasionally they would go sailing on the Sound with David Wyatt, a Magnolia Hi-Fi colleague who had a twenty-seven-foot sailboat named *Xocomil*, after the Mayan god of wind. "I thought I was happy," says Beem. "I fell so hard for Tanya. I thought she was the be-all, end-all. I thought being with her was all I had ever wanted, and would ever want."

Others weren't so sure, including Tanya. "For as long as I'd known Rich he wasn't happy unless he was playing golf," she says. "Even if he was unhappy because he had played bad, he was still happy. You know what I mean? Deep down I think he knew that's what he belonged doing, but it was so hard for him to admit it. I'm sure that had something to do with his relationship with his dad."

Though Beem wouldn't let himself play eighteen holes, it was clear he was still in the grip of the game. "He wouldn't go to the course, but he always had a club in his hand around the apartment," says Corey Thie. "He was forever checking his grip, checking his swing in the mirror, that kind of thing." From their second-floor balcony to the edge of Puget Sound was a carry of a couple hundred yards at least, all of it over a bustling industrial complex attached to the port. Beem used to delight in launching drives off the balcony, trying to reach the water.

On Easter Sunday in 1996 something finally snapped inside of Beem. He spent the better part of the weekend screaming at his TV, watching the PGA Tour's BellSouth Classic. Paul

Stankowski was in contention. Stankowski had gone to the University of Texas-El Paso, a mere thirty miles from New Mexico State's campus, and Beem had always counted him as both a friend and a healthy rival. By 1996 Stankowski was in his third full year on tour and showing considerable promise. At BellSouth he shot a final round 71 to force a playoff with Tour veteran Brandel Chamblee, and then birdied the first extra hole to win it. The victory was worth $234,000 to Stankowski and an immeasurable amount to Beem. That afternoon he went sailing with Wyatt, who was quickly becoming his best friend. It was just the two of them, and after a spin around the Sound, Beem grew reflective.

"David," he said, "I think I feel like playing golf again."

IN HIS FIRST ROUND OF GOLF since landing in Seattle, Beem played in only 2 over par, and that was all it took to push him off the wagon. Overnight he began bingeing on the game, in whatever form was available—the driving range over lunch, a quick nine holes after work, and thirty-six-holes-a-day benders on the weekend. Predictably, Beem's relationship with Tanya began fracturing almost immediately. A scant three weeks after that first fateful round, Thie suggested she get her own apartment and that they take a little break. "Tanya was very clear it wasn't a breakup, just a break," says Beem, but Thie still returned the engagement ring. It was supposed to be symbolic—Beem was going to slip it back onto her finger again when they were both ready. But with Thie going in her own direction Beem decided to do the same. The day after getting the rock back Beem quit at Magnolia Hi-Fi and began tuning up for another run at the Dakotas Tour. "I just had to know," he says.

Beem played seven tournaments in as many weeks up in the Dakotas, making the cut in all seven, and finished second in a triumphant homecoming in Sioux Falls. But while he was falling in love with golf, maybe for the first time, Thie was rapidly falling out of love with him. By the middle of the summer "her tune had changed completely," says Beem. "One day, out of the blue, she says, 'I don't think this is going to work.' I was like, 'Excuse me?' "

Says Thie, "It's a hard thing, to follow a golfer around. It's not a stable life, and it's not what I wanted. Hats off to him, but it's not how I envisioned my life." By the summer of 1996 Thie was well on her way to a bachelor of arts in human services, with a minor in counseling, and was volunteering at a group home for disenfranchised youth.

"As Rich once put it, 'She wanted to save the world and all he wanted was to save par,' " says Larry Beem. "They just didn't understand each other after a while." One person with whom Thie connected was a fellow volunteer at the group home, whom she would eventually marry. By the time Beem returned home from the Dakotas Tour to pick up his stuff in early September, "There was a closet full of this other guy's clothes," says Beem. "I fuckin' freaked. Total meltdown." Beem called his friend and colleague Wyatt and they found a quiet slice of shoreline along the Sound and proceeded to pump hundreds of purloined range balls into the water.

"Thank God for David," says Beem. "Without him I might have wound up at the bottom of Puget Sound, too."

DAVID WYATT GREW UP in Alexandria, Minnesota, a tiny town in the state's central lakes region, 130 miles from Minneapolis. When he was three years old his dad skipped out on the family and was never heard from again. When he was five he was molested by a baby-sitter. "I was basically programmed at an early age to be fucked up," Wyatt says with a hard, little laugh. When he was eight Wyatt got high for the first time, and he says, "It was like, 'This is the answer to my life right here.' To this day that was the best experience of my life. It was the most peace I've ever felt." By nine he was actively using a cornucopia of drugs. "I liked speed and Valium, but I wasn't picky," he says. Wyatt dropped out of school after ninth grade; by then he was in and out of foster homes and often living on the streets. At fourteen he got his GED while, he says, "a guest of the state of Minnesota." And what was he arrested for?

"You want the whole list, or just the partial?"

By fifteen Wyatt was sober but still living like a junkie, stealing to survive. He would often disappear for months at a time on wild hitchhiking jags across the country—by the time he was sixteen Wyatt had visited forty-seven of the lower forty-eight states. "How I missed Pennsylvania," he says, "I'll never understand." Wyatt spent one long night on the road picking the brain of his ride, a gent who happened to install security systems for a living. After that, breaking and entering became a way of life. That is, until, "The state of Minnesota was kind enough to correct my wayward path," he says.

Beginning when he was seventeen, Wyatt spent two and a half years incarcerated or in halfway houses, and upon his release he got tangled up with a woman eight years his senior, the daughter of one of Alexandria's most prominent families. "She was an alcoholic, I was in recovery, it was all part of the charm," Wyatt says. They were married in October of 1984, and divorced eight months later. In the interim a daughter, Cady, was born, and Wyatt earned his certificate of chemical dependency counseling. He was thrilled to finally have some decent job prospects—to that point he had already worked as a beekeeper, fishing guide, tire repairman, cook, waiter, motor boat repairman, and construction worker.

Wyatt spent the next ten years wandering, living like the Unabomber in a tent in Helena, Montana, spending a year exploring Guatemala, where he became a vegetarian and embraced meditation, and along the way working at various counseling outposts to earn pocket money. In September of 1995 he somehow washed ashore at Magnolia Hi-Fi, where during orientation he told the following two truths and a lie: 1) he had ridden a motorcyle at 178 miles per hour; 2) he had been to forty-seven of the lower forty-eight by the time he was sixteen and 3) he had a six-year-old son named Jacob.

After bonding at that orientation it took little time for Wyatt and Beem to become friends, and accomplices. "It was definitely pandemonium when they were around," says Bobby McCory, a coworker at Magnolia Hi-Fi. "They were quite a combo—like powerful opposite forces that somehow kept the other in check." Beem and Wyatt used to delight in cranking up the display stereos to ear-splitting volumes, and they quickly developed a language so dense with inside jokes and obscure references that customers had no idea when they were being made fun of, which was often.

Nevertheless, "If it weren't for strippers, we wouldn't be best friends," says Wyatt. "Maybe buddies, but not the blood brothers we are now." It seems that during his Magnolia days Wyatt was dating a dancer at Club Déjà Vu. "She was the love of my life," he says. "She was my Tanya." One night, while hanging out at the club, Wyatt had "the big one," the kind of blowup that signals the end of any relationship. Wyatt stormed out of Club Déjà Vu and jumped in his car. Sensing the gravity of the situation Beem followed him outside, and, uninvited, parked himself in the passenger seat. "Rich was afraid I might kill myself, and I probably would have," says Wyatt. Without so much as a word Wyatt raced out of the parking lot driving like a madman, and after running a series of red lights he finally pulled over, screaming at Beem to "fuck off and get the fuck out of my car." Says Wyatt, "I was shaking, crying, and Rich grabbed my hand and touched my heart. He said he wasn't going to leave me, no matter what I said or did. It was a very special thing for him to make himself so vulnerable like that. When I finally cooled down I said, 'From this day forward you and I are forever best friends,' and that's exactly how it's worked out."

AFTER COLLECTING HIS THINGS at his old apartment Beem crashed with Wyatt for a spell, assessing his options, such as they were. He finally accepted what everyone else had known all along: "The only thing I really knew, the only thing I was special at, was golf," he says. His dad made a few phone calls and, per usual, Rich was taken care of, this time in the form of a job offer at El Paso Country Club, just down the road from Las Cruces. The assistant pro position didn't pay much, but Beem could work on his game, and, more importantly, start right away. After a lifetime of running away—from golf, from his dad, from Las Cruces—Beem was heading home, to the life he never wanted.

CHAPTER

• 2 •

When Steve Duplantis was growing up in Brampton, Ontario, he loved golf so much he used to sleep with his clubs. "Literally," says his mom, Sandy Cantin. "We used to hear them fall out of his bed and onto the floor when he would stir at night." Duplantis loved golf so much that, at age nine, he would ride his bike to the neighboring city of Georgetown because it was the only place he could play. Brampton to Georgetown was twenty minutes by car, so for a pint-sized kid like Duplantis it must've taken at least an hour of dogged pedaling. When he was older he took a job delivering pizzas late into the night so he could reserve his afternoons for golf. Once Duplantis got a junior membership to North Halton Country Club in Brampton, nothing could keep him off the links. "Steve considered a couple inches of snow to be playable conditions," says John Mitchell, Cantin's husband from the time Duplantis was six to nineteen. "He'd play thirty-six holes a day in weather that was below freezing, and then complain that he only got in thirty-six before he lost feeling in his hands and toes." When the snow got too deep, Steve and his father, Stephen Duplantis, would travel to an indoor driving range in Toronto. After hitting mountains of balls they would retire to the practice green, to have cutthroat putting contests. "He would grind over those putts as if it were the U.S. Open," says Stephen.

Eventually Duplantis graduated from his grudge matches with his father to some bona fide tournament action. In the summer following his junior year in high school he teed it up in a handful of American Junior Golf Association events, in such glamorous, faraway places as Hilton Head, Aspen, and Lake Tahoe. Duplantis was blown away to see the video cameras, swing gurus, and sports psychologists that the other kids had at their disposal. "We never saw any of that until we came to the States," says Mitchell. "In Canada there are no junior programs to speak of. The access to courses for kids is very limited, and there's almost no coaching. Steve had the dedication, but that's all he had." In his case, that was enough.

There had always been a touch of the obsessive in Duplantis. When he was a preteen he was an eater of almost cartoonish specificity. When Duplantis decided he liked something, he would gorge himself on that one food until he grew sick of it, then move on to another. Those close to him remember in particular a period of months when he ate virtually nothing but Eggo waffles at every meal. So when Duplantis got it in his mind he was going to play college golf in the United States, he set about making it happen. Blindly culling addresses from a guidebook, he sent out dozens of letters to small schools across Florida, Texas, and South Carolina, selling himself and his accomplishments, such as they were. No one in his family knew he had sent the letters until a smattering of replies trickled in. The only school that showed genuine interest was Spartanburg Methodist Junior College, in Spartanburg, South Carolina, which came through with a half scholarship offer, sight unseen. When Duplantis visited the campus for the first time the coaches were surprised to find out he was left-handed. Apparently the form letters and various applications hadn't asked about that particular bit of information. Duplantis had two decent seasons in Spartanburg, though he never won a tournament, and never really threatened to. "I knew I loved golf," he says. "Maybe I wasn't as great as I wanted to be, but I loved it."

Duplantis became equally passionate about exploring the brave new world south of the forty-fifth parallel. "Steve was always amazed with the things that I think of as uniquely American," says Cantin. "He loved the spectacle, the excess. He would go to these high school football games, where he didn't know a soul, and just sit in the stands and marvel at the thousands of fans, the bands, the cheerleaders, the whole bit. And this was just a high school football game." Duplantis was always jumping in his beat-up sky blue Chevy Cavalier to spend long weekends exploring Charleston or Charlotte or Savannah or Hilton Head, and more than once he roadtripped cross country. In the summer of 1993, following his sophomore year at Spartanburg, Duplantis drove to Greeneville, South Carolina, to take in the action at that week's Nike Tour event, the Greater Greeneville Classic. He had an old friend he wanted to see.

A GOOD OL' BOY BORN and raised in Goldsboro, North Carolina, Clarence Rose was a mainstay on the PGA Tour throughout the 1980s, especially from 1985 to 1989, when he never finished lower than 63rd on the money list (though he never managed to get that elusive first victory). Rose has a Carolina drawl thick as barbecue sauce, and a distinctly down-home sensibility. When he and his wife, Jan, his college sweetheart, first set out to travel the Tour in 1981, they weren't forty-five minutes outside of Goldsboro when they pulled the car over for a good cry. "We had never been away from home before," says Clarence.

In 1990, with Jan five months pregnant, the Roses found out that their eighteen-month-old son, Clark, had been diagnosed with testicular cancer. Over the next four years Rose would play in a total of only eighteen PGA Tour events, consumed with caring for his family. Clark eventually had a malignant tumor removed and went on to a full recovery, and by the summer of 1993 his father was haunting the Nike Tour, trying to bring his golf game back from the dead. (The Nike Tour, now known as the Buy.com Tour, is the equivalent of baseball's Triple-A minor leagues.) Rose didn't know Duplantis was going to drop by the Greater Greeneville Classic, but then he certainly wasn't surprised to see him.

Duplantis had long been like Rose's second shadow.

"I vividly remember the day it all started," says Stephen Duplantis. "It was a Tuesday practice round at the 1985 Canadian Open, at Glen Abbey Golf Course. Steve was twelve years old, and this was his first pro tournament. I couldn't spend the day out there with him so we set a time and a place to meet and I dropped him off at the course. My parting words were, 'Be sure you don't talk to anybody.'

"So I come back in the afternoon and Steve pulls from his pocket a handful of beautiful brand-new balls.

" 'Where'd you get those?' I asked.

" 'From my friend Clarence Rose.'

" 'Who the heck is Clarence Rose?'

" 'Oh, you want to meet him? He's over there on the putting green.' "

It turns out that following Rose's practice round Duplantis had sparked a conversation, and they hit it off famously. Duplantis wound up taking his father over to meet Rose, who was as gracious as could be. Rose even posed for a photo with Steve, still a treasured keepsake. That night Steve returned home (he was living with his mother and John Mitchell) and, "He went on and on about Clarence Rose, who none of us had ever heard of, of course," says Sandy. "The only way I could get him to put a lid on it was to promise to take him to Glen Abbey the next day."

At 6:45 the next morning Sandy dropped Steve at the course, making a lengthy detour from her usual drive to work. Duplantis tromped along for all eighteen holes of Rose's practice round, sat in the bleachers at the range while Rose hit buckets of balls, and camped in the grass next to the putting green while Rose endlessly practiced his stroke. Rose was a solid player but hardly a marquee attraction. The number of fans that followed him during those practice sessions numbered two—Jan and Steve—and that didn't escape Rose's attention.

When the tournament proper began tickets weren't as easy to come by, but Stephen managed to secure a couple for Sunday's final round. "When I called Steve to tell him, I mentioned that I'd pick him up at ten," says Stephen. "All he said was, 'Why so late? Clarence goes off at eight-thirty.' I said, 'Hey, bud, it's my day off. I'll see you at ten.' "

When the Duplantises arrived at the course Steve beat a path to the 9th hole, where, having memorized the day's pairings, he calculated Rose would be playing. Sure enough, Rose was putting out on the 9th green. Duplantis positioned himself in the walkway between the green and the 10th tee, for maximum visibility. When Rose saw him, he said, "Hey Steve, where ya been? I missed ya, buddy."

"My boy lit up like a Christmas tree," says Stephen.

That was the start of a beautiful friendship. Duplantis and Rose began corresponding by letter, and every year when he rolled into town Rose would leave a complimentary pass to the tournament for his biggest fan. During practice rounds Rose would sometimes let Duplantis walk with him right down the middle of the fairway, and occasionally he would sneak Duplantis into the clubhouse for a meal, where they sat elbow to elbow with all the other players.

"He was like the tournament mascot," says Rose. "Every hole I played, everywhere I went that week Stevie was there. It was a little weird, I reckon, but it was kinda neat, too."

When Rose dropped out of golf to help care for Clark, Duplantis kept in touch and offered healthy doses of encouragement. "Not a lot of people picked up the phone, but he did, and that meant a lot," says Rose.

So, when Duplantis arrived at the 1993 Greater Greeneville Classic, Rose was just as happy to see Duplantis as the other way around. Over lunch Rose told Duplantis that he had had a falling out with his regular caddie, and that he was looking for another looper. That's when Rose broke into a sly grin.

"Steve," he asked, "you got any plans next week?"

DUPLANTIS HAD FIRST STARTED caddying at age eight, during therapeutic weekend mornings spent pulling his father's trolley. The wounds from his parents' divorce were still fresh, and, says Steve, "The golf course was one of the few places where I could feel close to my dad, where we could come together." (When Steve was sixteen he and the old man won the Ontario father-son tournament, which both count among the highlights of their athletic lives.) In his middle age Stephen still played to a mid-single digit handicap, and was often a factor in the club championships at North Halton. Steve would caddie for his dad in the championships, and he proved a natural.

The younger Duplantis had an analytical mind; when he was twelve he was given a Commodore 64 for Christmas, and would stay up until the wee hours of the morning punching archaic codes into that museum piece of a computer. On the golf course he loved crunching the yardage numbers and doing the cost-benefit analysis that went into every shot. By the time Duplantis was in his early teens he had displayed such an aptitude at caddying that another North Halton member, Gary Notar, hired him away for the club championship. When Notar took the trophy in their first outing together, much to-do was made about Duplantis's contribution. (Thankfully, for the sake of family tranquility, Notar and Stephen Duplantis were in different flights.)

So when Rose, back in Greeneville, offered him the chance to caddie for a week, Duplantis was quick to accept. His summer plans were wide open, and there was plenty of time to tune up his game before the fall, when he was due to enroll at High Point (North Carolina) University, where another half scholarship was waiting. One week on the bag with Rose would be a hoot, and a good chance to earn some spending money.

Off went Duplantis, to Knoxville, Tennessee, site of that week's tournament. In their first practice round together Duplantis performed admirably, and Rose enjoyed their easy chemistry. Following the round Rose turned to Duplantis and asked, in that courtly drawl of his, "Say, Steve, what are you doing the rest of the summer?"

DUPLANTIS JUMPED AT ROSE'S OFFER to caddie for the rest of the summer of 1993, and three weeks into the job something serendipitous happened: Rose was granted a sponsor's exemption into the PGA Tour's Anheuser-Busch Golf Classic. Duplantis, greener than a Masters jacket, was heading to the big leagues. "I shit a brick when Clarence told me," says Duplantis. "I mean, I was only a couple years removed from asking these guys for their autographs."

The Anheuser-Busch (now known as the Michelob Championship) has long been played in Williamsburg, Virginia. With a nod to the oppressive summer weather the PGA Tour has, in recent years, scheduled the tournament in the fall, but back in 1993 it was played in the middle of July. Duplantis remembers the heat index hovering around 140. "People were dropping like flies," he says. To that crucible Rose added even more heat. For Thursday's opening round the group immediately behind Rose and Duplantis was a trio of crusty, old-school veterans—Ed Fiori, Leonard Thompson, and Barry Jaeckel. At the driving range prior to the round, Rose made a point of mischievously telling all three that this was Duplantis's first PGA Tour event. Implicit was that hazing was to be encouraged.

On the first hole Rose dumped his approach shot into a greenside bunker, and Duplantis raked it without a thought. After all, in his golfing life he had raked thousands of bunkers. While idling on the fourth tee Duplantis spied a cart-bound PGA Tour official cutting a swath through the gallery toward the tee, and his stomach began doing somersaults. Sure enough, the official approached Rose and Duplantis's threesome and said, with the gravitus of Cronkite announcing JFK's assassination, that the group behind them had complained about the rake job on a bunker back on the first hole. Duplantis meekly kept his mouth shut, but Rose volunteered that his man was the culprit. Duplantis was informed that one more slipup would result in Rose being fined, per PGA Tour regulations (players can also get zinged if their caddies violate the dress code or are seen driving courtesy cars, which are off limits). For the rest of the round Duplantis scurried around in a caricature of the overzealous rookie, ignoring both the heat and the snickers of the other caddies in the group. His ardor reached its zenith at the 17th hole, Kingsmill Golf Club's signature. The 17th is a 177-yard par-3, framed by the James River, which runs the length of the right side of the hole. Between the green and the river is a cavernous bunker, the bottom of which is some thirty feet below the putting surface. Rose slashed his tee shot into that bunker and, after a nifty explosion shot onto the green, left Duplantis with a sizeable cleanup job. Still smarting from his rebuke, Duplantis smoothed the sand like a Japanese monk tending to his Zen garden.

"When I finally hiked up to the green the pin was already in and everyone had split for the eighteenth tee," says Duplantis. "Clarence just deserted me—he took his driver and left the bag on the side of the green. When I caught up to him on eighteen he laughed and said, 'Well, at least you took your time on that one.' " Rose had shot a solid 70 on Thursday and followed with a 67, putting him within shouting distance of the leaders. (Duplantis also acquitted himself nicely on Friday, though at one point Rose's playing partner David Toms complained that the rookie caddie was standing too close to the hole while tending the flag. This led Rose to make a big deal of demonstrating the proper technique, much to Duplantis's mortification.) For Saturday's round Rose was paired with three-time U.S. Open champion Hale Irwin, who was still swaggering from his win a couple months earlier at the Heritage Classic on Hilton Head Island, the twentieth victory of his illustrious career. Prior to the round Rose gave Duplantis his version of a pep talk: "I don't want no star-gazing out there, rook," he said. "You do your job and Hale Irwin will do his."

Both Rose and Irwin brought their A-game that day, and as the round wore on Duplantis sensed a little competition building between them. At the University of Colorado Irwin was the rarest of two-sport stars—the 1967 NCAA golf champion and twice an all-conference defensive back during the glory years of Big Eight football. He is famously competitive and aloof on the golf course; in an anonymous poll of the players some years back he was named, along with Nick Faldo, the Tour's least favorite playing partner. Irwin did not deign to give Duplantis even the courtesy of eye contact throughout the round, but Duplantis, and Rose, got the last laugh. With a strong finish Rose posted a 67 to Irwin's 68. Tied for eighth place, Rose was only four strokes back of the leaders. Alas, after such a long layoff Rose's game couldn't withstand the final round pressure, and he shot a 76 to fade to thirty-ninth place, good for $4,290. Duplantis's 5 percent cut was worth $214.50 (the standard agreement throughout all levels of golf is that caddies get 5 percent of their man's check, which increases to 7 percent for Top 10 finishes and 10 percent for victories). On top of that Duplantis got his usual weekly salary of $300 (a number that is subject to negotiation between every player and caddie). As a bit of a bonus Rose rounded the two numbers up to $600. "It was the most money I had ever seen," says Duplantis.

The rest of the summer wasn't quite so heady, but it went well indeed. "Steve was a quick learner because I was a bad teacher," says Rose. "I explained it was pretty simple—get to the ball first, have the yardage ready, and don't speak until spoken to." Dehumanizing, perhaps, but Duplantis had never felt more alive. "It was a blast, just an incredible time," he says. "I loved the travel, I loved seeing the world, and I loved being around golf at that level."

In August Rose called it a season, discouraged by his desultory play and anxious to get home to his family. Duplantis, too, should have been on his way to North Carolina and High Point University, but by then he had the fever. Duplantis was so caught up in caddying he granted himself a little sabbatical from the university, withdrawing with the promise that his spot on the golf team, and his half scholarship, would be waiting.

The Nike Tour season stretched into November, and he caddied in nearly a dozen more tournaments. Duplantis would simply show up at the host course and bird-dog players in the parking lot to see who needed a looper, a process he likens to turning tricks. At the Nike Cleveland Classic that summer, Duplantis hooked up with a twenty-three-year-old kid with a rapidly receding hairline and a swing funkier than Isaac Hayes. He and Jim Furyk hit it off that week, even though they missed the cut. Duplantis and Furyk wouldn't work together again that season, but they remained friendly.

It was during his time on the Nike Tour that Duplantis's future in golf began to crystallize. "I think Steve finally recognized that those guys were playing at another level, a level he would never reach," says Stephen Duplantis. "Desire will take you so far, but so many of those guys just have so much natural talent. Clarence used to say, 'If you gotta try hard just to hang around Triple-A, you're not ready for the big leagues!' He was talking about himself, but I think that sunk in with Steve in regards to his own playing career."

At the end of the 1993 season Steve's family informed him that money was a little tight and they wouldn't be able to help him pay for his half of the room and board of High Point U. With the dream of a playing career fading fast, Duplantis returned to Brampton and spent January through early May taking special prerequisite courses necessary for Canadian universities. Rudderless without golf in his life, this seemed like the thing to do. In late May of 1994, just as classes were finishing up, the Nike Tour swung through the northern Midwest, and Duplantis couldn't resist driving down to try to pick up a couple of jobs. It was there that he bumped into Bobby Cole, a friend of Rose's who happened to need a caddie for the PGA Tour's upcoming Anheuser-Busch Golf Classic.

Cole has long been married to Laura Baugh, once a player of great promise on the LPGA tour. In her 1999 autobiography Baugh went public with a series of startling tales about how she almost drank herself to death. At the 1994 Anheuser-Busch Classic Cole mysteriously withdrew late Wednesday night, saying nothing to Duplantis, though it's reasonable to assume now that he had to tend to his wife. Left in the lurch, Duplantis spent the morning of the first round in a familiar place—the player parking lot, trolling for a job. He was surprised to see Furyk casing the lot as well. Earlier that morning Furyk had been at the driving range warming up for his round. One of the perks of playing the Anheuser-Busch is that the players and caddies get free tickets to Busch Gardens, a sprawling amusement park. It seems that the caddie Furyk had hired for the week had been caught Thursday morning trying to scalp his complimentary tix, and was subsequently barred from the grounds.

"There were a lot of guys looking for bags that day," says Furyk. "I was young and didn't know many of the caddies, but Steve was a familiar face." Furyk hustled over and offered Duplantis the loop, which he gladly accepted.

"Let's go then," Furyk said. "We're on the tee in five minutes."

Furyk had come into that tournament in the throes of a grinding slump, having missed seven of his last eight cuts. Something clicked for him that week, and with a 66–69 weekend Furyk tied for tenth. "Steve was really into it," says Furyk. "He would get excited over the good shots, and he was leaning on every putt, trying to coax it in." Furyk's finish was worth $28,600, which was, to that point, the third biggest check of his rookie year. More significantly, the dough propelled him high enough up the money list to all but guarantee his playing privileges for the following season, always a big accomplishment for a rookie (players finishing among the top 125 money winners earn exemptions). Duplantis's cut for the week was just over $2,000, which at the time was "mind-boggling." There were even richer rewards. After coming off the course on Sunday, Furyk's dad, Mike, who handles many of his son's affairs, put his arm around Duplantis and said, "We were talking last night at dinner, and we want you to come work for Jim."

GROWING UP IN WEST CHESTER, Pennsylvania, Jim Furyk played quarterback, catcher, and point guard. He's one of those guys who wants the ball. As a senior he led the University of Arizona to the 1992 national championship, upending the prohibitive favorite, Arizona State, and its pretty boy leading man, Phil Mickelson. Straight out of college Furyk landed on the Nike Tour, and in his only season out there he won the Mississippi Gulf Coast Classic, which shot him to the PGA Tour. For all of Furyk's impressive credentials, his swing was the thing that set tongues wagging when he arrived on tour in 1994. The late Jim Murray, the Pulitzer Prize-winning columnist from the *Los Angeles Times,* wrote that he'd seen "more form from a guy fighting a swarm of bees." TV funnyman David Feherty described Furyk's swing as looking like "an octopus falling out of a tree," and said that Furyk appears to write "Merry Christmas on the backswing and Happy New Year on the follow through." In the pages of *Sports Illustrated* Gary Van Sickle wrote of Furyk having a flying right elbow that appears to be "doing the macarena."

While most players strive to take the club straight back, on the same line as their target, Furyk's backswing strays far to the outside, forcing him to move the clubhead in a circular motion at the top of his swing and drop the club way inside on his downswing. This unorthodox locomotion has become known far and wide simply as The Loop. It is so instantly recognizable that Furyk used to boast that he was one of only two professional golfers identifiable from across the golf course, along with the late, great Payne Stewart and his trademark plus-fours. Coaches at every level have tried to tinker with Furyk's mechanics but he has resisted heroically. Growing up in blue-collar eastern Pennsylvania has not only left him unpretentious and thrifty but also with a stubborn streak as wide as the Allegheny Mountains. Then again, Furyk has had good reason to be protective of his swing; he has always been a deadly straight ballstriker, making up for a lack of distance with consistency and precision. Keeping the ball in play is a sound game plan because that allows him to take advantage of a putting stroke that was recognized as one of the game's best the minute he set foot on tour. "People have always doubted me because of my swing," Furyk once said. "I don't mind that at all. I have always enjoyed proving them wrong."

THE NEGOTIATIONS didn't last long. When Furyk confirmed his father's offer, Duplantis said, "My intention is to make enough money this summer to allow me to go back to school."

"I need the whole year."

"If you can promise me that you'll keep me the whole year, barring some idiotic screwup, then I'll do it, because that will allow me to make enough money so I wouldn't ever have to worry again about school bills."

"Deal."

The rest of 1994 was a blur—new golf courses, strange towns, and then, at season's end, a near jackpot at the Las Vegas Invitational. The LVI is a ninety-hole birdie-a-thon, played on a trio of wide-open desert courses rendered defenseless to accommodate the amateurs that play alongside the pros during the first four rounds. In 1994 the LVI was the last official tournament on the schedule, and Furyk let it all hang out. He fired at every flag and attacked every par-5, putting together rounds of 67-64-69-66 to take a one-shot lead heading into the final round. Late Saturday night Furyk's parents and then-girlfriend flew into town, and Duplantis spent the better part of his evening calling home to remind his family to set their VCRs.

"The excitement was unbelievable," says Duplantis. "Jim and I went to dinner, just the two of us, and though we were trying not to think ahead to the final round too much we couldn't help it. Every now and then we would be like, 'Can you believe we're gonna be on TV tomorrow?' It was a weird feeling to know that our friends and family all over the world were going to see us."

Sunday morning Duplantis was so nervous, "I was just trying not to step on any rakes or fall in any bunkers," he says. "Jim was definitely steering the ship that day." Though Furyk was in control of his emotions he never got in a groove with his putter.

The fifteen-footers that had been diving into the hole like gophers earlier in the week simply wouldn't fall. He wound up shooting a two-under par-70, ordinarily a respectable round, but in this track meet it was like stopping to tie a shoelace. The players who went on to finish 1-2-3 in the tournament—Bruce Lietzke, Robert Gamez, and Phil Mickelson, in that order—blistered the TPC at Summerlin with scores of 65, 64, 63, respectively. Furyk played in the final group with Lietzke, a wily old vet, and says Duplantis, "We got to see somebody win a tournament, and that was a huge learning experience for both of us. We never forgot it."

Furyk wound up tying for fifth, earning the biggest check of his rookie season, $54,750. That scooted him all the way to seventy-eighth on the season-ending money list, and further convinced Duplantis that university life could wait.

It was a no-brainer, really. Once Duplantis saw Furyk's myriad skills and cerebral course management, his single-minded dedication and puritanical work ethic, he knew he would be crazy to give up the job. Duplantis also recognized that he enjoyed a rare chemistry with Furyk. "The single most important part of caddying is relating to your player," he says. "That means everything. The yardage guides have gotten so good everyone's got the same numbers. Most players read their own putts. What caddying boils down to is knowing what to say and when to say it. You also spend more time together than with your wife, so you better get along." Such a personal relationship can lead to outsized showings of appreciation. Nick Faldo once gave his caddie Fanny Sunesson a new Jeep Wagoneer as a token of his esteem, and, back in the days when the purses were significantly smaller, Steve Elkington promised his bagman, Dave Renwick, a $100,000 thank you if Renwick could shepherd him to a major championship. After winning the 1995 PGA Championship, Elkington kept his word.

Though not yet in a position to do anything that lavish, Furyk always requested a hotel room with two beds and let Duplantis crash with him, free of charge. Furyk also picked up the check for some of their many meals together. A couple weeks before the 1994 season ended, during a triumphant homecoming at the Canadian Open, Duplantis got to play host when Furyk tagged along to Duplantis's grandparents' house for dinner one evening. Furyk, memorably, wore his Callaway cap at the table throughout the meal. "My dad still hasn't gotten over it," says Cantin, Duplantis's mom. "He thought it was the rudest thing, but he didn't say a word, because he didn't want to hurt Jim's feelings."

Duplantis had always pictured for himself a life in golf. If he couldn't play for a living, caddying was the next best thing. "Steve was so proud of what he called his new profession," says John Mitchell. "So proud. It wasn't hacking a bag around to him, just handing a guy a club. He saw it as a noble calling, that he was akin to a skilled craftsman. He really felt like he was part of a team with Jim, a good team. Once he got a taste of that partnership, none of us expected to see Steve hanging around Canada for a while."

THE 1995 SEASON started off with great promise for Furyk and Duplantis. At the second tournament of the year, in Tucson, they finished a strong fifth, and a month later, at the L.A. Open, a third-round 65 on venerable Riviera Country Club led to a tie for ninth. In all, Furyk made his first seven cuts of the season, a terrific start toward his goal of playing more consistently after having missed fourteen cuts in thirty-one tournaments as a rookie. After a little lull in March—when he failed to reach the weekend in his only two tournaments—Furyk rode into Fort Worth, Texas, for the Colonial National Invitational on another hot streak, having made five of his last six cuts. The Colonial is one of the more prestigious tournaments in golf, played on what Fort Worth native Dan Jenkins calls the "best track in Texas, a golfing state." Another Fort Worth local, Ben Hogan, was the man who put the tournament on the map, winning it the first two times it was played, in 1946 and '47 and then on three other occasions, including 1959, at age forty-six, the sixty-fourth and final victory of his legendary career. A seven-foot bronze statue of Hogan looks down upon the golf course, like a stern grandfather waiting to pass judgment on those who would trespass across his legend.

The Colonial, played in late May, was the exact midpoint of Duplantis's season, and so far it had been like a dream come true, only more so. Already he had visited such glamorous locales as Hawaii, Pebble Beach, Los Angeles, and New Orleans. Just as significantly, Duplantis was earning the respect of his peers. He had picked up the affectionate nickname "Kid," but more and more he was being treated as an equal. "There are a lot of random guys who come and go on tour," says Duplantis. "When you first start out the established caddies don't give you the time of day. You gotta pay your dues, prove you're not just another guy who's gonna disappear after a month." Furyk's fine play also helped boost Duplantis's standing. "As a caddie, you're only as good as your player," he says. "That's the perception, anyway."

There were some practical benefits to this acceptance. "One of the ways the veterans make you eat shit when you start out is by never helping you on the course," Duplantis says. "They won't ever pitch in and rake your bunker, or clean your player's ball, even if they're standing right there and you're one hundred yards away. As you get to know the guys, and they get to know you, they'll help you out in little ways like that." Rule 8-1 prohibits players from asking "advice" of each other, defined as "any counsel or suggestion which could influence a player in determining his play, the choice of a club, or the method of making a stroke." The behavior of caddies is a gray area, and among friends loopers will "tip the bag" toward each other, allowing a caddie to ascertain what club the other players are hitting. Occasionally, from across a fairway, fingers will be flashed. Such information can be crucial in club selection, and being privy to it was an advantage Duplantis was increasingly enjoying.

Off the course he was also beginning to find a niche in the hard-living caddie culture. Owing to Furyk's success, Duplantis had plenty of money in his pocket, and he had found more than a few buddies to waste it with. On the Tuesday night of Colonial week Duplantis and a couple of other caddies went in search of some burlesque-style entertainment. What Duplantis found would change the course of his life forever.

Her name was Vicki Gristina. She was, as Duplantis delicately puts it, "a titty dancer." That night they flirted for a while, no big deal, and then during Thursday's first round Duplantis spotted Vicki in the gallery. She was, after all, hard to miss. Following the round, Duplantis happened to bump into Vicki and kibitzed with her and one of her friends, and the three of them made plans to go out that evening. "Vicki was trying to fix me up with her friend, but it wasn't her friend I liked," says Duplantis.

He and Vicki had an intoxicatingly good time that night, and in the wee hours they rented a hotel room. As usual, Duplantis and Furyk were sharing a room that week. On this night, Duplantis needed his privacy.

"What you need to emphasize is that up until then I was as pure as the driven snow," says Duplantis. "I had never really had a girlfriend before Vicki. I was extremely, extremely innocent."

The next morning Duplantis awoke with a start, eyes immediately settling on the clock in the room. It read precisely 8:04. That wiped the perma-grin right off his face, as Furyk's second-round tee time was scheduled for 8:17. The Colonial is one of the few events on tour where the majority of the housing is within walking distance of the golf course. Duplantis was lucky to have shacked up in a hotel not far from the first tee. He bolted the room in a frenzy and made it to the front of the clubhouse just as Furyk was being announced to the crowd by the starter. Furyk, out of desperation, had already pulled some lucky schmo out of the crowd to carry his bag for the day. With Ben Hogan's likeness looking on, Duplantis wormed his way to the tee and snatched the bag away—not that he looked much different from the paying riffraff. Duplantis was wearing leather dress shoes and a long-sleeve polo shirt, which happened to be on inside out. His hair was at roughly Don King altitude, despite his best efforts to comb it with his hands in the reflection of the bronze plaques that frame the first tee. In perhaps the most egregious breach of conduct, his yardage guide was nowhere to be found.

Furyk never said a word.

Duplantis spent the better part of the front nine pawing through the bag, desperate to hide his mop top under a visor that he remembered stuffing deep into one of the pockets the week before. Finally, on the 6th hole, Furyk said, "I took the visor out of the bag on Tuesday." That was the sum total of their conversation for the round. That Furyk shot a 70 is testament to his laser focus, but he still wound up missing the cut. After the round apologies were made, and accepted. It was an aberration, the kind of mistake that would never happen again, an epic, once-in-a-lifetime blunder.

Duplantis's contrition lasted all of two days.

The week after Colonial brought the Memorial Invitational, and Furyk was being allowed past the velvet rope for the first time. The Memorial is played in Dublin, Ohio, at Muirfield Village Golf Club, one of the best tracks the tour visits. Throw in Nicklaus as host and master of ceremonies, and it is not a tournament to be taken lightly. Ever fastidious, Furyk was quick to line up a practice round for Monday morning, at nine o'clock. Following Friday's round at the Colonial, Furyk's parting words to Duplantis were, "Don't be late." So, of course, Duplantis missed his flight Sunday evening, which conveniently allowed for another night with Vicki.

Duplantis arrived in Columbus the next afternoon and tracked down Furyk on Muirfield Village's 16th hole. This time he got two sentences: "Dude, you're fucking up big time, and it's got to stop. Now go back to the room and get some sleep." The rest of the week went off without a hitch, though Furyk finished a distant fifty-third. This was followed by a missed cut the next week at the Kemper Open. Vicki had come to suburban Maryland for that tournament, and Friday night she and Duplantis jetted to Key West, Florida, for a romantic weekend away.

Did we mention that was where they got married? Under a coconut tree? In their swimsuits? By a notary? They had known each other all of nineteen days.

To be sure, there was a certain amount of love and passion in the air . . .

"It was mostly passion," Duplantis says. "Gawd, those big fake titties . . ."

The morning after the wedding Duplantis's family back in Canada awoke to the sound of a ringing phone.

"That was the worst," he says. " 'Hey Mom, how you doing? Guess what, I just got married . . .'

" 'Hey Dad, how you doing? Guess what, I just got married . . .'

" 'Hey, Grandma . . .' "

This all created a certain amount of head-scratching up in the Great White North.

"I remember that phone call very clearly," says Sandy Cantin. "I said, 'You got married!? To who!?'

" 'To Vicki.'

" 'Who's Vicki?'

"We hung up," says Cantin, "and I was just lying there in bed thinking, Did that really happen, or was it a dream?"

"The whole thing was just a reminder that Steve's always been a free spirit," says Stephen Duplantis. "I guess that's a nice way of putting it."

On the way back from Key West, Duplantis dropped by Goldsboro, North Carolina, to show his new bride off to Rose.

"I sat them down and started right in with the questions," says Rose. " 'Vicki, do you love Steve?'

" 'No.'

" 'Steve, do you love Vicki?'

" 'No.'

"I said, 'This is the stupidest damn thing I've ever heard,' " Rose continues. "I told Steve they should get it annulled the very next day, but oh no, he had to do it the hard way. Call me old-fashioned, but I believe you should love each other when you get married. He said they would learn to love each other. What a crock that was!"

As to why Steve and Vicki would rush into such a quickie marriage, there are competing theories. Rich Beem, who knows of these things, says, "You don't get to pick who you're going to love in this life." Shannon Pennington, the woman to whom Duplantis would later propose while still married to Vicki, is more dubious. "They used each other," says Pennington. "She saw a great big dollar sign over Steve's head, and he saw a green card over hers." Duplantis, as a Canadian citizen, faced certain work-related issues once he decided to stay on with Furyk. Marrying Vicki may have seemed like a simple solution, but things quickly turned complicated. Six weeks after the wedding Duplantis, twenty-two years old at the time, had another round of phone calls to make. Vicki was pregnant.

"Un-fucking-believable," he says.

CHAPTER

• 3 •

THE EL PASO COUNTRY CLUB was inaugurated on June 1, 1906, some three months before the city's first paved road appeared. In 1921 the club relocated to El Paso's Upper Valley, where it remains today, a stately presence surrounded by the sprawl and mall of an expanding city. To understand the club's current culture you must first know some of its history: In 1929 stables for fifty horses were built on club grounds, so members could park their horses while they played; throughout the 1930s, '40s and '50s "bathing beauty revues" were a staple of the social calendar, as El Paso's young lovelies would put on shows for the enjoyment of the membership; finally, with the club deeply in debt due in part to the Great Depression, slot machines were installed in the clubhouse in 1937, even though their legality was in question. The one-armed bandits were such a hit that within a year the club had paid off its mortgage, and the slot machines endured until 1951, when they were removed in a surprise raid by the local police.

The stables are long gone now, but it still feels very much like Texas around El Paso Country Club. "The emphasis is on country here," says Bill Eschenbrenner, the head pro emeritus, who has been part of the EPCC firmament since 1961. "Just a bunch of good country folks, nobody trying to outdo anybody else." The bathing beauties are but a fond memory, but the membership still has, by all accounts, an active interest in the town's young women. "At El Paso Country Club everyone has a girlfriend, or three or four," says Larry Beem. "Even the married guys. It's like some kind of game of oneupsmanship, to see who can coax whom into bed. Those guys need to grow up." And in lieu of the slot machines, the gambling action has been moved onto the course. Everybody plays for money at El Paso Country Club.

There are two institutions around EPCC (three if you count Eschenbrenner): the Wednesday game and the Friday game. On those afternoons all comers (usually six or seven foursomes) tee it up in sprawling, boozy pseudotournaments, during which heavy betting is mandatory and woofing encouraged. The Wednesday game is a little more loosey-goosey, often set to the soundtrack of country music, as a couple of the regulars are known to throw boom boxes in the back of their carts for added ambience. On Fridays the greenskeepers are instructed to set tougher pins and move the tees to the back of the box. It is a day for bloodletting. All the best players in the area show up for the Friday game. PGA Tour veteran J. P. Hayes, a resident of El Paso, plays whenever he's in town. Another local boy, Rick Todd, a two-time winner on the Buy.com Tour who topped the Asian Tour's Order of Merit in 1996, is also a regular. Cameron Doan, the EPCC head pro who was on the same powerhouse University of Texas-El Paso teams as Paul Stankowski, never misses a Friday. Kristi Albers, a winner on the LPGA Tour, often plays as well, from the men's tees. "If somebody thinks they're ready for the Tour, tell 'em to come out and play the Friday game," says Eschenbrenner. "They'll find out real quick how good they are."

The professionals from the pro shop are not encouraged to play in the Wednesday and Friday games, they are required. At many clubs the staff of teaching pros are considered little more than hired help, shopkeepers whose primary role is to make sure the sweaters are neatly folded. Around El Paso Country Club the pros are expected to be players. Doan, the head pro throughout much of the '90s, hired his assistants based in large part on the strength of their game and their ability to mix with the members. It was this milieu that awaited Beem when he arrived in El Paso in October of 1996, and he dove in headfirst. Seattle had been an unhappy experience, and not just because of the way things ended with Tanya. Beem had few friends there besides David Wyatt and Corey Thie, and this was hardly enough to sustain him. He is a social animal. "Rich began to display his overt need for companionship by sleepwalking as a kid," says Larry Beem. "He still can't stand to be alone. You want to kill Richard, just lock him in a room, alone, with no phone. He'll be dead by the morning. The coroner's report will say he died from a lack of social interaction."

When he arrived at El Paso Country Club Beem suddenly had dozens of new best friends, because the Wednesday and Friday games all revolve around a team betting game, the two-man quota (though it is routine to have numerous side bets between individuals, involving skins games, Nassaus, and low gross). Not that it was all fun and games—the Wednesday and Friday action was potentially an important subsidy for Beem, what with a starting salary of a meager $15,000. Playing poorly, however, could be costly. EPCC is a players club—of the 425 gents on the handicap list over a hundred are single digits and forty-five of them are 5s or less. The pros, even the new guys, are nonetheless obliged to give away enough strokes that, says Doan, "If you're playing out of the shop and you shoot only sixty-nine you're toast."

In this environment of camaraderie and competition Beem's game, and his desire to play, flourished. "I played every chance I got," he says. "Part of it was because I just wanted to get the hell out of the golf shop. Part of it was because I was having more fun on the course than I'd ever had before." Within a few months of arriving in El Paso Beem was playing some serious golf. "I remember the day it all started," says Doan. "It was in March of '97. We played thirty-six at a place called Painted Dunes, a pretty strong track here in El Paso, and Rich dropped a sixty-five–sixty-four on me and the boys. After that his confidence was incredible. He began looking for his own games."

Beem didn't have to look very hard. The golfing community in the El Paso–Las Cruces area is as insular as high school, and when word got out that Beem was the man to beat, the pigeons began flocking to EPCC.

"There was this guy who we all knew locally who liked to shoot his mouth off about what a great player he was," says Greg Johns, one of the alpha males among the EPCC membership, with whom Beem would become close friends. "For weeks he was after Rich, and finally he basically embarrassed Rich into a game, by questioning what you might call his manhood in front of some other people. Well, Rich overloaded the boat a bit, agreeing to a minimum of one hundred dollars a hole, which was money he didn't have at the time. He came to me and asked if I would be willing to help him out, just in case something happens. So I wrote him a check for one thousand eight hundred dollars on the spot and said, 'Hell, go have a good time and play your game.' The next day I see Rich and he gave me back my check and then peeled off twelve hundred-dollar bills and said, 'Here's half my winnings, which you deserve for backing me.' I told him to put the money away—knowing that he kicked this guy's ass was reward enough."

Beem's chutzpah occasionally proved expensive. During a lazy summer day in 1997 Beem, Doan, and three members found themselves locked in a mortal struggle at the El Paso Country Club. They were playing a betting game called wolf, which happens to work best with five players. There are numerous permutations of the game, but on this day Beem and the boys were playing with fairly standard rules: Each player got three holes where he was designated as the wolf. After all the drives had been struck on each hole the wolf was allowed to choose who he wanted as a partner for that hole, and they would take on the other three players, team best ball. (It takes an army of Big Six accountants to keep track of all the bets.) Generally, after fifteen holes the player who is shaping up as the big loser gets to be the wolf over the final three holes. Beem was getting spanked on this particular day, so he was the wolf to close out the round. On the 16th tee, before any drives had been struck, he announced, "I'm wolfing it." That meant he was playing on his own, one against four, a situation where a player can make up a lot of money in a hurry or lose even more. On the sixteenth hole Beem made par while someone in the foursome produced a birdie, a costly loss. Beem stalked to the 17th tee and again announced that he was wolfing it. The 17th was halved with birdies. "We get to eighteen," says Doan, "and we all know what's coming." Sure enough, Beem wolfed it again. Doan made birdie at the last, while Beem narrowly missed his own birdie putt. "Beemer gets killed in the bets," says Doan. "He loses five, six hundred dollars, easy, which you gotta remember is his entire paycheck back then." At first glance Beem's behavior would seem reckless or foolhardy or both, but Doan sees it another way. "Oh, I think it's a great story," he says. "It shows he thought he could get it done. That belief is by far the most important thing when it comes time for the nut-cutting."

It is this bulletproof self-confidence that tends to separate the men from the boys in golf, and Rich developed his while growing up and competing against his father. On the occasions when Larry could talk Rich into teeing it up with him it was less a golf match than a Freudian drama.

"Oh, I was just terrible to him," says Larry. "My favorite line was, 'You can't even beat an old man, you no-playing puke.' I abused him on purpose, because if he could learn to handle my mind games, then he would be ready for anything else that happened to him on a golf course."

"My dad was always so much better than me, and he just beat me like a drum," says Rich. "Losing like that gives you a determination you can't get anywhere else. When I finally started beating my dad in college it was a big deal. Once I broke through and beat him a few times I almost never lost after that, just because I finally believed I could do it. After a while my dad basically stopped playing with me. It stopped being fun for him."

Still, for all that ferocious competition, Larry says, "It was the gambling games he had to go through at El Paso CC that really made Rich into a player. That first Friday he had to put down a couple hundred dollars he didn't have, and that scared the hell out of him. The only thing he was missing as a player was the toughness, and you get that when you're playing for your rent money. I know from experience."

LARRY BEEM GRADUATED from Venice (California) high school in 1954 and was drafted into the army in 1958. In between, he says, "There was a lot of stuff I'm not very proud of." Beem was a hustler back then, committing so many robberies that his putter may as well have been a switchblade. Beem and a couple accomplices used to enjoy what he calls "making sandwiches." The three of them would go to a golf course, acting as if they didn't know one another, and pick up an unsuspecting fourth. They would then talk the dupe into a betting game of two-on-two, which was really three against one. "We were the meat, and whatever poor sucker we found provided the bread," says Beem.

That was small-time stuff, though. Beem routinely played in big-money games arranged by third parties. How big were the stakes? "Oh, three or four thousand dollars," he says with an air of studied nonchalance. Of course, the money wasn't his exactly. "We hung out with professional gamblers—every club had 'em. You didn't have to worry about finding them, they found you." One of Beem's favorite haunts was the Western Avenue Golf Course in Gardena. "It was known as a haven for the black criminal element in L.A.," says Beem. "Racketeers, numbers guys, pimps, thieves—it was one-stop shopping. The best black players hung out there, too, guys like Bill Spiller and Charlie Sifford. It was a great scene, and I was the token harmless white kid. So I go out there one day, and like all the guys looking for a game I wore my worst clothes, got out a bag with a big rip in the side, certainly didn't clean my clubs. There was one guy at the course famous around L.A., known only as Mad Dog, at least to me. I was pretty friendly with Mad Dog, so I asked him if anybody was looking for a game. He pointed to this guy on the putting green, and said, 'He'll give you one.' 'What's he do?' I asked. 'He's a thief,' Mad Dog says. 'You tell him what you want and he'll steal it for you.' 'Oh, that's nice,' I say. Mad Dog says, 'He'll bet you whatever you want. I'll cover your game and you can keep ten percent of what we win.' I said fine. Mad Dog told me to say I was an eight handicap. He knew that's what this other guy would claim to be.

"So we decided to bet a great big dollar on the front nine. Both of us played that nine trying to hit it as bad as we possibly could. We get to number ten he says, 'You're no eight handicap.' I say, 'Neither are you.' He says, 'I tell you what, I'll play you even on the back nine for one hundred dollars. I'll play you with one stroke for another one hundred dollars, two strokes for another one hundred dollars, three strokes for another one hundred dollars, and four strokes for another one hundred dollars.' I say, 'You're on.' So he starts the back nine birdie-birdie-birdie"—here Beem pauses dramatically—"and loses all five bets and two presses. I shot a twenty-eight and beat him seven ways. We finish on the eighteenth green and Mad Dog is there waiting for us. Of course he wants to know how we did. Before I can answer, this guy walks over with a fistful of hundred-dollar bills. He says, 'You know what I do for a living, don't you, Dawg? If this kid ever needs a job you send him to me, because he's the biggest thief I ever seen.' "

Beem's golf swing was homemade, held together by paper clips, duct tape, and an unbendable belief in himself. He had learned to play before the glossy centerfolds in *Golf Digest* began displaying the golf swing in almost pornographic detail, before swing instructors became multinational corporations, and in the days when Hogan, the greatest ball-striker who ever lived, sat astride his throne. The secret, Hogan used to grumble, is in the dirt—you gotta dig it out. What he meant was that golf swings were built not through esoteric philosophizing but through playing and practicing, experimentation and repetition. Beem learned the nuances of the game as a boy by caddying at swank Fox Hills Country Club in Culver City, and until the age of twenty he moonlighted at a separate driving range, just so he could hit an endless number of balls for free. Beem discovered the secrets of golf on his own, and along the way he became a true believer. When he talks about the game he sounds more like a mystic or a shaman than an accredited PGA of America instructor.

"Golf to me is an art form," he says. "It's a cross between Baryshnikov and Salvador Dali. It takes the discipline, the strength, the grace, the beauty of the finest ballet, but also demands the eye and the imagination of the surrealist painter. I see the golf course in curves, not straight lines, in color, not black and white. The course is a canvas, best maintained by an artist, not an agronomist. You play golf through your eyes, you have to interpret with your senses. The only way to play is with your heart, and not your damn brain.

Having become New Mexico State's golf coach in 1998, Larry has had the chance to observe a number of players with diverging approaches to the game. "The problem with these kids today is that they're too computer literate. They think they can just put the information in and an acceptable answer will be spit out. There's so much analysis now. Kids ask me what's wrong with their games, I don't talk about the angle of their downswing or the pronation of their wrist. I tell them, 'You got no fucking imagination, that's what's wrong.' They think their swings have to meet some imaginary industry standard. They don't understand this isn't a game of swings. It's a game of shots." This was the gospel Beem preached to his son whenever he could bend his ear, and it forever shaped the way Rich would play golf.

Rich remembers an afternoon around the course in Berlin, when he wanted to learn how to play a soft pitch shot. He asked Larry for his counsel, and class was convened behind a sizeable hedge adjacent to the practice putting green. Rich had to hit over the hedge but stop his ball on the green.

"I asked him how to play the shot," remembers Rich.

" 'Keep your hands soft,' said Larry.

" 'How do you do that?'

" 'You just feel it.'

" 'How do you do that?'

" 'You just feel it.' "

Larry showed his son where to play the ball in his stance, how far he should open the face of his wedge, and then he said no more. "He'd always watch me and let me figure it out on my own," says Rich. "Later he might explain the mechanics to me, but I had to figure out how to hit the shot on my own. The only way I would know if I was doing it right was when he'd grunt and mumble, 'Not bad, kid.' "

EL PASO COUNTRY CLUB was the perfect canvas for Rich to perfect his art. Baked by the sun, parched by the west Texas winds, EPCC plays hard and fast, closer in character to the ancestral homeland of golf, the Scottish linksland, than the lush, immaculately manicured courses common to this country. At 6,781 yards from the tips it is a relatively short par 71, flat (as is virtually every course in Texas), but with devilishly undulating greens and plenty of sand. The layout is stern enough to have hosted the Savane College All-American Golf Classic since 1974, a tournament with a past champions list that reads like a Who's Who of the last quarter century of collegiate golf: Jerry Pate ('74); Scott

Simpson ('76); Davis Love ('84); David Duval ('91); and Tiger Woods ('95). Still, El Paso Country Club is a course where birdies can be had in bunches, if you play aggressively enough.

Just as valuable as the hundreds of rounds Beem played at EPCC was the time he spent on the driving range, the province of Doan and Eschenbrenner. Doan, though still in his twenties, was quickly establishing a reputation as a premier teacher, relying heavily on videotape and the latest theories. Doan, however, recognized Beem was different and treated him accordingly. "The way he grew up with his dad, he plays so much by feel," says Doan. "You take a guy like Rich and try to get too mechanical, you're gonna ruin him." Nevertheless, Doan was forever harping on the basics that sometimes betrayed Beem—lining up square, keeping his ball position correct, and staying on balance (Beem had, and has, a tendency to put too much weight on his left side at the address position, which gets him ahead of the ball and leads to his trouble shot, a block to the right, or, if he overcompensates with his hands at the last moment, a crash hook). "I've never known anything about the golf swing," says Beem. "It's like, okay, that went too far to the right. So now I have to try to hit it to the left. I would know if it didn't feel good, but I couldn't tell you why. Cameron opened my eyes to some things. I've basically had the same swing since college, I've just learned how to manage it a little bit better." With Doan's help Beem began to supersize his game. To compensate for his relatively small stature, Beem lengthened his swing arc, and, in concert with a powerful shoulder turn, he began killing the ball off the tee. This unlocked the rest of his game, which has always been built around a flammable putter.

While Doan was fixated on swing mechanics, Eschenbrenner offered a different perspective. He was old school. He had grown up in that cradle of American golf, Fort Worth, and learned to play among the colorful characters who were immortalized in Dan Jenkins's classic *SI* piece "The Glory Game at Goat Hills." Esch, too, had been captivated by the Hogan mystique. As a teenager he worked at Rivercrest Country Club, a favorite haunt of Hogan's, and Hogan, even with his Garbo-like reclusiveness, took a liking to the young pro. Eschenbrenner was one of the few people Hogan allowed to watch when he hit balls at the range, an honor akin to being able to observe Michelangelo mix paint. Eschenbrenner saw in Beem a rare sort of free-wheeling genius, but he had an almost Calvinistic belief in the virtues of hard work. He hectored Beem constantly with stories about Hogan's practice ethic, little parables about the sacrifice and the dedication it took to be a champion, and these, too, began sinking in.

As 1997 bled into '98, Beem's golf game had gone to another level. It was something else that was holding him back.

CHAPTER

• 4 •

A MONTH AFTER WAKING to the news of her son's marriage, Sandy Cantin went south to meet Steve and Vicki. They were to rendezvous in Williamsburg, Virginia, at the Anheuser-Busch Golf Classic, where, a year earlier, Duplantis had had his fateful encounter with Furyk in the parking lot. Much had changed in Duplantis's life since.

"All Steve told me about Vicki was that she was very pretty and she was from Texas," says Cantin. "I expected her to have lots of blonde hair and be bubbly like a cheerleader. She didn't quite turn out to be that way."

Though she had been adopted by a family in Fort Worth as a baby, Vicki was born in the Philippines, and had dark hair and eyes and skin the color of peanut butter. She was extremely shy, at least around her mother-in-law.

At the family's first meal together Duplantis was oddly insistent about Vicki having a glass of milk, though she clearly didn't want one. Finally he begged her to at least have some *chocolate* milk. Duplantis had planned to tell his mother about the pregnancy that night at dinner, but Sandy figured it out on her own. "I just thought, Holy cow," she says. "I knew that would make the marriage more challenging. Steve loved what he was doing so much, and I knew he was never gonna give it up, even if that meant not being at home. I just thought, Whoa, something's got to give."

That turned out to be domestic tranquility. The road was an isolating place for Vicki. While virtually all the players have their wives or girlfriends traveling with them, these women were not viable options for companionship because the lady of a lord does not deign to mix with that of a serf. Few, if any, of the other caddies brought their significant others on the road. The added expense was a factor, as was the prevailing culture—having the ball and chain along would only get in the way of all the carousing. The stereotype of the besotted caddie is as old as golf itself, and like most stereotypes, it is grounded partly in the truth. A defining moment for the profession came late one night at the Players Championship, in the mid-'90s, when two caddies were arrested in separate incidents, one for solicitation, the other for cocaine possession. "If the question is, Are there still plenty of caddies who do drugs and act like idiots, then the answer is, Yes," says Duplantis. "But it's not like it was. The money is getting too big, the job too respectable. Every year more and more of the screwoffs get weeded out." No pun intended.

With her husband often held hostage by Furyk's marathon practice sessions, Vicki quickly grew restless with the vagabond life that comes with following the Tour. From the outside it may seem glamorous and fun, and occasionally, when the Tour caravans through a place like Pebble Beach, it is. But most weeks it is a numbing life of cheap hotel rooms, lowbrow chain restaurants, and soul-sucking suburban settings, each indistinguishable from the next. In 1995, Duplantis's first full season with Furyk, he was still traveling predominantly by car, like a lot of caddies. (Duplantis was still rolling his battle wagon, the sky blue Cavalier.) In August, with Vicki already beginning to show her pregnancy, she and her hubby drove from the Buick Open in Flint, Michigan, all the way to Los Angeles for the PGA Championship at the Riviera Country Club. They left Sunday evening and arrived just in time for Furyk's practice round Tuesday morning, despite frequent stops necessitated by a urinary tract infection Vicki was suffering through.

The long drives were only one of the indignities that came with the job. "There aren't too many professions where you can make the money caddies do and still be treated like a second-class citizen," Duplantis says. At tournament sites the caddies are usually given what Duplantis calls "shit parking," and they are never allowed to enter the clubhouse, as if they are somehow subhuman. Maybe a dozen tournaments provide the caddies with food, on the order of sandwiches and potato chips. At these Tour stops, "It never fails, there are always guys filling up plastic bags full of food," Duplantis says. The penny-pinching ways of caddies are legendary. "Having a hotel room to yourself is considered the ultimate luxury," says Duplantis. "If the rooms are expensive—and seventy-five dollars a night would be considered expensive—there are usually three guys crammed in there. Even if there are only two beds. Caddies aren't too proud to sleep on the floor." Who gets the floor? "Usually whoever's man shot the high round that day," says Duplantis.

Vicki never felt at home in these surroundings (is it any wonder?), and before long there was trouble in paradise. (It is a measure of how delusional both parties were heading into the marriage that Vicki saw suburban bliss in the caddie's gypsy lifestyle, while Steve was looking for domestic tranquility in a party girl who took off her clothes for a living.) "When I met Vicki she told me she wanted a white picket fence and two-point-five kids and a whole new life, and I believed her," says Duplantis. "But she was a wild person at heart, and she couldn't leave behind her old party life. She just gravitated to those kind of people, those kind of situations, and she couldn't let it go. All I wanted was for her to be a good wife, and so we fought like cats and dogs."

Reached at her parents' home in Fort Worth, Vicki says, "I don't care what Steve says about me because I know none of it's true." She declines to comment further.

The summer of 1995 brought other changes, and other challenges, as well. At Jack Nicklaus's Memorial, the week after Duplantis met Vicki, Furyk was signing autographs behind the 18th green when he noticed a fetching blonde hanging around the green trying to catch the players' eye, as so many fetching blondes seem to do at PGA Tour events. Furyk had just recently broken up with his girlfriend, so, despite his inherent shyness, he introduced himself. The woman, Tabitha Skartved, was a local elementary schoolteacher. With school out for the summer Skartved had plenty of time on her hands, and, after spending much of the week of the Memorial with

Furyk, she accepted his invitation to accompany him to the following week's Kemper Open. After missing the cut Furyk flew back to Columbus with Skartved to pursue the burgeoning romance. He wound up taking three weeks off. When Furyk returned to action, at the Western Open in early July, his head was obviously not in the ball game. He opened the Western with a shocking 82, and promptly withdrew, sparing himself further embarrassment. The next week, at the Anheuser-Busch, Furyk shot a first-round 79, followed by a 73, and was down the road. A week later he hung up an opening-round 80 at the Deposit Guaranty Classic, assuring he would miss another cut. By now Skartved was traveling with Furyk nearly every week, and the nature of the relationship between player and caddie changed dramatically.

In their first year together Furyk and Duplantis spent an almost unnatural amount of time together. "There is usually a distance between players and caddies," Duplantis says, "but Jim and I were both young, and we had a lot in common, and we enjoyed hanging out together. All of sudden, I'm married, he's dating Tabitha, and everything changed."

Furyk's struggles throughout the middle of the summer added a layer of strain to everyone's relations. It was a relief, then, when he began righting himself in August, including a solid thirteenth at the PGA Championship at the Riviera Country Club in L.A., only the second Grand Slam event he had competed in. Furyk continued to play well throughout the fall, and in October he returned to the Las Vegas Invitational, scene of his near-miss the year before.

Again Furyk got off to a torrid start, opening with a 67 and then following with a pair of 65s to go into the weekend with the lead. A flawless 67 on Saturday kept him in front. In contrast to the giddiness of the previous year, Furyk and Duplantis were calm and composed as the final round began. "The first time around we had been hoping to kinda sorta get lucky and maybe sneak away with a victory," says Duplantis. "This time we expected to win." A victory was especially important to Duplantis, because he had picked up a host of squatters at his hotel room, within the Maxim casino. The unofficial rule on tour is that the winning caddie pays the rent for the week, and as Furyk sat atop the leaderboard throughout the tournament, more and more displaced caddies found their way into Duplantis's care. By Sunday he had four roommates in his tiny room (Vicki had not made the trip). "These pricks weren't just sticking me with the room charges, they were running up the bill," he says. "Room service, long-distance phone calls, pay-per-view porn, you name it. I guarantee you I haven't stayed with any of those cocksuckers ever again."

Furyk got off to a solid start on Sunday and then, on the par-5 9th hole, he jarred a long pitch-and-run from a greenside bunker for an eagle that all but assured the victory. "It was pandemonium," says Duplantis. "We were high-fiving and hugging and screaming at the top of our lungs, not that we were even able to hear ourselves, because the crowd was so loud. Then we remembered where we were, and it was like, okay, I'm cool, I'm cool."

After the final putt dropped Duplantis cried for an hour. "I was just so happy," he says. "Yeah, the victory was a great paycheck, and it secured our future, but that wasn't it. I cried because it felt so good to have won." At the trophy presentation, where Furyk collected an oversized cardboard check for $270,000, Duplantis was overwhelmed by one thought: Holy shit, we're going to the Masters next year. Back then every tournament winner snagged a coveted invitation to golf's most glamorous tournament (the entry guidelines were modified following the '98 Masters).

After sharing a congratulatory beer with Furyk, Duplantis took a redeye home to Fort Worth, where he and Vicki were now living with her parents. "I would have loved to have stayed and partied," he says, "but I had to get home."

Three weeks later Duplantis and Furyk traveled to Maui for the Kapalua Invitational, where Furyk shot a carefree 21-under to blow away the star-studded field, collecting another $180,000. As Kapalua was an unsanctioned off-season event, the cash didn't count toward the official money list, but it spent the same. The week was memorable for other reasons. Vicki, despite being five months pregnant, came along for what was a belated honeymoon. The Duplantises luxuriated at the Ritz-Carlton and enjoyed one of their happiest times together. "Because Vicki was pregnant she couldn't have any alcohol," says Steve. "We probably fought less that week than any other time in our marriage."

Kapalua put an exclamation point on Furyk's sophomore year, and as the 1996 season began he showed no signs of cooling off. At the Hawaiian Open in February, Furyk survived gale-force winds and a series of shocking putts from Brad Faxon to prevail in a four-hole playoff. Furyk's style was already beginning to emerge: he played with a joyless efficiency and clinical precision that was numbing to watch and difficult to beat. Emotionless as a Buckingham Palace guard, and just about as stiff, he had a perfect demeanor to combat the hardships doled out by the game. In a little over three months Furyk had won a trio of tournaments and some three quarters of a million dollars, and, at the tender age of twenty-five, his reputation was soaring along with his tax bracket. After the victory in Hawaii, *Sports Illustrated* opined, "It's time to stop talking about Furyk's funny swing and start celebrating him as one of the best young players in golf."

"It was like, ho hum, another victory," says Duplantis. "Things were just coming so easy."

Two days after the Hawaiian Open, Sierra was born.

THE MASTERS, played every year since 1934 at the Augusta National Golf Club in Georgia, is one of the few things in life, let alone sports, that exceeds expectations. Everything about the tournament is done in an effort to preserve the memory and the legacy of the tournament's founder, Robert Tyre Jones—Bob to his friends, Bobby to an adoring public. Jones was many things, the winner of the Grand Slam in 1930 being only one of them. He was a gifted writer with a keen intellect, not to mention a law degree from Emory. As the archetype of the golfing gentleman, he abhorred the idea of golfers playing for money. Not only did he compete throughout his career as an amateur but, upon birthing the Masters, Jones set out to create a tournament that was a shrine to tradition and decorum, not capitalism. There has never been any advertising allowed on the grounds of Augusta National, no Japanese car companies as title sponsors, and since its initial television contract the tournament has allowed only four minutes of commercials per hour, instead of the sixteen that is standard today. A few years ago there was great hand-wringing among the tournament leadership as to whether the price of a sandwich should be raised from fifty cents to a dollar, a quaint debate these days considering Madison Square Garden extorts six dollars from its patrons for a lousy hot dog.

To make sure its traditions are kept alive, the Masters extends a lifetime invitation to each of its champions, which is why Arnold Palmer, now in his seventies, still patrols the hills of the National, proud merely to be a part of the proceedings. A past champions dinner was created in 1952, and every Tuesday of the tournament week three or four generations of golfing history gather to share a meal and a couple of toddies and tell the same old stories one more time.

The course itself is beyond compare. Working with Dr. Alistair MacKenzie, the legendary Scottish architect, Jones crafted a layout for the ages. Nevertheless, it is Augusta National's conditioning that tends to produce the most heavy breathing from first-timers, as the course is more heavily manicured than a Brentwood trophy wife. Paul Stankowski, a Masters rookie in 1996, still discusses sotto voce the little patch of clovers he found in one of the fairways—the offending flora had been circled with white paint and declared ground under repair. Duplantis had a similar epiphany during his first round at the National. Furyk, with the eagerness typical of Augusta virgins, had arrived the Friday afternoon before the tournament, to allow at least a full four practice rounds. During their first round on the hallowed grounds, Duplantis encountered a lone greenskeeper at the 10th hole, on his knees with a pair of kitchen scissors meticulously trimming the grass around the lip of one of the bunkers. "That sums up the Masters right there," he says.

On Wednesday of every Masters week there is the annual par-3 tournament, played on a short course behind the clubhouse that is every bit as beautiful as its big brother. Furyk happened to be in the group behind Palmer, and he reached the 8th green just as the King was striking his tee shot on the adjacent 9th hole. Palmer's ball hit the cup and nearly went in for an ace. "It was one of the loudest roars I've ever heard on a golf course," says Duplantis. "I got goose bumps, and this was just the frickin' par-three tournament."

Furyk was similarly overwhelmed by the experience of his first Masters, or so it seemed, because he opened the tournament with a jittery 75. He rallied with a second-round 70 to make the cut on the number, but a 78 on Saturday put him in the very first group to go out for the final round. Done by lunchtime (Furyk shot a 71 to move up to twenty-ninth), Duplantis stripped off his caddie gear and went out to watch the leaders play (1996 was the year Greg Norman spit the bit). "My whole life I would've cut off my right arm to have a pass to the Masters on Sunday," says Duplantis. "No way I was gonna waste the opportunity."

Two months later, at the U.S. Open at Oakland Hills, Duplantis found himself in the thick of the action. On Sunday Furyk birdied the 16th hole to pull within one stroke of the lead, part of a furious final-round charge. To get to the tee of the 17th hole, a sharply downhill par-3, required a long walk up a hillside, and, "I just floated all the way to the top," says Duplantis. "It was an amazing feeling, to be in contention at the U.S. Open. I still remember that feeling." Alas, Furyk's 4 wood to the 17th green trickled off the back of the putting surface and into a gnarly patch of rough. He gouged out a chip and then missed the par putt, ending his chances at victory. He went on to tie for fifth.

Three victories, a trip to the Masters, a near miss at the Open—things could scarcely have been going better for Duplantis. In August he got another thrill when his old friend Clarence Rose finally won the first tournament of his seemingly endless career, at the International. Rose eagled the 71st hole to force a playoff, and then, as he was standing over another eagle putt on the same hole in sudden death, a rainbow filled the skies above Denver's Castle Pines Golf Club. An omen if there ever was one,

Rose rammed in the putt for the victory. Duplantis called him that night for an emotional congratulations.

However thrilling all of this may have seemed, in reality Duplantis's life was beginning to crumble. Vicki was not inclined to go through the hassle of traveling with a baby. She preferred to stay behind, at the home the Duplantises had purchased in the spring of 1996, on a lake in a quiet golf course development in Plant City, Florida, outside Tampa. All the time spent apart only complicated an already volatile relationship.

"What did we fight about?" asks Steve. "Everything and anything."

By January of 1997 things had reached a crisis point. (Following the U.S. Open Furyk had played steady if unspectacular golf the rest of the way in '96, finishing twenty-sixth on the money list.) Duplantis was in Pebble Beach for the Crosby Clambake, and he was unable to reach Vicki on the phone. Hours turned into days, which turned into nearly a week without any contact. "I was getting hysterical," he says. "I was always telling Vicki that if she didn't dress in a more respectable manner she was gonna have some psycho follow her home from the mall someday and something bad was going to happen. I thought that's what had happened. I was expecting to come home to two dead bodies."

In fact, Vicki had gone to Fort Worth to stay with her parents, taking Sierra with her. Duplantis finally reached her there, and, with Furyk idle for a couple of weeks following Pebble, he flew to Texas straightaway. Steve and Vicki were able to patch things up and she returned to Florida, along with Sierra. Soon, however, Duplantis was back on the road. Early March brought the L.A. Open. "Sunday morning I'm strolling out of the Brentwood Motor Inn on my way to the course," says Duplantis, "and some sleazeball comes up to me and says, 'Are you Steve Duplantis?' I say yeah, and he throws a stack of wadded-up paper at me. Vicki had filed for divorce. It was like right out of a movie—a bad movie."

Vicki, according to court transcripts, had slapped a restraining order on her husband, which was granted in absentia in both Florida and Texas. "I had to get a lawyer in both states to get that thrown out," Steve Duplantis says. "I didn't get to see my daughter for three months. I finally said, 'Fuck this,' and filed for divorce."

Throughout all of this drama Furyk was in the middle of a torrid streak during which he would finish in the Top 10 in an incredible eight straight tournaments, including a fifth at the U.S. Open, a fourth-place finish at the British Open, and a sixth at the PGA Championship. It was a stretch that would solidify his standing as one of the premier players in the world. Duplantis seemed to get little joy from these dizzying achievements, and it was obvious to Furyk something was seriously wrong with his caddie. "Jim would be like, hey, I'm your friend, you can talk to me," says Duplantis. "Yeah, he was my friend, but first and foremost he was my boss. If I told him any of this stuff he was gonna wonder how I could ever do my job, so I kept my mouth shut."

Says Furyk, "I don't think anyone in the world could have been aware of everything that was going on. In the beginning, I probably knew ninety percent. I even called it when he got married. Steve phoned me right after it happened and said, 'Are you sitting down?' I said, 'Let me guess, you got married.' With Steve nothing ever surprised me. But after maybe his first year with his ex-wife I knew about a decreasing percentage of that stuff. He didn't want to talk about anything. I tried to be there for him, but he just clammed up."

Duplantis's divorce papers were filed in mid-August, the week of the PGA Championship, which was played at Winged Foot Country Club outside New York City. He went out to celebrate that week with a couple of Furyk's agents. They wound up at a dive bar in the town of White Plains, and it was there that Duplantis met Sollange Lewis, a Bronx Mona Lisa who worked in the burbs. Lewis would become an important figure in his life. "Our first night together we both revealed a secret," says Duplantis. "I told her I had a kid, and she told me she was really seventeen."

ON AUGUST 27, at the Hillsborough County Courthouse in Tampa, the family law division of Florida's 13th Judicial Circuit Court convened to determine temporary custody of Sierra Duplantis. Steve Duplantis was the petitioner, Vicki Duplantis the respondent. The Honorable Katherine G. Essrig presided over the hearing, case number 97-10120, which is part of the public record.

The 249-page transcript reads like the screenplay to a bad Aaron Spelling drama. It tells the long, sordid, tragic tale of the undoing of a volatile marriage. There are charges and countercharges of infidelity, boozy bar fights, and public urination, as well as detailed chronicles of domestic disturbances and police intervention. A lot of personal effects seem to get thrown from hotel room windows, or wind up floating in the swimming pool at the family residence.

In the end, Judge Essrig cut short Steve Duplantis's lawyer's final rebuttal. She awarded custody of Sierra to the petitioner, and offered a stern rebuke to the respondent. Of Vicki, the judge said, "I have some serious problems with her credibility before this court today on a number of issues."

THREE WEEKS AFTER the custody hearing Steve Duplantis boarded the Concorde, bound for Spain's Costa del Sol. (Duplantis's grandmother Dorothy came down from Canada to stay with Sierra in Florida.) Furyk had played his way into his first Ryder Cup, the trans-Atlantic match that was founded in 1927 to promote goodwill within the game but that has, since the mid-1980s, turned into the most compelling, pressure-packed event in sports. In 1997 the Ryder Cup was being played on the Continent for the first time, and the European squad was being captained by Spain's own Seve Ballesteros. There have been few players in golf history more charismatic or contentious than Ballesteros, and his presence, in his homeland, all but guaranteed this Ryder Cup would turn into a win-at-all-costs grudge match. Still, the Americans couldn't have known what kind of ambush they were walking into.

In Spain golf is still not a game played by the common man, and the great unwashed that turned out for the Ryder Cup showed little understanding, or appreciation, of traditional golf etiquette. They cheered wildly for every American miscue, and repeatedly broke into the national soccer fight song, which is heavy on the word *olé*. Some American players later complained that folks in the gallery tried to trip them with umbrellas as they were walking through some of the narrow corridors between green and tee. The host course, Club de Golf Valderrama, was already short and twisty and vaguely claustrophobic, with every fairway choked by towering oaks, but Ballesteros tricked it up to further negate the American long-hitters.

In this cauldron U.S. captain Tom Kite showed a tremendous amount of confidence in Furyk, sending him out in the match's third pairing, along with the Americans' emotional leader, Tom Lehman. The Yanks were matched up in team best ball against Jesper Parnevik and Per-Ulrick Johansson, a couple of nutty Swedes who were just beginning to emerge as players of note. Furyk played well, but not well enough, as Parnevik rolled in a mile of putts and the Swedes won, 1-up. Kite seemed to lose a little trust in Furyk after that, benching him until the next day's afternoon alternate shot, when he played with Lee Janzen against one of Europe's strongest and most experienced teams, the standoffish Scot Colin Montgomerie and Bernhard Langher, the ultimate driving machine from Germany. Janzen and Furyk battled furiously and the match was dead even as it arrived on Valderrama's 18th green, where both teams had birdie putts. Rain had disrupted the Ryder Cup's schedule throughout the first two days, and the sun was disappearing fast behind the Andalusian Mountains as Janzen stood over his uphill forty-footer. That Saturday had been devastating to the Americans. Between the delayed day-one matches that were completed in the morning and the day-two scrums that followed, the U.S. hadn't won a single match. Furyk's match was even more critical than usual, then, and dozens of players, caddies, and wives from both teams crowded behind the 18th green to watch Janzen's birdie attempt. Ordinarily one of the best putters in golf, an overly excited Janzen blasted his putt ten feet past the hole, leaving Furyk a terrifying downhill comebacker with nearly a foot of break. The Europeans tapped in for their par, and now the weight of two continents was resting on Furyk's shoulders.

"I could barely breathe," says Duplantis.

Furyk never threatened the hole. It was a tough putt under any circumstances, virtually impossible under the ones he was facing. Furyk and Janzen lost the hole and the match, 1-up, completing the U.S.'s Saturday skunking.

If Furyk was hoping to reclaim his reputation during the Sunday singles, he couldn't have gotten a tougher draw—Nick Faldo, the stiff-upper-lipped Brit who will go down as the greatest player in the post-Watson, pre-Tiger era (a nose ahead of Ballesteros). Faldo was playing on his record eleventh Ryder Cup team, and earlier in the week he had won the twenty-fifth match of his career, another all-time mark. Furyk hardly seemed intimidated. "It was the most focused I'd ever seen Jim," says Duplantis. "He had fire in his eyes." Playing in a steady drizzle and a stony silence with Faldo, Furyk forged a 1-up lead after thirteen holes. On the 14th hole, a tough par-4, Faldo stiffed a long iron to what Duplantis calls "dick length," although we'd like to know whose member he's referring to, considering Faldo was some eighteen inches from the hole. Furyk conceded the birdie putt, and then from the thick, wet rough in front of the green, dramatically holed his birdie chip to halve the hole. On 15, a long, downhill par-3, Faldo again produced a brilliant iron shot to three feet, while Furyk's tee ball was sucked into a gaping greenside bunker. Digging his feet in the sand, having already addressed the ball, Furyk looked up at Duplantis and said, "What do you think, two in a row?" Seconds later his ball traversed some fifty feet of green, clanged off the flagstick, and disappeared for another birdie and another halve. Furyk then looked at Faldo and nonchalantly said of his putt, "That's good." A shellshocked Faldo then three-putted the next hole to lose the match 3 and 2. The victory would become one of the defining performances of Furyk's career.

At the conclusion of the match Duplantis and Furyk jumped in a cart and began crisscrossing the course to cheer on their teammates, who were staging an inspired rally. Down five full matches at the start of the day, the U.S. won seven of the twelve in singles, and halved two others, taking the Ryder Cup to the brink before losing by the narrowest of margins. Still, the spirit of the week, and the sense of team, touched Duplantis deeply and the Ryder Cup was, to that point, the most thrilling experience of his career.

Duplantis floated home from Spain. His divorce was in the works, he had custody of his daughter, and the future with Furyk seemed endless.

"I thought all the drama was behind me," Duplantis says.

CHAPTER

• 5 •

As part of Rich Beem's newfound commitment to golf he began working with a personal trainer named Bob McDonald in the fall of 1997. McDonald is a no-nonsense kind of guy, a burned-out accountant who got into training athletes late in life. When, after a couple of months of working together, he saw something was holding back Beem in his workouts, he called him on it. "I confronted Rich and told him straight up he was drinking way too much," says McDonald. "I could see it in his face. You know that look drunks get? Leathery skin, a face that's about six shades too red? That was Rich. I told him he was blowing it big time, and if he didn't shape up he could forget about ever reaching his potential as a golfer."

These were words Beem needed to hear. His problems with alcohol dated at least as far back as when he got kicked off the golf team at Heidelberg high school, and they only seemed to intensify in the years that followed. Talking casually about her son's college friends, Beem's mother, Diana, says, apropos of nothing, "I will always be eternally thankful for Max Schroeder. He was always the designated driver when the guys would go out, and he's the reason Rich is still alive." At Westward Ho Country Club, in Sioux Falls, Beem's nickname among the pro shop staff was Bagroom Billy. Says Jeff Brecht, the Westward Ho head pro, "Rich was always coming into work hungover, and the last thing I wanted was for him to be interacting with the members, so I'd stick him in the bagroom till he was ready to be seen. After a while I just stopped scheduling him for the six A.M. opening shift, unless I wanted to punish him." Corey Thie, reminiscing about his party days in Seattle with Beem, says, "I'd love to tell you some of our stories, but I don't remember any of 'em, and I'm sure neither does he."

Like so many of his attributes, Beem's thirst can be traced back to his father. "When I was younger I drank to escape, to get away from all the strife, all the turmoil," says Larry. "I'd order sixteen ounces of tequila, a bowl of limes, and just go to it. It was a salve for the daily wounds. Rich is like me, he drinks to get happier."

Around El Paso Country Club there were always plenty of folks looking to elevate their spirits with spirits, and they were usually buying. Partying with the young, cool guys from the pro shop was the source of some pride amongst the graying membership, and so they were not inclined to lecture Beem about the hazards of excess. Beem's father, with his share of drunken escapades in his past, had also ceded the moral high ground, and Beem's sisters were hardly teetotalers either. (Tina has a footlong zipper on her left knee, thanks to three surgeries resulting from a gnarly accident on a four-wheel all-terrain vehicle. "She was drunk when it happened, of course," says Susie.) So for McDonald to get in Beem's grill was an especially important development, because he was one of the few people in Beem's life whose words would carry some weight.

"Rich took it like a man," says McDonald. "He took it well, and he went on to do the things that needed to be done. To me that was a turning point—it showed what kind of heart he had. He could've chucked it and said, 'Screw you,' but he found some dedication."

Drawing Beem to the bar was not just the drink but also his fellow barflies. Still rebounding from Tanya, Beem was doing brisk business at the meat markets around El Paso and Las Cruces. "All the girls are a big blur," Tina Beem says of those days. "It was like, okay, Rich, which one is it this week?" Around the time of McDonald's lecture Beem met a woman who would further help get him on the straight and narrow. Her name was Amy Onick, and she was, somewhat uncharacteristically, out on the town with a group of friends when she was sucked into Beem's vortex. Onick had shocks of red hair that seemed to spill out of a Pantene shampoo commercial, and, says Beem, "She was wearing this black outfit that made me sweat." But Onick wasn't destined to become just another story told around the bar at El Paso Country Club. She was the girlfriend type, an elementary schoolteacher with solid family ties in the El Paso area. She didn't like hanging out with Beem's EPCC cronies, and with a room full of fifth graders waiting to ambush her every morning she wasn't inclined to keep Beem's vampire hours.

"Amy was a terrific influence on Rich," says Larry. "She got him out of the bars and allowed him to concentrate on some other things."

Like winning golf tournaments.

THE SUN SECTION of the PGA of America comprises El Paso as well as the whole of New Mexico. Any member of the PGA of America—which is to say, virtually every employee in every pro shop—is eligible to play in the Sun Section tournaments, and throughout the Southwest these events are known for their high-caliber competition. In April of 1998 one of the Sun Section's biggest tournaments was played at El Paso Country Club, the Pro-President, which pitted the pro shop staffs and club president of some fifty country clubs against one another over two days of stroke play.

Beem came roaring into that tournament with both his golf game and his personal life in perfect order. He had settled into a contented domesticity with Onick, and had been working hard on his game so he could make a good showing during the Sun Section season, which runs throughout the spring and summer. During the first round of that Pro-President Beem got off to a good start with a couple of quick birdies, but then, on the eighth hole, he realized he had a 15th club in his bag, leftover from a practice session when he was fooling around with some new sticks. This was a violation of USGA rule 4-4(a), which sets the legal limit at fourteen clubs, and calls for a two-stroke penalty for each hole that the rule is breached, maximum of four strokes per round. Beem went on to shoot a 67, which became a 71 with the tariff. This left him far in arrears of Doan, who was leading with a 66. That Doan was atop the leaderboard was hardly a surprise. He had already set the course record at El Paso Country Club, an achievement memorialized in his email prefix, Doan62. "Cameron was the big dog in the Sun Section," says Beem. "To win anything you always had to go through him." The following day Beem did exactly that, posting a scorching 65 and blowing away Doan, who shot 73, for the victory.

Two weeks later was the Sun Section match play championship in Albuquerque. Beem and Doan shared a hotel room that week, as well as the same draw in the tournament. They met in the quarterfinals, and again Beem trumped his boss, with a decisive 3 and 2 victory. He breezed through his remaining matches to win yet again. "Rich had never beat me twice in a row in anything," says Doan. "I think the match play was a big victory for him."

"It was huge," says Beem. "After that I felt bulletproof."

And that was exactly how he played. Beem went on to win five more tournaments in a row, making him a unanimous choice for Sun Section Player of the Year. As trivial as that honor may sound, to that point it was by far the most glittering entry on his résumé. As the victories piled up throughout the summer the drumbeat grew louder and louder: it was time for Beem to test himself against stiffer competition.

Deep down Beem was also beginning to feel like it was now or never. That summer he was going on twenty-seven years old, and it had been nearly two years since he arrived in El Paso, which was supposed to be a springboard to better things. Still, there was no yellow brick road stretching to the horizon, showing him the way. Beem had taken his lumps on the minitours, and was not inclined to go that route again. Those around Beem were pushing him to attempt to qualify for the PGA Tour, a quixotic notion that he had trouble even discussing with a straight face. For a guy like Beem there was only one realistic route to the Tour, the annual Qualifying Tournament, known far and wide as Q School. Every fall a thousand or more dreamers pony up $4,000 to enroll in Q School, and then the examinations begin in earnest. Two rounds of prequalifying whittles the field down to 160 players, which is only a prelude to the final stage of qualifying, a six-rounds-in-six-days death march where the low thirty-five players (and ties) become full-fledged members of the PGA Tour and everyone else heads to therapy, or the Buy.com

Tour. The stories are legion about the grinding pressure of Q School, where men are not playing for trophies or checks but rather their very livelihood. Beem had never forgotten a yarn he once heard about veteran Billy Ray Brown, a two-time PGA Tour winner in the early '90s who fell on hard times after a serious wrist injury. In the fall of 1995 Brown was forced to go back to Q School for the first time since his rookie year. Brown had a wife, a baby daughter, and a mortgage hanging in the balance, and was so overwrought by the circumstances that he is reputed to have thrown up every morning for six straight days before heading out to play. Whether or not the tale is true is beside the point (though, it should be said, Brown did gut out a spot among the Top 35, and he went on to win another Tour event, in 1997). Q School didn't sound like any kind of fun to Beem, and he was reluctant to throw away four grand on such a longshot.

Then, in the midst of Beem's winning streak, his perspective was altered dramatically.

JOHN PATRICK HAYES turned pro out of the University of Texas-El Paso in 1989, and then spent the next ten years as so many touring pros do—struggling. J.P. bounced around the minitours for three years before finally reaching the PGA Tour in 1992, thanks to a strong performance at the preceding Q School. He spent his rookie year as so many rookies do—struggling. He made only ten of twenty-seven cuts and earned just $72,830. That barely covered his expenses, and at one hundred fifty-fifth on the money list he was demoted to the Nike Tour, where he spent the next two seasons. There was never any doubt Hayes could play. At the 1994 Nike Boise Open he shot a second-round 61, the low round of the year on the tour. Plenty of El Paso Country Club members had lost money to performances like that in Friday games over the years, as following UTEP Hayes decided to make his home in El Paso, along with his highly supportive wife, Laura, and make EPCC his home club. But in 1995 and '97 Hayes made it back to the PGA Tour (with yet another year on the Nike Tour sandwiched in between), and his play showed no signs of improving. Hayes may have been maturing as a player, but every year that went by brought more young, hungry kids onto the

Tour, and intensified the pressures on him to try to keep up and earn a living. In the fall of 1997, after having finished one hundred thirty-fifth on the money list that season, Hayes was forced to stagger through Q School for a fourth time. Once again he emerged with his playing privileges on tour, but he started the 1998 season like a man thinking about getting into another line of work.

When Hayes arrived at the Buick Classic in mid-June, at stately Westchester (New York) Country Club, he had broken 70 only twice all year and had earned a paltry $16,712. Westchester is one of the best golf courses on tour, and the list of past champions reads like a Who's Who of golf glitterati. On this grand stage Hayes summoned the kind of unlikely performance that makes sports so compelling. He opened the tournament with a surprising 66, tying for second place, and then had to stew on it for nearly forty-eight hours. A rainstorm of biblical proportions had swept through Westchester County on Friday, forcing the cancellation of the second round. Hayes got in sixteen holes on Saturday before darkness fell, playing some lights-out golf along the way. On Sunday morning he finished up his second round with back-to-back birdies for a 67 and a piece of the lead, along with none other than Jim Furyk. They would play together in the final round

"I remember thinking, Oh, we'll crush this guy," says Duplantis. "I know Jim was thinking the same thing. But J.P. played awesome. He never cracked."

By the 15th hole a hard rain had begun to fall, and Furyk and Hayes were dead even. On 16, Furyk's ball found a puddle in a bunker, but he elected not to take relief, and went on to make a costly bogey. Hayes was still one shot up heading to the 18th hole, a long, uphill par-5. Hayes put his second shot just off the green and got up-and-down for a clutch birdie, leaving the tournament in the hands of Furyk, who had smote a 3-wood from 265 yards out to within twenty feet for eagle. The situation was beautiful in its simplicity—miss the putt and lose, or make it and head to a playoff. Furyk rammed it in the center of the cup.

Back to 18 they went for sudden death. Hayes drove perfectly, but Furyk lost his tee ball into the left rough, where it settled into a nasty lie. He stood over his ball for what seemed like an eternity, agonizing over whether or not to go for the green. Finally, Duplantis said, "If you don't feel comfortable with the shot, just lay it up and make birdie with a wedge."

"I won't be able to look at myself in the mirror if I lay up," Furyk said.

He took a mighty rip with his 3-wood but the ball squirted low and left and ever deeper into the rough. From there he had to struggle to make par. Hayes, meanwhile, had left himself a five-footer for birdie. He drilled it to win the tournament, a two-year exemption onto the Tour, and, oh yeah, $324,000.

Back at El Paso Country Club, they just about blew the roof off the place.

A couple weeks later a party was thrown to honor Hayes. Elegant tents were set up in front of the clubhouse to accommodate the two hundred or so guests, a down-home dinner was served, toasts were made, and highlights of Hayes's victory were shown on a big-screen TV. Beem had been given the late shift that day, and he was forced to watch the first half of the party through the pro shop windows, frantically closing down the registers, vacuuming, dusting, and putting away the stray merchandise. Finally he rushed out to join the party, where, like everybody else, he gave Hayes a sloppy hug and some kind words.

"Winning a PGA Tour event always seemed like a million miles away," says Beem. "It was like trying to reach out and touch the stars. What J.P. did somehow changed that. I mean, he's a helluva player, don't get me wrong. But he was also a friend, and somebody whose pocket I got into more than a few times. I guess that whole deal really opened my eyes." Within a month after Hayes's shindig Beem sent in his application for the 1998 Q School. Once again he was chasing the dream, a step ahead of a familiar ghost.

JUST BECAUSE LARRY BEEM was drafted, in 1958, didn't mean his golfing days were over. Stationed at Fort Lewis, Washington, he quickly sized up the army golf team as just another hustle of which he could take advantage. "If we were playing golf that meant we didn't have to play soldier," says Larry. "Avoidance was our only goal." One of Beem's teammates on the army squad, and his roommate for the better part of a year, was Lee Elder, who had made a name for himself as a shark around Dallas. Elder would go on to win four tournaments on the PGA Tour and another eight on the Senior Tour, where he still occasionally competes today. Beem could more than hold his own against Elder, and after being discharged in 1960 he had little trouble landing a scholarship at New Mexico State. In Beem's first season at NMSU, he won the individual championship of the old Border Conference. Following his freshman year he had to put in another year in the army, and upon returning to school in the fall of 1962 he began dating Diana Parker. They had met cute in Biology 101, flirting over a petri dish. "Back then New Mexico was a real cow college," says Diana. "Larry was one of the few guys on campus who didn't dress like a cowboy. He looked like one of those old golfers—very natty. I couldn't resist him." Diana was the yin to his yang, a nonstop talker bursting with life and good cheer, a social butterfly forever floating from one societal engagement to the next. Within a year they were engaged.

In the spring of 1964 Beem squared off against Marty Fleckman in the quarter finals of the NCAA Championship, back when it was still match play. Fleckman was one of the longest hitters of his era, a player tabbed for greatness before he had even reached his teen years (in 1999 *Golf* magazine would name him one of the busts of the century). Beem battled Fleckman for twenty holes before losing in sudden death, but the heroic performance helped land Beem on that season's All-American team. Later that spring, after only three years of schooling, Beem completed his degree in business. Following graduation he turned pro, but, he says, "I didn't have the money to go out on tour, and I didn't know how to go get it."

There was another reason Beem didn't hit the road. "The story I've always been told," says Rich, "is that my dad was afraid he would lose my mom if he went out on tour. That wasn't the life she wanted." In the summer of 1964 Larry and Diana were married, and they settled near her parents in Phoenix, where Larry had lined up a job at tony Phoenix Country Club. He lasted all of seven months. "I had become burned out on the game," he says. After Phoenix CC he took a job selling insurance, and in

1966 Beem was reinstated as an amateur, so he could compete in local tournaments. A year later he quit the game cold turkey, not touching a club for eighteen months. Near the end of 1968 Beem took a job as a pharmaceutical salesman, a position that came with a membership to the Century Country Club in North Phoenix. Beem spent the next four years playing client golf and haunting the local amateur events. He had a comfortable life, his nice new house filled with a loving wife and three little cherubs.

Then he woke up one day and, in his words, "chucked it all." At the 1972 Phoenix amateur Beem had battled a couple of college stars, Tom Purtzer and Howard Twitty, down to the wire, finishing second. (Both Purtzer and Twitty would go on to become multiple winners on the PGA Tour.) Something was rekindled within Beem that day. Shortly thereafter he quit his job, cashed in his stock options, loaded up the family Datsun, and lit out for Texas. He was thirty-five years old. "The minitours were a brand-new concept back then," says Larry. "For those of us who had missed out on playing professionally the first time around, they offered a welcome second chance."

Beem played seven tournaments in seven weeks at courses around San Antonio and Houston. It was an educational experience. "I found out I was well past my playing days," he says. "I also found out there was no way to survive out there. It was one of those deals where the entry fee was like three hundred dollars and first place was worth two hundred ninety-five dollars. But the biggest thing I learned was that I didn't love it enough."

After the seven-week jag Beem headed home. At loose ends for a while, he finally landed a job as head pro at the nine-hole course at White Sands (New Mexico) Missile Base in the spring of 1974. He would stay there until 1981, followed by the similar positions in Panama and Berlin. "Like they say in the ad, I found myself in the army," Beem says, sardonically. Beem did find a life in golf, though it was in teaching, not playing. "No regrets," he says.

Others are not so sure.

"If anybody should have gone out on tour it was my dad," says Rich. "He could putt and chip like a demon, and he could play any shot. He had the balls and the attitude but he didn't have the backing. I know that ate at him for a long time, and maybe it still does."

If the success of J. P. Hayes persuaded Rich that he was good enough to compete on the PGA Tour, his father's story convinced him that he owed it to himself to try, before it was too late.

AT THE END OF SEPTEMBER 1998, Beem quit at El Paso Country Club. The first stage of Q School was the following week. "I was done working," he says. "If Q School didn't work out, I had no plan. Maybe play overseas or in Canada, or who knows where. I was just gonna see what came up." Just as with U.S. Open qualifying, there were multiple sites for the first stage. Beem elected to play at Talking Stick Golf Club, in Scottsdale, Arizona, where there were eighty-eight players for twenty-three spots. In the first round he shot an even par 70, and then over the next two days it blew a gale. Beem eked out rounds of 72-72, putting him in twenty-fifth place heading into the final round. Instead of hitting balls or putting until dark following the third round, he went out for pizza, relaxed in the hotel room, and hit the sack early. The next day Beem played the first eleven holes even, putting him squarely on the bubble. On number 12 he rolled in a twenty-five-footer for birdie, the first long putt he had made all week. He stiffed it on the next hole for another bird, and then on the par-5 17th he reached the green in two and two-putted easily for his third birdie in six holes. In the kind of clutch performance that would become a trademark, Beem wound up shooting a 67 to move up to fourteenth place, and move on.

The second stage was played two weeks later. On the advice of J. P. Hayes, Beem traveled to Deerwood Country Club in Houston, reputedly a tough track that played to Beem's strengths, straight driving and putting on fast greens. Again it was eighty-eight players for twenty-three spots, although this time the competition would be considerably stiffer. Hayes had given Beem some other advice. "If you go through all three stages you'll play a total of fourteen rounds," says Hayes. "I tried to impress upon Rich that fourteen rounds of seventy gets you on tour. You don't have to be a hero at Q School. Good, steady golf is what it takes."

Beem was -1 after two rounds at second stage, and then in the third round he shot a smooth 68 to put himself in good position. On the morning of the final round Beem was "unbelievably tight," he says. "I think for the first time it hit me how much this all meant." He three-putted the first hole for a bogey, and then made another bogey on number two. After escaping with a par at the third he came to Deerwood's fearsome 4th. This was the hole that was used as number 18 of the fictitious U.S. Open course in *Tin Cup*, the Waterloo of Roy McAvoy. In the movie the hole played as a par-5, while in reality it's a beastly 470-yard par-4, with a lake fronting the green. Beem ripped a drive on number 4 then smoked his approach pin-high, setting up a stress-free par. That settled him down, but two holes later, on the short par-4 6th, Beem caught a flier lie out of the rough and pumped his approach shot a mile over the green. He had no shot from there and did well to run his pitch back off the green, some fifty feet from the hole. Putting from the fringe, he banged his par effort off the flagstick and into the cup. "It was the biggest hole of my life," he says. "No joke." Thoroughly pumped up, Beem proceeded to birdie the next two holes, and he played flawlessly on the back side, shooting a one-under par-71 to sneak into the Top 23 by two strokes.

By the time Beem reached the final stage of Q School, played the week before Thanksgiving in Palm Springs, he was feeling invincible. Before the first round, on a Tuesday morning, he turned to his college-buddy-turned-caddie, Gus Braunschweig, and said, "See you on Monday." That was Beem's way of indicating how focused he was going to be. "I didn't know how I was going to handle the pressure," he says, "but I could guarantee I was going to grind my nuts off for six days." Playing at Weiskopf Private Course at PGA West, he opened with a solid 69. There was no key shot, or crucial putt. "Just steady golf, hole after hole," says Beem. He came back the next day with a 68, putting him among the early leaders. While everyone around him seemed to be throwing up on themselves, at least metaphorically, Beem continued to churn out error-free rounds—a third-round 70, followed by a 71, and then a 69. It was the kind of golf that those around El Paso had become accustomed to seeing. "Once Rich gets on a roll he gets tunnel vision, where the only thing he sees is the flag," says Doan. "It's like he believes he's incapable of making a mistake, and so he doesn't."

On Sunday, always a day of heavy melodrama, Beem shot a bloodless 66 to tie for eighth, good for $25,000 of the $1.1 million purse. As it turned out, Beem could have shot a final round 75 and still finished among the Top 35. He was one of only four players to finish under par in every round.

After the completion of the final round, PGA Tour commissioner Tim Finchem presided over a ceremony where the forty-one Q School graduates (there had been a seven-way tie for thirty-fifth) received little plastic cards emblazoned with their name and the Tour logo. It was proof that each player was now officially a member of the Tour. Those cheesy plastic cards probably cost no more than a dollar to manufacture, but they represented a potential fortune to the recipients.

Following the ceremony a couple dozen of the Q School grads convened at a bar in Palm Springs to whoop it up. Beem slipped away for a while to call his loved ones back in El Paso and Las Cruces.

"Wow," Rich told his father. "What a vacation this is going to be."

CHAPTER

STEVE DUPLANTIS didn't have long to get over the emotional hangover from the Ryder Cup, as upon his arrival back in Florida he was confronted with some sobering realities. With Vicki now back in Fort Worth, Duplantis was all alone with Sierra, who was not yet two years old. Duplantis had been drawn to Tampa by the weather, the affordable housing, and the convenience with regards to traveling. He had no family there, and a very small support group of friends. With his grandmother having returned to Canada, Duplantis was forced to do the Mr. Mom thing, and from the beginning it was far more difficult than he expected. Compounding his anxiety was the cruelty of the calendar—three weeks after the Ryder Cup he had to report back to work, for the Las Vegas Invitational. He had no idea what he was going to do with Sierra then. It is a measure of Duplantis's desperation that he turned to Sollange Lewis, the barfly he had met at the PGA Championship in New York. Duplantis and Lewis had been burning up the phone lines in the two months since the PGA Championship, though they hadn't seen each other. With winter coming to Rosedale Avenue in the Bronx, Lewis was happy to escape to Florida, so she accepted Duplantis's invitation to come for a visit.

"At that point Steve and I were just enjoying a nice friendship," says Lewis, the lovely lilt in her voice betraying the fact that she grew up on the island of Antigua in the Caribbean. "He was a really nice person and I wanted to make the effort to get to know him better. And—how to put it?—Steve, being a single parent and a guy, he was very inexperienced in how to deal with a little girl. I mean, Sierra was still in Pampers, and I knew he needed the help."

Lewis had grown up with younger brothers and was a caregiver at heart. When Duplantis asked her to stay in Florida with Sierra during the week of the Vegas Invitational she couldn't say no. The week after Vegas brought the Tour Championship, the last official event of the PGA Tour schedule. It was being played at Champions Golf Club in Houston, and per the terms of the custody ruling Duplantis was compelled to leave Sierra with her mother. At that Tour Championship Furyk finished second by a shot to David Duval, earning a whopping $432,000. That propelled him all the way to fourth on the season-ending money list, with more than $1.6 million, and Duplantis's $30,240 payday pushed his year's earnings well into six figures. The next week brought the Kapalua Invitational where Furyk was now a featured player. Because it's a mellow event Duplantis decided to bring Sierra along, for what would be their first trip alone together.

To get to Kapalua, father and daughter had to fly from Tampa to Denver to L.A. to Honolulu to Maui. Duplantis had purchased only one ticket, to save on the hefty fare, which meant Sierra was sitting in his lap most of the way. This became a particularly acute problem when she crapped her diaper on the approach into Honolulu. "I was trying to get out of my seat and go to the bathroom but the stewardesses wouldn't let me," says Duplantis. "It was nasty, and the people in my row were not happy about it. Finally we landed and I sprinted off the plane into a john, and that's when I realized I'm out of diapers. I must have had a look of sheer desperation, or terror, because some guy asked me what was wrong. I told him and he sent his wife to go buy some diapers. She was there and back in about two minutes, thank God. The diapers were like nine dollars, but this couple was so nice, they wouldn't take any money. It turned out the guy was a golfer, and I had a bunch of Jim's gloves and balls with me, so I gave all that stuff to him. But the whole thing was crazy."

Little wonder that upon returning from Kapalua Duplantis hired a nanny to help him with Sierra. The young woman, Shannon Artz, was the daughter of a neighbor, and she was looking to take a little sabbatical from nursing school. She stayed with Sierra in Tampa when Duplantis went to the Abierto de Argentina in December. At that tournament Furyk birdied the 18th hole during the final round to tie Eduardo Romero. The playoff would have been wild, as Romero is Argentina's favorite son, but it never happened. Romero was disqualified for signing an incorrect scorecard, and Furyk was declared the winner. It was that kind of a year for Furyk.

When the 1998 season kicked off Sierra and Artz were traveling with Duplantis full-time. Duplantis had graduated from sharing rooms at the Motel 6 to caddie-free suites at Extended Stay America (though strictly platonic, Duplantis and Artz did share the same unit). In addition to paying Artz $300 a week, Duplantis was also kicking down for three plane tickets per trip, as Sierra was too big to sit on anybody's lap anymore. Not only was he paying for the hotel room himself, he was also on the hook for all of the expense of a rental car, which caddies usually split two or three ways. It was the fabulous financial rewards that came with Furyk's bag that made all of this possible. "I was burning up money, but who cared," says Duplantis. "I knew every time Jim teed it up I was gonna make a check for three or four or five thousand dollars, minimum. I used to pull into short-term parking at the airport, leave the car for two weeks, and then come home and the bill would be like three hundred dollars. No big deal—it was just paper back then."

Though Duplantis was known as "Kid" to the other caddies, he was now more like the big man on campus. "If you want to know who are the best caddies on tour, just look at the top of the money list—the cream rises to the top," Duplantis says, a theme fleshed out in the writer Michael Bamberger's chronicle of his year packing on the PGA Tour, *The Green Road Home.* "If you have a big bag, you're a big man," Bamberger quotes another caddie as saying, and then he continues, in his own voice, "Years on the Tour, curiously, played little role in determining a caddie's status. Caddies were not bound by history. Three weeks was the typical perspective: how much you made last week; how you're playing this week; and what you have lined up for next week."

Furyk had now played himself into the very best events and pairings. His practice rounds were increasingly spent with the other elite players, thanks to friendships forged at the Ryder Cup. "It's funny how your life changes," Duplantis says. "One day you're having dinner at McDonalds with some Q Schooler's caddie, and the next day you're eating at a steakhouse with Fred Couples's caddie, or Phil Mickelson's, or whoever. You wind up losing touch with your old friends. It just sorta happens, mostly because you're playing a totally different schedule. Also, you stop sharing rooms, because why do that unless you have to?"

Duplantis was feeling his oats enough to start playing the occasional practical joke on his more established colleagues. A doozy involved John (Cubby) Burke, Brad Faxon's then-bagman, known for his cocksure manner. During a practice round Duplantis became so irritated with Burke's schtick that he stealthly removed Faxon's sand wedge, stashing it in his own bag, under the putter cover. "The next hole Brad needs his wedge, and Cubby is going nuts trying to find it," Duplantis says. "He looks in my bag but he doesn't think to look under the putter cover. He checks every bag in the group, and everyone is playing dumb. Next hole Fax needs his wedge again, and now he's all over Cubby. I'm starting to feel bad at this point, so I give the wedge to Rich Mayo, a new caddie Paul Stankowski had just hired who Cubby would never expect to pull a prank. I tell him to say he found it in the rough on the last hole. I think from the look on my face Cubby knew what had happened, and of course he ratted me out to Brad, like the crybaby he is."

With Duplantis growing fat and happy, punctuality increasingly began to be a problem. "You can count on one hand the number of times I was more than ten minutes late to meet Jim, for our entire time together," he says. "But it's true, I was always a couple minutes late to everything."

"You can count the number of times he was more than ten minutes late on one hand?" an incredulous Furyk says, on the phone from his home in Florida. "Hold on, I've got some people laughing here in the background. Let me explain this to them."

Pause.

"No matter what I say here it's gonna sound like I'm trashing Steve or tarnishing his reputation, and I don't want to do that," Furyk continues. "Put it this way—he was late a lot. I couldn't begin to speculate about how often or by how much, but I think it's safe to say you would need more than one hand to add it all up."

To be sure, living on the road with a stubborn little girl in her terrible twos presented challenges, and though Artz was helpful, she never seemed to grasp how valuable every minute was when Duplantis was trying to get to the golf course. Still, Duplantis admits, "Probably half the time I was late it was because of things beyond my control involving Sierra. The other half of the time it was just an excuse I could use."

Furyk was enjoying so much success that he was not inclined to make a big deal of things, and so Duplantis eventually earned a new nickname from his colleagues—"Asbestos," because he was seemingly fireproof. (A word on nicknames: like ex-wives, every caddie's got at least one. Among the best are Dave "Unabomber" McCloud [player: Bob Gilder], whose huge shades recall artist's sketches of the infamous terrorist; Anthony "Ant Man" Knight [Robert Allenby], who as a boy would wade into stinging nettles to fetch balls; John "Wheelbarrow" Sullivan [Hale Irwin], who is hauling away loads of money on the Senior Tour; Dave "Munster" Mince [Glen Day], who looks so much like the old TV character he has been known to joke about having had the plugs removed from his neck; Ron "Bambi" Levin [Per-Ulrick Johansson], who was but a babe in the woods when he started caddying at the age of seventeen; and, our favorite, Tommy "Burnt Biscuits" Bennett, who packed for Tiger Woods at the 1995 Masters, and, as a kid, once singed his hand while trying to steal biscuits.)

By May of 1998, when the Tour began its Texas swing, Artz had called it quits to go back to school. (Heading into the Texas swing Furyk was putting together his usual fine season, having made eleven straight cuts, with five Top 10 finishes.) For the week of the Byron Nelson Golf Classic in Dallas, and the Colonial Invitational in Fort Worth, Sierra again stayed with Vicki, and Duplantis made up for lost time by hitting the bars with a vengeance. "Where else can you meet girls?" Duplantis says. "You're in a strange city, it's not like you can go to a church social. You're on the road every week, what are you supposed to do, sit in the hotel room and stare at the walls? So you end up going to a bar, because there is nowhere else to go. Naturally, you end up trolling."

It was at a honky-tonk watering hole in Dallas that he first felt Shannon Pennington's gravitational pull. They hung out throughout the two week Texas swing, and for a couple of weeks afterward kept in touch by phone. At that point, Pennington came to Tampa for a visit. Duplantis, naturally, saw this as a sign of her romantic interest. Pennington claims other motives. "I felt sorry for him," she says. "I walked into a situation where my sympathy just got the better of me. There was this precious little girl and I felt so bad for her." Pennington wound up staying for the better part of a month and a half, remaining in Tampa with Sierra when Duplantis went back out on tour. "It was always like, 'Can you watch her for just one more week, please, just one more week?' " she says. "I was in a very vulnerable stage. I didn't have a job, and he was offering me all this money to take care of his daughter. All I had to do was sit around the pool and play with her. It was like, God, why wouldn't I do this?" Not that the situation was without its stresses. "The first time I walked into Steve's house every piece of clothing he owned, his ex-wife owned, and Sierra owned was scattered around the floor," says Pennington. "It was beyond disgusting. I called my mom and just bawled and bawled." Pennington conducted an archeological dig to locate the carpet, and then, at Duplantis's urging, filled the house with some furniture and decorative touches it desperately needed. Steve wasn't the only person who began to see Pennington as a surrogate homemaker.

"Sierra was calling me 'mommy' after two weeks," says Pennington. "It was a little bit scary. I think she was just desperate for some stability in her life. She was acting out a lot back then—a lot of screaming and temper tantrums, especially around bedtime. I'm sure it was because she had been in so many different hotel rooms, or tucked in by so many different people, that nothing felt like home to her anymore." Pennington, who harbored dreams of becoming an elementary schoolteacher, began taking Sierra to preschool two times a week, a new experience for the little one. "She was just dying to play with other kids, to do arts and crafts, to just be a normal little girl," says Pennington.

Duplantis could see how attached his daughter had become to Pennington, and that life surely was a lot smoother with her around. So, two months after they first met, Duplantis proposed. "All I could think was, 'This is perfect,' " he says. "I found somebody who loves me, somebody who loves my daughter, and all I gotta do is make the money." Of course, missing from that sentiment would be his love for Pennington. Asked about this, Duplantis shrugs his shoulders and rolls his eyes, but says nothing.

The proposal came at the airport, as he was scurrying around to catch a flight for the British Open. "I was running late, of course," Duplantis says, "so I ran in, dropped my bags, ran out, dropped to one knee, and pulled out the ring." What happened next is the source of some debate. "Shannon said yes," he says. "Of course she did."

"I never agreed to marry him," says Pennington. "I took the ring and told him I would think about it. I mean, we barely had a relationship at all at that point. The whole time I was at the house girls were calling continuously. I would just take a message or give them his cell number. It wasn't a big deal to me because we were just really starting to date. We never even had sex. It's very odd to me, but it just was not there. And I'm not a prude."

After Furyk put in his usual strong performance at the British Open, finishing fourth at Royal Birkdale, a scant two shots back of winner Mark O'Meara, Duplantis flew directly from England to New England for the PGA Tour's CVS Charity Classic. Pennington met him in Sutton, Massachusetts, along with Sierra. Following the CVS, the three of them drove to Buffalo to rendezvous with Steve's family. "He had told them all that I said yes," says Pennington. "It was so weird. They kept asking about the date of the wedding and stuff, and we just played the whole thing off." From Buffalo, Duplantis and Pennington returned to Tampa, and it was there, while doing laundry, that she found the incriminating evidence of Duplantis's British Open fling. She bolted for Dallas immediately.

"The little indiscretion at the British Open—that was the escape hatch Shannon was looking for," Duplantis says. "She got in over her head. I mean, she's nineteen, and all of a sudden she's supposed to be a wife and a mom? I can't say I blame her."

As for the phony ring that Pennington returned, Duplantis says, "She thinks I didn't know it was fake?! What am I, a fuckin' idiot?! It had MADE IN CHINA stamped on the inside of the ring! I knew, I just didn't care. By then I had become so hardened about being ripped off for money that I was like, 'Hey, what's six or seven grand?' "

There were still four months left in the season, and again Duplantis turned to Sollange Lewis for help. She agreed to watch Sierra, but this time it would be at her home, not in Florida. Throughout September, October, and November, as Duplantis was trekking across Washington and Colorado and Ontario and upstate New York and Georgia and Virginia and Las Vegas, Sierra stayed with Lewis, who lived in an apartment with her parents and two younger brothers. It was a happy place, filled with neighborhood kids and the smells of island recipes. "Sierra was here for two and a half months and she was so happy," says Lewis. "She got to be in one place, where there were kids to play with and parks to explore and just a lot of love. She is a really, really enchanting child. She is such a sweetheart and I love her dearly, as do my mother and father." To Sierra, they became known as Grandma and Grandpa.

Duplantis, in the midst of a full late season schedule, was rarely able to drop by New York City to see his daughter. He would call three or four times a day ("Thank God for one-rate cellular plans," he says), but in his absence it wasn't long before Sierra began calling Sollange "mommy," just as she had Pennington before her. "I cried the first time she called me that," says Lewis. "It meant so much to me. At the same time, she wasn't my child, and to be constantly reminded of that every time she called me 'mommy' was very painful. I tried to tell her that she should reserve that word for her real mother, but she wasn't having it. She wanted to call me 'mommy,' and so she did, and still does."

"Sollange has been an unbelievable friend," says Duplantis. "She puts her life on hold for weeks or months at a time to take care of Sierra, and never asks for anything in return. She is the kind of person who restores your faith in humanity."

"I have never taken a cent and never will," says Lewis. "That would be like taking money from Sierra. I would never dream of doing that."

With his child-care situation solved, at least temporarily, it would be reasonable to assume Duplantis's chronic tardiness abated over the latter parts of the 1998 season, but in fact the opposite was true. Free of wife and child for the first time in over three years, Duplantis was partying heartily, and he often had trouble crawling out of bed on time. Furyk, even with Job-like patience, finally became fed up. "It had become a joke on tour," says Furyk. "Other caddies would make jokes to Steve, and players would make jokes to me. It was frustrating, and I had had enough."

Near the end of 1998 Furyk sat Duplantis down and told him that all the little screwups and excuses had to end. There would be no more second chances.

CHAPTER

• 7 •

IT DIDN'T TAKE LONG for the giddiness of having survived Q School to wear off. The 1999 season was starting in a month, and Rich Beem faced the same money pressures that had shortchanged his dad's chances of playing professionally. Spending a season on the PGA Tour—especially these days, with so many far-flung events—is brutally expensive. Players must pay for their own airfare, hotels, meals, and caddies (the standard weekly salary is $600 a week, above and beyond any winnings). The only time rookies have access to the courses for practice rounds are Monday morning and Tuesday, which means arriving at a tournament site Sunday night (the course is closed Monday afternoon and Wednesday for a pro-am limited to the Top 52 players from the previous year's money list). It is not uncommon for a rook to spend five nights in a pricey resort area, shell out thousands of dollars for all the attendant costs, and then shoot 75-75, miss the cut, and not earn a nickel for his labors. It is this Darwinian calculus that explains why so many players spend one year on the PGA Tour, run out of money, and are never heard from again.

There is a little wrinkle in the golf culture that addresses the plight of the young, penniless dreamer. It is rarely discussed or reported on, maybe because indentured servitude was believed to have died with the eighteenth century. Call it what you may—backing, sponsorship, or fleshpeddling—but without this kind of an arrangement Beem would never have made it out on tour. In the weeks leading up to Q School he approached dozens of El Paso Country Club members with a business proposition, whereby they'd pay Beem's expenses in exchange for a generous cut of whatever money he made. A few years earlier a group of

EPCC members had worked a similar deal for Ryan Hietala, a two-time All-American at UTEP who was destined to go bust professionally.

"Rich was so popular among the membership that he had no trouble rounding up supporters," says Greg Johns, one of the members who accepted Beem's offer. Johns is a self-made man who has earned his fortune owning and operating retirement communities. Twice a week he commutes across Texas to check on his properties in a single-engined Cessna that he pilots himself. Johns is typical of the EPCC membership, except for the bit about the plane. There's not a drop of oil in El Paso, and so there is very little money around town that is more than a generation or two old. The EPCC members are mostly local businessmen—car dealers, accountants, real estate developers, doctors, and lawyers. They have done well in life, but remember what it was like trying to climb the ladder. The support for Beem was so strong that by mid-December, thirty-five men had ponied up $75,000, with individuals contributing anywhere from $1,320 to $9,980.

Under the direction of John Butterworth, Beem's accountant and frequent playing partner in the Wednesday game, a two-year contract was drawn up establishing a general partnership, of which Beem would be the only "employee." The partnership would pay all of Beem's expenses, down to his dry-cleaning bills and skycap tips, every dollar of which was to be itemized in weekly expense reports that Beem would submit to Butterworth. Beem would be given a "company" credit card and checkbook to use against the expenses, as well as a $1,500 monthly "salary." He would also get to keep 10 percent of the prize money he won. Every other cent he made was to go into a pot. At the end of the two years (assuming Beem was able to stay on tour for a second year, which was hardly a sure thing) the money that was left in the pot would be paid out. Of the first $300,000, the partners would get 60 percent—$75,000 to repay the original investment and $105,000 to reward them for their gamble. For every dollar over $300,000 Beem would keep 90 percent, with the other 10 percent going to the partners.

Beem hadn't sold his soul, but he had signed away a large chunk of any future earnings. Still, he was eternally grateful for the opportunity, and the members were thrilled to play a part in his journey into the brave new world of the PGA Tour. "Maybe one or two of the guys were in it for the money," says Butterworth. "The rest of us never expected to see a nickel—we just wanted to give Rich a chance to chase his dream."

The 1999 season kicked off the second week of January with the Mercedes Championships, an elite field limited only to players who had won Tour events the previous season. On January 3rd, Beem drove his Ford Explorer to Phoenix, where he stayed with friends for a few days and tuned up his game. He continued on to Los Angeles, parking his truck in front of a buddy's house so he could use it to drive from tournament to tournament when the West Coast swing returned to the mainland. The week after the Mercedes brought the Hawaiian Open, on Oahu, where Beem was to make his PGA Tour debut—a perfect spot to begin a working vacation.

BEEM LANDED IN HONOLULU on the Saturday before the tournament, jumped in his rental car, and blazed up to the North Shore, eager to see its unsullied beaches and famous surf spots. He had always dreamed of visiting Hawaii and didn't plan on wasting a second. On Sunday Beem and Gus Braunschweig, who had signed on indefinitely as caddie, patrolled Waikiki and sucked down a few piña coladas at Duke's Canoe Club along the beach, what would become a favorite hangout. Monday morning Beem finally made it to Waialae Country Club for the first time. He was sporting his lucky Chicago Cubs hat, a nondescript polo shirt and an off-the-rack canvas bag with the El Paso Country Club logo emblazoned on it.

"I wandered around aimlessly for a while before I finally found the locker room," Beem says, "and when I got there I realized I had no idea what to do. No clue. I didn't know my locker number or even how to find it. I didn't know anybody in there. I was starting to sweat because I was so nervous. So this Maxfli rep—I forget his name—he walks in, takes one look at me, and just starts to laugh. I mean, he's cracking up, right in my face. I was so lost it was unbelievable, and it must have been written across my forehead. You talk about somebody being ill-prepared for the PGA Tour, that was me. The whole thing was so overwhelming I can't even describe it."

It's true that Beem couldn't have been more of a greenhorn. Most players, by the time they earn their full playing privileges on the PGA Tour, have managed to sneak into at least a handful of Tour events for reconnaissance, and surely they've knocked around the Buy.com Tour for a while. Owned and operated by the PGA Tour, the Buy.com mimics all the policies and procedures of its big brother, helping to ease the culture shock of arriving in the major leagues. Beem would be one of the few rookies in recent years to shoot straight to the PGA Tour. His only preparation for the bigs came from flipping through the 124-page *Player Handbook* he was given at Q School, and a few conversations he had had with J. P. Hayes around Christmastime. Beem remained so clueless that for his first two days around Waialae he bought lunch at the concession stand, gorging himself on overpriced hot dogs and hamburgers. Beem didn't know the players were provided with a free gourmet buffet in the clubhouse (as they are at every tournament).

On that first, eventful afternoon around Waialae, Beem eventually found his way to the driving range, where he spied veteran Tom Byrum hitting balls. Byrum hasn't made a ripple on tour since winning the Kemper Open in 1989, but Beem was starstruck nonetheless. "I was thinking, Man if I can meet this guy, a New Mexico State grad, a PGA Tour winner, shoot, what a great deal this would be," he says. So Beem sidled up to Byrum, introduced himself, and after a few minutes of small talk he staked out a spot of his own on the range. Moments later Curtis Strange—two-time U.S. Open champ, three-time leader of the money list, member of five Ryder Cup teams—plunked down his rocks next to Beem. "I just took a deep breath and went, 'Oh baby,' " says Beem. "I was just trying not to bounce any shanks off Curtis's ankle." A few moments later Mark O'Meara—sixteen-time winner on tour, the reigning Player of the Year and Masters and British Open champ—set up shop on the other side of Beem. "I just stepped back for a second and Gus and I actually started giggling, right there on the range," says Beem. "It was like, I can't believe they actually let me out here."

From the range Beem cruised over to the putting green,

where a Titleist rep was showing off every model of Scotty Cameron putter under the sun, including a Bullseye with a head dipped in platinum. After successfully navigating Q School Beem had signed a bottom-of-the-barrel endorsement contract with Titleist that was to pay him $15,000 to play the company's balls and wear its shoes and gloves, and another $10,000 to wear the Titleist logo on his hat. Putters weren't part of the deal, but Beem wanted to get in on the so-called tee-up programs, the weekly bonus pools that pay players to use certain brands of equipment. (The golf business is so cutthroat, and involves so many billions of dollars, manufacturers are desperate to carve out market share on the PGA Tour, which often affects what equipment the weekend hackers spend their money on.) Titleist was offering $750 a week to use one of its putters, which Beem had been doing for years and years anyhow. (Callaway, meanwhile, began paying Beem $500 a week to use its drivers, which, again, he already had in his bag when he arrived on tour.) Beem was fondling a cutting-edge Scotty Cameron prototype when the man himself showed up. For years Cameron has been crafting the finest handmade putters, and he is a revered figure among serious golfers. Cameron noticed Beem's interest in that particular putter, and said he would hand-deliver one to Beem the next day, a promise he kept. ("Scotty Cameron! In my hotel room!" says Beem. "It was mind-boggling.") Another bonus: the Titleist rep, spying Beem's conspicuously unlogoed shirt, told Beem he would set him up with two dozen of their shirts on the house. Beem wouldn't be paid extra for wearing the logo, but hey, a free shirt's a free shirt. (The polos arrived the following week.)

Beem finally stumbled to the first tee for a practice round with another rookie, Mike Weir, with whom he had become friendly at Q School, and an acquiantance of Weir's, Mike Reid, a twenty-three-year veteran who had won twice in the 1980s. "Having Reidy along made me a little nervous," says Beem. On the first tee Beem was also introduced to none other than Steve Duplantis, a buddy of Weir's caddie. With Jim Furyk under the weather Duplantis had come out to walk the course and get a look at a few modifications that had been made in the preceding year. "Man, that really impressed me," says Beem. "I was just thinking, This guy is a real pro." As opposed to Braunschweig, who, having never before seen the course, was frantically stepping off every daisy and anthill on the property, hoping to make sense of the yardage.

Beem acquitted himself nicely during his first spin around Waialea, and he felt even more comfortable the next day, playing another practice round with Doug Dunakey, a fellow Q School grad and refugee from the Dakotas Tour. There is no formal system determining practice round pairings. Beem had simply bumped into Dunakey in the locker room, and both were looking for someone to play with. It is not uncommon for pros to simply show up on the first tee and wait around to see who has room in their group, much like hopeful singles at a crammed muni.

Frozen out by the Wednesday pro-am, Beem practiced around Waialae for a bit and then repaired to Duke's. For his first-round pairing, Thursday afternoon, he drew two other anonymous Q School graduates. There is a four-tier system used by the Tour to decide who plays with whom over the first two rounds and when they tee off. The categories break down as:

1. Major championship winners; tournament winners within past three seasons; players among the Top 25 on the career money list;
    a. Tournament winners whose exemptions have run out, which is to say, their victories occurred more than three years prior;
2. Career nonwinners who: a) were in the Top 125 of the previous year's money list; b) have at least $750,000 in career earnings; or c) are in the Top 50 in the World Rankings.
3. Q School graduates; Monday qualifiers; and sponsor's exemptions (if the player does not fall into any of the above categories).

Group 1's play with other Group 1's, 1a's with other 1a's, etc. The 1's get the best tee times, in the middle of the morning and afternoon pairings. Group 3s get only the very first or, more commonly, the very last times in either session, what Beem calls the "ass end" of the draw. By then the greens are spiked up and often drier and faster from having been baked by the sun, the wind has usually stiffened, the tee boxes and fairways are littered with divots, play is slower because of the sheer number of golfers on the course, and the fans are drunker and rowdier. Of course, Beem didn't know any of this back at the Hawaiian Open. He was just happy to be there.

For the first shot of his PGA Tour career Beem killed a drive down the middle. He followed with 17 pars and a bogey to shoot 71, a commendable score on a very blustery day. The next day Beem struck the ball with more authority and made some timely putts, shooting a smooth 68 to make the cut easily. "I didn't think it was a big deal, but everybody else did," he says. Back in El Paso and Las Cruces the real-time scoring on pgatour.com got more hits than Ty Cobb.

On Saturday Beem let his round get away from him, shooting a 74, but he hardly minded because David Wyatt was in the gallery cheering every shot. Wyatt had always told Beem that no matter where he was or what he was doing he would make it to Beem's first PGA Tour event, should such a thing ever come to pass, and Wyatt made good on the promise, flying in from Seattle on Friday evening. They had a blast in Waikiki over the weekend, and Beem closed with a 71 to finish fifty-third. His first paycheck was for $6,084.00 (though "check" is an abstract concept on tour; all earnings are electronically deposited in a player's bank account Monday morning). "If my plane had crashed on the way home I would have died a happy man," he says. "I know it's a cliché, but that week truly was a dream come true."

Beem couldn't get into the field at the next two tournaments on the schedule, the Bob Hope Desert Classic and the Phoenix Open. Four days before the Phoenix tournament began Beem had moved up to third alternate, luring him out to the desert. He played a practice round on Tuesday, beat balls on Wednesday, and spent his evenings enjoying the scenery at the Bird's Nest, an enormous on-site tent-turned-watering hole that is far and away the best party of the PGA Tour season. Beem never moved up any farther than third on the waiting list. There is a thirty-two-tiered pecking order to decide who gets to fill out the field at each tournament (156 players is the standard size, though the number can vary in either direction) and graduates of Q School are twenty-fourth from the top, just north of those with minor medical extensions. In 1999, a year of tremendous purse inflation, there were easily a couple hundred players with priority ahead of Beem, and only if enough of them decided to take a week off at the same time would he be able to sneak into any tournaments.

In the season's fourth week Beem squeezed into the Pebble Beach National Pro-Am because of its bloated 181-man field, made possible by a three-course rota. The week couldn't have started any dreamier. Beem's dad's dentist's sister owned a swank house near Spanish Bay, and after a few phone calls Beem secured some accommodations that were not only deluxe but delightfully free of charge. On Monday morning Beem was contacted by a couple of El Paso's most popular DJs, Buzz and Patty from KLAQ 95.5 FM, who had come to the tournament on a boondoggle involving a sister station in nearby Salinas, the dusty farming town that birthed John Steinbeck, among other writers. On that Monday Beem did the first of what would be daily on-air bits on the life of a Tour rookie. (His call-in Q & A's created such a stir back in El Paso that a couple of EPCC members, Rick and Cathy Taft, heard one on Thursday morning and were inspired to fly out in time for the second round.) On Tuesday, Beem played a practice round at Pebble Beach Golf Links, his first spin around the famous course. "It was like one of those MasterCard commercials," he says. "Priceless. I took pictures, the whole bit. I just kept saying to myself, I can't believe I'm playing Pebble. For free!" The round was all the sweeter for the company. Beem played with J. P. Hayes, Dunakey, and Woody Austin, another Dakotas Tour acquaintance. This would become a regular game for Beem, a two-man team best-ball that paired El Paso's finest together. At Pebble Beem and Hayes lost forty bucks apiece, about the usual stakes in a practice round. "No one bets a lot out there, even the guys who love to gamble," says Beem. "There is plenty of pressure beginning on Thursday. We don't need any more on Tuesday. If you play a ten-dollar Nassau or two-dollar skins it's just for fun, to keep your interest."

Beem's first round in the tournament proper was at Poppy Hills, a quirky layout that drives the pros batty with a number of blind shots and confounding doglegs. "I didn't hit it bad at all," says Beem. "All those courses just take so much knowledge, which I didn't have." There is no room to write excuses on the scorecard, just numbers. Beem took a 78. He came back with a 71 at Spyglass Hill, which Peninsula regulars will tell you is the toughest of the three courses, and then the skies opened up, unleashing a particularly virulent strain of Crosby weather. (The Pro-Am used to be known as the Crosby Clambake, honoring its founder, Bing Crosby.) Saturday was, quite simply, one of the most miserable days in the long, cold history of the tournament. "It was old Clambake weather," said Clint Eastwood, a regular at the tournament since the early 1960s. "None of this El Niño shit." Gusts blew upwards of fifty miles per hour, and a series of squalls soaked the players to the bone. Beem had the misfortune to be playing at Pebble Beach, which, with its treeless oceanside holes, played the nastiest of the three courses. On the 7th hole, the downhill 107-yarder that usually calls for an easy sand wedge, Beem was compelled to hit a 6-iron into the teeth of the gale. "A good six-iron," he says. Though he fought valiantly, playing the first thirteen holes in only four-over, Beem got pummeled on the way in, finishing with an 84. "I thought that was a pretty good score," he says, in all seriousness. The final round wound up being cancelled and prize money was paid out based on the existing standings, not that it mattered—Beem had missed the three-round cut by a mile.

The following week he went to San Diego and put together four rounds of par or better to finish forty-fifth and earn $7,567.71. The highlight of the week came well before the tournament even began. On Monday Beem showed up at the course without having lined up a practice round. Loitering around the first tee, he noticed a threesome about to tee off—Fultom Allem, Tommy Armour III, and Frank Nobilo. All three were longtime Tour veterans, and all three were Tour winners. After much internal deliberation, Beem finally asked to join. "Absolutely I was hesitant," he says. "To those guys I was just another rookie, and they see fifty new ones a year. I knew I would have to prove myself with every shot. I was nervous over my first drive, and the butterflies never left me." Beem played well on the front nine, and at the turn Nobilo dropped out. On the 10th tee the threesome picked up a new player—(Long) John Daly, past champ of the British Open and PGA Championship, and a player of cartoonish length and personality. "Now I was really nervous," Beem says. But he continued his solid play, and Daly, with his downhome Arkansas sensibilities, took a shine to Beem. Coming up the 18th hole Daly asked Beem if he'd like to do it again the next day. On Tuesday they played a full eighteen holes together, along with Fulty and TA3. "It was cool to be accepted like that," Beem says. "Daly's won major championships and he's one of the biggest names out here. I mean, I used to watch him on TV when I was in college."

The week after San Diego brought the L.A. Open at the Riviera Country Club, the course Beem calls his favorite on tour. On Thursday he played the front 9 even and then birdied 10, 11, and 12. When he reached the 13th tee his name was alighting the electronic on-course leaderboards. "Oh yeah, absolutely, I was rattled," Beem says. "It felt different than I imagined it would. You spend your whole life dreaming about something like that and then it happens. It's very weird. It meant a lot to me at the time because the biggest thing, for me, when I set foot on tour, was earning the respect of the other players, proving I belonged. All the big boys were in L.A. that week—Tiger, Ernie Els, Davis Love, you name it—and I wanted them to see my name and remember it."

The L.A. Open was only Beem's fourth tournament, but already he was becoming aware of the chasm that separates the PGA Tour's haves and have-nots. "It's almost like there's two Tours," he says. "The big names, you hardly even see those guys during the week if you're a rookie. Because all the top players are in the Wednesday pro-am, they don't have to play practice rounds on Monday. On Tuesday, they've already got their games lined up. Guys like Fred Couples or Tom Lehman or whoever, they've been out here so long they've got a group of guys they always play with. It's hard just to go up and say, 'Hey, y'all want to tee it up?' When the tournament starts you're playing at such radically different times that by the time you've finished your round those guys have already gone home. If you do happen to be in the locker room or at the range at the same time, they're always surrounded by swing coaches and agents and manufacturers' reps and God knows who. It's a weird deal. You almost feel invisible sometimes."

Beem wound up with an opening-round 70 at L.A., a score he matched on Friday to make the cut easily. Following the second round Beem went to a Los Angeles Kings hockey game with a sprawling group of players and caddies, including Steve Duplantis. They chatted a bit before Duplantis big-timed the group, tapping a connection to move to some better seats rinkside. A 75–77 weekend sent Beem skidding to seventy-seventh place (worth $5,208), but his season was nonetheless off to a promising start—three cuts in four tournaments, and already plenty of war stories.

"I was playing pretty good because I was so focused," he says. "I was trying so hard on every shot." Amy Onick had flown in for the weekend at both Pebble Beach and San Diego (at the latter, Beem had stayed with her mom's boyfriend), which had helped Beem keep his head in the game.

The next week, at the Tucson Open, Beem seemed to be concentrating on everything but golf. A dozen of Beem's sponsors roadtripped to the tournament, and, playing hooky from their wives and workaday lives, they collectively released their inner frat boy. Beem made a few token protestations but was all too happy to join in the revelry. Tucson was basically a weeklong party, and Beem, predictably, opened with a 76, taking himself out of the tournament. He scarcely did any better on Friday, shooting a second round 74 to miss the cut. At least Beem had a few laughs between the ropes. At one point during his round on Friday he looked over at his gallery—basically a dozen sunburned middle-aged guys with bloodshot eyes—and spied Cotter White, a buttoned-down financial adviser, walking at roughly a forty-five-degree angle to the ground. Beem called over to the group and then imitated White's stooped carriage. That sent the boys into spasms of laughter.

One missed cut would not be a big deal if Beem's lack of focus had merely been an aberration. But Tucson was hardly the last time his life off the golf course would compromise his performance on it. "He always has to feel like the star of the party," says Larry Beem, who traveled to Tucson for Tuesday's practice round, the first time he had seen his son play on the PGA Tour. He didn't bother to stick around for the rest of the week. "Rich surrounds himself with a lot of people and a lot of drama, and then he suffers from social life overload. He OD's on people, on fun, and on drink. If you want to be outrageous, be a rock star. If you want to be a golfer, copy Arnold Palmer. He had his fun on the side, but he always projected an image of class, and he never let anything get in the way of his golf."

THE WEEK AFTER TUCSON the Tour began its Florida swing, and Beem found himself at the Doral-Ryder Open in Miami. More to the point, he found himself in South Beach, that nexus of late-model sports cars and scantily clad models, trendy restaurants and chic clubs, the entire scene illuminated in neon and set to a pounding salsa beat. Five of Beem's college buddies showed up early in the week at Doral, and Beem and his crew were determined to paint the town crimson. He particularly enjoyed an encounter he had in the wee hours of Tuesday night with Tim Hardaway, the Miami Heat star who had played his college hoops at the University of Texas-El Paso. Beem spied Hardaway at a late-night grub spot and, ever the jock sniffer, strolled over and introduced himself. "What was cool was I wasn't just another fan but a fellow athlete, you know?" says Beem. "I told him I was in town for the tournament and that got his attention. It felt good to say I was part of the Tour."

The Florida swing was the beginning of Beem's intensive traveling, and this brought a whole new world of complications. Booking plane tickets was the least of it, as the PGA Tour has an in-house reservation system offering good zone fares, though there is no magic discount as is widely believed. Where to stay was a far dicier proposition. Beem knew the cities on the West Coast, and often had friends or family in town to offer suggestions, if not a spare bed. Florida and the rest of the Southeast was a new frontier. As would become his practice, Beem called the player relations desk at Doral and got a fax of all the hotels where rooms had been blocked on behalf of the players. "I would just look at the list and take the cheapest one," Beem says. Those rooms usually ran around $100 a night, at chains on par with Best Western or Courtyard by Marriott.

As for meals, "My dad told me if I ate McDonald's I would play like McDonald's," Beem says, but his tastes were nonetheless downmarket. "Outback Steakhouse, Chili's, those would be what I considered nice," he says. "More often than not I would go to Boston Market, take it back to my room, and pop on the TV." Ah, the glamorous life of a pro golfer.

To Beem's way of thinking, packing was the worst part of the job. He traveled with four bags—a backpack he carried on, a "huge" garment bag, a duffel, and, of course, his golf clubs, which once cost him a tariff from the airlines because it weighed in excess of a hundred pounds, thanks to so many spare clubs, trial putters, and backup drivers. Beem would become so flummoxed trying to plan two or three weeks' worth of outfits he would sometimes lay them out on his bed in advance of packing, like a fashion-conscious teenage girl. "Packing, to me, is about as much fun as three-putting," Beem says.

Once he got settled in at Doral, Beem opened with a 70, continuing his relatively strong play in the first round of tournaments. He slipped to a 74 on Friday but just sneaked under the cut line. Rounds of 75-71 followed, leaving him in seventy-fourth place, worth $5,730. If Beem wasn't exactly tearing up the Tour, he could at least take comfort in the fact he had made four cuts in six tournaments. "It took me a long time to realize how important it is to make cuts as a rookie," he says. "It's not just because it means you're gonna get a check at the end of the week, although that is nice. What's important is that you get to play two extra rounds. The experience you get, and the course knowledge that comes with it, is worth a lot more than money."

Following Doral, Beem went to the Honda Classic, outside Fort Lauderdale. It was his sixth tournament in as many weeks. Never knowing when the next opportunity might come, Beem says, "I wasn't going to skip a thing. Every tournament they let me into I was gonna play." Beem shot a first-round 71 at the Honda, followed by a 74 to miss the cut. "I fought hard," he says, "but I was just wiped out. Just exhausted physically and mentally. I hadn't traveled in two and a half years, and never on this scale. The golf was a lot more stressful than the Dakotas Tour, too, as you might imagine. So was living. I didn't know the cities, I didn't know how to get around, and I was sweating every dollar. I was ready for a break."

Beem got one in the two weeks after Honda, as the schedule

brought Arnold Palmer's Bay Hill Invitational and The Players Championship, A-list tournaments reserved only for the top players. Beem headed back to El Paso to hang out with Amy and catch up on his rest. He would need it. Nearly a third of his season was already in the books, and things were about to get interesting.

CHAPTER

• 8 •

THE 1999 SEASON was not a good one for caddies. Before May had rolled around more than a dozen loopers had been fired, including those of such world-class players as Tiger Woods, Mark O'Meara, Ernie Els, and Jesper Parnevik. South African David Frost even made history, of a dubious sort, when he became the first player to confirm his man's termination via email. Caddying is a fickle business, and those who ply the trade have only the security of a handshake deal. In 1999 the PGA Tour was flooded by the riches of a new TV contract, and the huge money added a layer of strain to the already delicate player-caddie dynamic. In April, O'Meara—coming off his Masters-British Open double dip in 1998—fired his longtime bagman Jerry Higginbotham, in part because he wanted to bring in a new caddie that he could pay less. "I find it hard to believe I will ever again pay a caddie ten percent of a win," O'Meara said at the time.

The most stunning victim of the caddie purge was Mike (Fluff) Cowan, who had been the Tenzing Norgay to Woods's Edmund Hillary ever since young Tiger began scaling great heights as a pro in September of 1996. They were a hilariously disparate duo—Woods young and slick, with the athletic gait of a puma, while Fluff was more than twice his boss's age, built like a duffel bag, and, with his graying Wilford Brimley mustache and shaggy haircut, bore an arresting resemblance to rock legend/sperm donor David Crosby. Fluff has long been a die-hard Deadhead, and for nineteen and a half years he and Peter Jacobsen, the noted jokester and lead singer of the bar band Jake Trout and the Flounders, had made up the most colorful team in golf. "He was living in his car when he came to me," says Jacobsen. "He had this huge beard with lunch from four days ago in it and this old Pontiac and his dog, Shivas. I thought, Why not?" Fluff cried like a baby when he told Jacobsen he was taking the job with Woods.

Woods's phenomenal success got him and his caddie an unprecedented amount of network TV face time, and Fluff soon developed a cult following. There have been well-known caddies before—Bruce Edwards, who packed for Tom Watson in his heyday, and Angelo Argea, Jack Nicklaus's longtime bagman, both earned a certain measure of renown in their day, but this was confined to golf circles. Fluff was the first caddie to crossover into the mainstream. He began doing nationally broadcast TV commercials for a well-known hotel chain, put out an instructional video (on playing, not caddying), was the subject of a profile in *Sports Illustrated,* and began signing more autographs than most of the players. In May of 1997, in the wake of Woods's epic win at the Masters, Tour veteran Jeff Sluman called Fluff "the second-biggest celebrity out here."

This all made for hot copy, but Woods eventually grew tired of the act. He created enough hullabaloo on his own; he didn't need sodden fans shouting "Touch of Gray" lyrics to his caddie while he was trying to make million-dollar putts. Fluff didn't help himself by participating in a round-table discussion with three other caddies for *Golf Digest,* which hit newsstands in January of 1999. Caddies, like old Italian mobsters, live under a coda of *omertà.* To reveal details, no matter how trivial, about one's player is considered professional suicide, and the compensation issue is especially touchy. Fluff was shockingly candid in the *Digest* interview about his pay. (Woods, though notoriously cheap, gave Fluff a generous base salary of $1,000 a week, plus the elevated percentages of 8 percent for making the cut, 9 percent for a Top 10, and 10 percent for a victory.) Fluff's candor pissed off Woods royally, adding to what were already strained relations. In February of 1999, prior to the final round of the L.A. Open, Woods informed Fluff that he was going to use a college buddy who needed help paying for medical school as his caddie at the following week's Match Play Championship. This was to be the first of the glitzy new World Golf Championship superevents, which boasted record $5 million purses, including a cool mil to the winner (which meant a hundred large to the winning caddie).

Fluff was miffed at the snub, and the final round at L.A. was played in an awkward silence. With a strong charge on the back nine Woods had a chance to force a playoff with a birdie at the last. The 18th hole at Riviera is one of the great finishing holes in golf, and on that Sunday it was playing into a stiff breeze. Standing in the middle of the fairway Woods was deliberating between clubs, and for the first time all day he asked his caddie for his opinion. Fluff mumbled something to the effect that he wasn't really sure which was the right club. It was the wrong time to quit on your man. When Woods got over his ball he must've still been hot, and he proceeded to uncork a monstrous slice, sending his ball skidding down an embankment, where it came to rest next to an ice-cream cart. Woods didn't get his birdie, and Fluff never worked for him again.

EVEN IN THIS CLIMATE Duplantis, amazingly, continued with his usual shenanigans. Over the first two months of the '99 season—when Sierra was again back in the Bronx with Sollange Lewis—he was late "maybe a dozen times," Furyk says. "Maybe two dozen. It all blends together."

Making Duplantis's laxity all the more shocking was his awareness of the ferocious competition for bags, especially among the top players. The big money pouring into golf had all of a sudden turned caddying into a respectable profession, and a new breed of looper was beginning to show up on tour—the former white collar professional. Dick Christie, Fred Funk's caddie, gave up a judgeship for the pleasure of toting a forty-pound golf bag; Don Thom, Notah Begay's man, was formerly a high-ranking police officer in Ontario; and Ken Dawson, caddie to his brother Marco, had been a practicing lawyer. With all the jockeying for work, "It's one big ratfuck out there," says Duplantis. "Guys will stab you in the back in a second. Jim was constantly getting notes in his locker or messages on his cell phone from these sharks who wanted my job. If he was at a bar, guaranteed some caddie would pay for his drink, even the tightwad bastards. These fuckin' guys would knife their mother in the heart for a bag like Jim's. People were always whispering in his ear about bullshit involving me. It was like a dozen guys were always standing around with stopwatches, just waiting for me to show up late."

On this account, Duplantis did not disappoint. As to why the ax never fell, Furyk says, "I don't really have an answer for that, other than to say it was a hard decision to make. Steve and I had had a lot of success, and I considered him a friend."

In the third week of March Furyk played at the Bay Hill Invitational, Arnold Palmer's tournament in Orlando. The Bay Hill Club is some fifty miles from Duplantis's house, and he was thrilled to be sleeping in his own bed and commuting to the tournament. On the morning of the first round Duplantis was cruising on Interstate 4 when he hit a monumental traffic jam. A couple of tanker trucks had wrecked, shutting down the Interstate, though Duplantis didn't know that immediately. "As soon as I hit the traffic I called Jim, and he was like, 'Don't worry about it, I saw the whole thing on the news,' " says Duplantis. "As it got later I kept calling. I talked to him personally twice, and two other times I had the locker room attendant take him messages on the driving range, to give him updates. I don't know what more I could have done."

By the time Duplantis arrived at the course Furyk was hitting his approach into the 8th green, having grabbed another loooper for the day, a friend of Jeff Sluman's. Duplantis snatched Furyk's bag on the 9th tee and caddied the rest of the day. "Jim was like, I don't want to talk about it, let's just play," says Duplantis. "He had said he saw the report on the news, so I thought he understood. We never really talked about the whole thing." Duplantis caddied the rest of the tournament and the following week as well, at The Players Championship in Ponte Vedra Beach, Florida, where Furyk was now living. In the parking lot of TPC at Sawgrass, following the final round, Furyk told Duplantis, "We gotta have a talk, and you're not gonna like it. I'm letting you go."

"My knees buckled," says Duplantis. "It was shock, disbelief, fear, all at once."

They retired to Furyk's nearby house and talked for an hour. "Well, he talked and I listened," says Duplantis. "He said, basically, he likes me as a person, but I had too much stuff going on, too much turmoil."

Says Furyk, "Steve is a good caddie. That's never really been the issue. When it comes to doing the yardages, understanding strategy and the nuances of the game, he's very good. He does a great job of crowd control. But everything else that goes into the job—being on time, being prepared, being professional—that's where we had problems.

"I told Steve many times that he could take a month off here or there to handle the things in his personal life, and that the job would still be waiting for him when he came back. He never chose that route. He was making some money and he probably felt like he didn't want to miss out on any paychecks. Whatever. It was time for Steve to take care of his business, and for me to take care of mine."

Furyk handed Duplantis an envelope full of checks—one for every tournament dating back to the previous October. Players and caddies deal with the payment issue in a myriad of ways, and Furyk and Duplantis had always been casual about it. The last thing Duplantis said before leaving Furyk's house was, "Good luck at the Masters," which was to be played two weeks later.

Looking back, Duplantis spins a contradictory mix of contrition, disillusionment, and denial. "I fucked up and I wish I did things differently," he says. "Jim thought I wasn't working as hard as I had been and he was probably right about that. But I definitely was not as unprepared or as lazy as he thought I was.

"Your caddie is a reflection of you as a player," Duplantis adds. "If your caddie's a big fucking idiot it makes you look bad. I understand that." Finally, Duplantis says, "The one thing that really pisses me off is that for once I had a totally legitimate excuse. Is it my fault they shut down I-Four for like, two hours?"

AFTER RETURNING HOME from The Players Championship, Duplantis spent the next couple of days in seclusion, sitting around his house wondering what to do. The calm was shattered by a phone call from a *GolfWeek* reporter. Is it true Fluff is caddying for Furyk at the Masters?

Well, I'm not, so I guess somebody has to be, Duplantis had said.

"That was when it really hit me, because I knew word was going to get out," he says. "I knew I was going to have to call my family and tell them, and I knew that Jim wasn't going to change his mind. That was a tough day."

When Duplantis broke the news to his loved ones they reacted with something less than surprise. "My take on Jim is that he's a real perfectionist," says Sandy Cantin, Duplantis's mother. "He's very demanding of himself and those around him. He likes perfection, and I don't think Steve was delivering that. I thought it was a long time coming, actually."

"I still can't believe Steve let himself get fired by Furyk," says Clarence Rose, Duplantis's old friend and first boss. Rose could see the problems developing, but was reluctant to say something to Duplantis. "That's not my place," he says. Of losing Furyk's bag, Rose adds, "I reckon that's like letting a winning lottery ticket fall out of your pocket. Big-time player like that, how many weeks a year you gonna have to work? Twenty-three? Twenty-five? I mean, c'mon. That's not asking much. But I've been around golf long enough to know that these things happen all the time. There's no sense in blaming one person or the other. It's like when a marriage ends. It doesn't matter why—the important thing is moving on."

Fluff did in fact caddie for Furyk at that Masters, setting off a minor media frenzy. They finished fourteenth. Duplantis, meanwhile, was acting like a man undergoing a midlife crisis at age twenty-six. Sollange Lewis had flown down from New York to cheer him up, and they began talking about getting married (never mind that Duplantis's divorce was not yet final). Duplantis, however, didn't score any points with Lewis when he told her one evening, "By the way, I'm leaving for St. Martin in the morning." He jetted off to the Caribbean to play golf and hang out with a buddy, leaving Lewis behind with Sierra. "I'm sure I came up with some kind of rationalization, but in reality I was just being a dick," he says.

Through all of this Duplantis didn't get a single phone call from any players inquiring about his availability. "I was really surprised by the number of guys who shied away from me," he says. "It hurt my feelings."

"As a caddie all you have is your reputation," says Furyk. "It's kinda strange to say, but name any player you want and I can tell you what kind of person his caddie is, whether or not he is prepared every day, whether or not he shows up on time, you name it. Word travels fast on tour."

In early May, after nearly five weeks without a loop, Duplantis got a call from an old friend, journeyman David Morland, who needed a caddie for the New Orleans Open, which was to begin May 6. Duplantis jumped at the chance to get back out on Tour. "It was almost full-scale panic time," says Duplantis. "I had to take care of my daughter. I had a mortgage, power bills, car payments . . ."

Over the first two rounds Morland was paired with Rich Beem. "I didn't pay attention to his game at all," says Duplantis. "Nothing he did impressed me. He just seemed like a run of the mill rookie." Still, Duplantis and Beem were friendly from the hockey game in L.A., and knowing that Beem didn't have a regular caddie, Duplantis suggested they exchange phone numbers. When Morland missed the cut those digits were the only thing Duplantis had to show for his week's work.

The Texas swing began the week after New Orleans, and again Duplantis took Sierra to Fort Worth to stay with Vicki. He was out with friends at a cowboy bar one night in Dallas when, after returning from a trip to the rest room, one of Duplantis's buddies said, "Dude, you gotta check out this this insane waitress." It turned out to be none other than Shannon Pennington. "So she takes my friends' orders and then walks away without even acknowleding my presence," says Duplantis. "They were like, what's up with that? I said, 'Yeah, well, I almost married that chick. It didn't work out so well.' " They spent the evening ignoring each other, but as he was leaving the bar Duplantis pantomined to an off-duty Pennington, who was shaking her groove thing on the dance floor, to give him a call.

While in Dallas Duplantis spent a day poking around the Byron Nelson Classic, trying to figure out which way the wind was blowing. It was there that he bumped into Mike (Fluff) Cowan. "I saw Fluff and said, 'Are you sure Jim's in the field, because I didn't see his name on player's list,' " Duplantis says. "So Fluff calls Jim at home, and reaches him just as he was walking out the door for the airport. It turns out Jim had forgotten to officially commit to the tournament, and now it was too late, so he wasn't going to be able to play. So I said to Fluff, 'Hey, it looks like neither of us is working for Jim this week, so let's go play golf.'

"That's how it goes out here. I didn't see it as Fluff stealing my job. I viewed it as Jim wanting to make a change and Fluff was the best man available at the time. It can be an uncomfortable situation, though. Sometimes you just kinda walk by that guy with your head down and try to pretend you didn't see him."

Steve wasn't the only Duplantis hanging around the Byron Nelson. Four days after the tournament ended he filed a restraining order against Vicki back home in Hillsborough County's 13th Judicial Circuit Court. In legal jargon, it was an "ex parte motion to enjoin and prohibit Wife from Husband's job sites." According to the complaint, "Husband was at the Byron Nelson Golf Tournament which was held this past weekend. It was at this tournament that Wife intentionally interfered, interrupted, and embarrassed Husband, by direct contact with the professional golfers, caddies, and others, by exhibiting the following behavior:

a. Wearing scantily clad clothing with fake tattoos and telling the professional golfers and caddies to visit her where she is currently stripping (The Santa Fe Men's Club);

b. Telling the professional golfers and caddies intimate details about her and Husband; and

c. Drinking excessively and causing an otherwise embarrassing scene."

The petition was granted on May 21st.

A couple of days later, while lounging around at home, Duplantis got a call from Pennington. They got to talking and he mentioned that he was thinking of phoning a rookie named Rich Beem, whom Duplantis was pretty sure needed a caddie for the following week's Kemper Open. After some negotiations Pennington, bored with waitressing, agreed she would serve as Sierra's nanny if the job with Beem came through. She was careful to stress that the arrangement would be business, and nothing more. Before calling Beem, Duplantis had given little thought beyond the Kemper. "I was looking at it strictly as a one-week job, just to get to put my face out there and get back in circulation," he says. "From everything I had seen out of Rich I figured we would be lucky to make the cut."

CHAPTER

When Rich Beem returned to El Paso in mid-March for his first real break of the '99 season, at the top of his to-do list was find an apartment with Amy Onick. They had been dating for over a year now, and both felt they were ready to begin shacking up. Onick had been staying with her grandparents and was eager for some freedom. Beem, meanwhile, was aware that he would be losing a good deal of his own. One of the revelations of his first two and a half months on tour was the omnipresence of golf groupies. "In every town we go to I promise you there are always great-looking female fans that are interested in meeting professional golfers," he says. "It's not hard to meet them, if that's what you're interested in." On the golf course, "Of course we notice them," Beem says. "Every player on tour does, and if they tell you differently they're full of shit. But the whole time I was with Amy all I did was look and smile. I never went out and chased it, even though it was always there." After settling into a cozy apartment in El Paso, Beem went back to work, at the BellSouth Classic, outside Atltanta.

The BellSouth was to be Gus Braunschweig's final tournament on Beem's bag. It had been a fun experience, but Gus had never planned on making caddying his life's work, and Beem was becoming increasingly aware that he needed an experienced bagman to help navigate so many unfamiliar courses. He was slowly learning about life on tour.

Through his connections with the manufacturers' reps he landed another endorsement deal the week of the BellSouth. Beem signed with Odyssey putters, a division of Callaway, pocketing another $15,000 to use Odyssey blades and carry the company's logo on his bag. Fifteen grand wouldn't even fill up the tank in Greg Norman's G-V, but for Beem it was like found money.

Beem was hoping to send Gus out in style at the BellSouth, and he got off to a decent start, with a first-round 71. Beem was cruising along on Friday until his 14th hole (he was actually playing number 5 at TPC of Sugarloaf, as he had started the day on the back nine along with the rest of the Group 3 players). The hole position on Sugarloaf's 5th was as a sucker pin, so-called because only suckers would be foolish enough to aim for it. It was cut on the front left of the green, only a couple paces beyond a creek. Beem was even on his round to that point, and figuring he would need a birdie or two down the stretch to make the cut, he decided to go for broke. Unfortunately he misjudged the swirling wind, and dumped a 9-iron into the creek. He chipped on indifferently, to eight feet, and then missed that putt for a homely double bogey. He came back with a birdie on 6, and then made a thirty-footer to save par at the 7th. On number 8 he produced his best iron shot of the week, a 3-iron that rifled through the wind to fifteen feet. He missed the putt. After studying the leaderboard on the 9th tee Beem knew he needed a birdie on his final hole to make the cut. He drove perfectly, smote a 7-iron to eight feet . . . and then had the birdie putt horseshoe out of the hole. He was down the road, and so, too, was Gus.

Following the BellSouth, Beem drove to Augusta, Georgia, for the Masters (where Jim Furyk and Fluff were having their coming out party). He had not been invited to play in the tournament, of course, but he had lined up a pass to the grounds for Monday's practice round. Beem anonymously strolled Augusta National and soaked up the pageantry, brimming with so much aw-shucks enthusiasm even the azaleas blushed. "It was surreal," he says. "After a lifetime of watching that tournament on TV, to finally go there and see it for myself—wow, if that doesn't inspire you, nothing will."

From the Masters Beem returned to El Paso to see Amy, but somewhere along the way he misplaced his golf swing. In a series of casual rounds around El Paso Country Club he hit the ball sideways, and no amount of time at the range could cure him. After being forced to sit out the Masters and the following week's Heritage Classic at Hilton Head, Beem returned to action at the Greater Greensboro Open. "By the time I got to the GGO I was just a mess," says Beem. "I didn't have a lot of confidence, and it showed." During the first round Beem missed the first eight greens, something of an accomplishment for a guy with his name on his bag. He slashed his way to a 78. In a marathon practice session following the round, Beem discovered a little something, and he came out smoking on Friday. He made five birdies in his first seven holes, to get himself right back around the cut line. "On the back nine I went for every flag," he says. "I got in the mind-set where I had nothing to lose." Beem fought hard for his 69, and though he didn't make the cut he scored something of a moral victory. It was the first time since the second round of the San Diego Invitational that he had broken 70, a span of ten weeks and seventeen rounds.

The GGO faded into the Houston Open. For the second week in a row Beem hired a stranger in the parking lot to serve as his caddie, this time an LPGA refugee who had never seen the course. Due to heavy rains leading up to the tournament, the grounds crew at TPC at The Woodlands hadn't been able to properly mow the grass, and the rough was brutally thick. Beem opened with an even par-72, and then in the second round he turned in 1 over, what he felt was going to be the cut line. Playing cautiously, trying not to make any mistakes, Beem instead made a rash of them. Everything that could go wrong did—bad luck, bad swings, and a series of awful putts. He wound up shooting 77 to miss his fourth straight cut.

"That's when the doubts started creeping in," Beem says. "This was the first prolonged slump I'd had in two years."

There were a number of factors fueling Beem's downward spiral. One of the most basic was the difference in the caliber and setup of the golf courses. He wasn't playing El Paso Country Club anymore. "I remember early in the year him telling me he couldn't believe how tough the pins were, how high the rough was, and how hard and fast the greens were rolling," says Cameron Doan, Beem's old boss, whom he would often call from the road. "Every day there are a bunch of pins tucked on the front of the green, usually behind bunkers. To get at them he started trying to hit the ball high, with a lot of spin, which has never been his shot. It started affecting his alignment and ball position. When Rich gets his setup out of whack, he can really start hitting it crooked."

Beem was not helping himself by slacking off on his conditioning. "When Rich started the year he was in tip-top shape," says his trainer Bob McDonald. "He was ready for battle. After a couple of months he started big-timing it. He got lazy, at the worst possible time. With all the traveling, and the irregular meals and what not, he needed his strength, but it was disappearing fast."

For all of that, Beem's struggles transcended the physical.

WHEN SUSIE BEEM'S SON Aaron was just a little squirt he used to call Larry Beem "Grumps." It was his way of saying Grandpa, but Aaron had no way of knowing how right he was. Larry Beem has long been considered something of a curmudgeon by his family. "That's just part of being a lifelong manic-depressive," Larry says matter-of-factly. "The whole depression thing is hard to understand, even by me. My family has never made the effort, that's for damn sure."

Beem can find periods of melancholy in his earliest memories, but he grew up long before the sophisticated recognition of emotional problems. In recent years he has formally been diagnosed as bipolar, but for most of his life he had simply been considered grumpy or eccentric. Certainly Beem's condition explains his love-hate relationship with golf. "My depression has always been one where I run to dark places," he says. "I run from people, I run from events, I even run from things that deep down I know that I want."

Golf is, by its nature, the loneliest game, and that is amplified for a young touring pro, where life is a series of unfamiliar cities and empty hotel rooms. As Rich was heading out on tour his father worried less about his son's golf swing than his mood swings. "Rich's got a depressive problem, but he doesn't know it yet," says Larry. "Take his friends away, he gets like me—very depressed. You can see it when he plays bad, because when you play bad it's very isolating. You're all alone between those ropes.

If he gets on a downer, he gets very low. It's a form of depression and he's going to have to watch it."

As Rich's play worsened, the depressive problem that his father had warned of began to materialize. Beem wasn't having any fun, on or off the course, and was becoming increasingly withdrawn. "When I started missing cuts I stopped going out as much, even just to dinner with the other guys," says Rich. "I wanted to get away from the whole scene. I didn't want to have to talk about my round. I was beginning to be embarrassed about my golf game, thinking maybe I was just a fluke." Beem was so down after self-immolating at Houston that his mom sent him a bouquet of flowers, with a stuffed lion intended to remind him to be courageous. "She could hear in my voice how devastated I was," says Beem.

The isolation was compounded because Onick had been unable to travel to a tournament since February. "She couldn't get away from school," says Beem, "and the long-distance thing wasn't working out. We were trying to figure out how our relationship could survive." Beem had lost his wingman when Braunschweig gave up caddying, and during the Tour's swing through the Southeast he had few people with whom to hang out. At season's end Beem would say there were only four tournament sites where he didn't know a soul, and three of them were Greensboro, Houston, and New Orleans, the city he traveled to the week after the Houston Open.

In his first round at the New Orleans Open Beem was even through fourteen holes, and then he finished with a flourish, going eagle, birdie, birdie, par to shoot a 68 and earn a spot among the leaders. "It was like, wow, this is fun again," he says. In his second round Beem was one over par through fourteen holes, -3 overall, and figuring two under would be the cut line. On his 15th hole—number 6 at English Turn Golf and Country Club, because once again he had been consigned to the back nine first—Beem walloped a drive on the par-5, leaving 240 yards to carry a small pond and reach the front edge of the green. Two hundred forty yards is the outer limits of how far Beem can carry a 3-wood, but, "I said to myself, let's not think about the cut, let's make an eagle here and get back in the tournament," says Beem. "I promise you it was the best 3-wood I've ever hit." The ball came up a few feet short of the green, splashing down at water's edge. Visible just beneath the pond's surface, it was within the rules for Beem to attempt to play the ball out of the water, though hardly advisable. "All the weeks of frustration finally got me," he says. "I went in after it. I had maybe a one in one thousand chance of pulling the shot off, but I was damned sure gonna try. I got that attitude from my dad, that I'll-show-you-you-son-of-a-bitch thing. So I took off my shoes, rolled up my socks, got in that murky water, took a mighty swing. When I looked up there was mud all over me, but I didn't see the ball on the green." It hadn't moved an inch and was still lying in the water, mocking him. Beem finally ate the penalty stroke, took a drop, and went on to make double bogey on a birdie hole. He would miss the cut by one stroke, naturally.

"I truly was starting to believe I didn't have what it takes," Beem says. "I thought I was gonna be just another one of those guys who spends a year on tour and is never heard from again."

After the round Beem had gotten some kind words from Steve Duplantis, who had witnessed Beem's train wreck while caddying in the same group for his friend, David Morland. "Steve was really nice about it," says Beem. "He was like, hang in there, you can be a great player."

Says Duplantis, "I don't even remember that. I must've been on autopilot."

Beem flew from New Orleans to Dallas, to attempt to Monday qualify for the following week's Byron Nelson Classic. Every noninvitational tournament on the PGA Tour reserves four spots for open qualifying, which is available to any professional (or amateur with a handicap of 2.0 or less) who coughs up $200 to give it a shot. Monday qualifying is a one-round shootout, where it is not uncommon to have a dozen or more players in a sudden-death playoff for the final one or two slots. Beem lasted all of ten holes at the Nelson qualifier. Three over par and at wit's end, he simply walked off the golf course, the first time he had ever quit in the middle of a competitive round. "I packed it in," he says. "It had reached a point where I didn't want to think golf, see golf, or smell golf."

•

BEEM RETURNED TO EL PASO, tail between his legs, but Amy Onick wasn't having any of his moping. "She gave me a pretty good talking to," says Beem. "Basically she just reminded me how lucky I was to be on the PGA Tour and that I owed it to myself to do everything in my power to succeed. I was feeling a little bit sorry for myself, but Amy took care of that real quick."

Beem had two weeks off until his next tournament, the Kemper Open, and he set about reclaiming his golf game, and his competitive spirit. His dedication showed up in his workouts—Beem made nine appointments with McDonald over the two weeks and showed up for every one. Beem also set about getting his golf clubs in shape. Arriving on tour was, he says, "Like being a kid in a candy store." Pro golfers are just like weekend hackers—they love to fiddle with new golf clubs. The only difference is the sticks are free to the pros and being handed out at every tournament. Beem had changed clubs more often than underwear throughout the season's first four months, but upon his return to El Paso he decided to simplify. He went back to his old shafts—Memphis 10 stock, cut down a quarter inch, 1 degree upright. (He had been trying out stiffer shafts throughout much of the year.) Beem had been rotating three or four putters ever since signing with Odyssey at the BellSouth Classic. He finally picked one and decided he would stick with it come hell or high water. After spending months experimenting with wedges—different models, different shapes, different lengths—he went back to an old set of Clevelands that had served him well in his journey through Q School. Finally, Beem put in his bag a prototype of a new 8.2-degree Greatest Big Bertha, which had a different shape and design than those on the market. Now armed for combat, Beem began playing every day around El Paso Country Club.

On the first hole of his first round with Cameron Doan, Beem took one putt and Doan said, "Jesus, Rich, what happened to your putting stroke?" Beem's once long, languid action had become a short, quick, defensive jab, without his even knowing it. Doan and Beem began putting in man hours on the practice green. Around this time Beem saw some tape of David Duval, who to that point in 1999 had already won four tournaments, and shot a historic 59 at the Bob Hope. Beem made note of how Duval took the putter back close to the ground, helping to keep it on line, and he began incorporating that motion into his takeaway. As for his long game, Beem's old problems at address—alignment, weight distribution, ball position—were also corrected with the help of Doan and Bill Eschenbrenner.

A week into this spring training Beem teed it up at regional qualifying for the U.S. Open. Twenty-three players were competing for two spots at Painted Dunes, the course where, two years earlier, Beem had dropped that 65-64 on Doan and the boys to begin his ascent to the Tour. For the qualifier an army of supporters turned out to cheer Beem on—Amy, a dozen of his sponsors, and bunches of friends and family from across Las Cruces and El Paso. Duly inspired, Beem says, "I fought like hell." He wound up grinding out a 68 to nab one of the two top spots, sending him on his way to sectional qualifying, which would be played in Memphis nine days after the Kemper Open. "Making it throught the qualifier was a big deal," says Beem. "It was the first positive thing to happen to me on a golf course in a long time." After that Beem was up to his old tricks at El Paso Country Club—shooting 65s and getting in people's pockets.

"It was important for me to get back to making birdies again, which you can do at El Paso Country Club," he says. "Just getting on a roll, making eight or nine birdies in a round was great for my confidence."

During Beem's second week in El Paso he had a couple of important conversations. The first was with Doan, who circled back to Beem's earlier laments about his struggles with the tight pins and hard greens. "Rich had gotten in his head he had to balloon these irons into the greens and hit it next to the flag," says Doan. "I said, 'Rich, if you hit your normal shot, that low slider, how many feet past the hole will your ball go?' He said probably about fifteen. So I said to him, 'Don't you think you can make a couple of fifteen-footers in a round?' Well, of course he can. So what's the problem here? If he plays his game, the worst he's going to do is two-putt from fifteen feet for par, and he's definitely going to make some of those fifteen-footers for birdie. If he tries to play their game, firing at sucker pins, he brings bogey or worse into play. You know, it's really not that difficult a concept. I think he finally grasped it."

Beem also rang up his dad. "He'll call once in a while," says

Larry, "but I never know if he wants a lesson or if he's just being condescending." On this occasion, Rich wanted a lesson.

Even at the highest levels of golf there are players with only one ball flight, and they use it like a crutch, even if a given shot dictates they should work their ball the other way. Beem is AC/DC. He can go both ways. Under his dad's tutelege he learned to hit a high, soft cut; a low, hard hook; and everything in between. This versatility in his shotmaking was a key to Beem's game, particularly in his wedge game, where creativity can most readily be expressed. Because El Paso Country Club plays so short Beem had ample opportunity through the years to work on his play from 125 yards in. "At Q School if you gave me a wedge, it was a done deal. Birdie every time," he says. "Out on tour I just don't have nearly as many wedges. The courses were longer, the rough higher, and the greens were so severe, so at the start of the year I was playing a lot more defensively, playing away from pins. My wedge game had basically disappeared." That was why Rich needed to talk to his father.

"I told him he needed to get back to playing golf the way Satchel Paige used to pitch—junk all over the place," says Larry. "He had always had a fastball, a slider, and a curve. When he got on tour he stopped doing that. To be a great wedge player you need eight or ten different shots, which means you have to have eight or ten different speeds you swing the club. Rich had lost that. Instead of making different swings he was making the same full swing, and just using different wedges, like all those other robots out there. That was something we talked a lot about, because it was clear to me he needed to be reminded."

With the Kemper Open only a couple of days away everything was falling into place for Beem. The only unsettling thing was his caddie situation. The constant turnover on his bag had affected his rhythm, as well as his preparation. Not trusting the opinion of the randoms he was scrounging up, he was forced to figure out the yardages and strategies on his own during his limited access to the tournament courses. Beem desperately wanted to find a regular looper, but even after talking to mentors like J. P. Hayes and Paul Stankowski he was unable to come up with any candidates. Besides Steve Duplantis, that is. Beem had been kicking himself for the better part of the previous two weeks, because following the New Orleans Open he had somehow misplaced Duplantis's phone number. Duplantis had said to keep in touch, and Beem was of the mind to see if he wanted to work together, if only he could find that damn phone number. On Friday, May 21, two days before he was heading to Potomac, Maryland, for the Kemper Open, Beem's phone rang. It was Duplantis, wondering if he needed a caddie for Kemper.

When Beem got off the phone he was, he says, "doing jumping jacks," much to the bemusement of Onick, who happened to be there when her boyfriend took the call.

"I told Amy, 'You don't understand—this is one of the best, most experienced caddies in golf,' " says Beem. "I was just so excited because finally things were breaking my way. I knew having Steve by my side would be an advantage, and that *he* would call *me* only gave me even more confidence. I was already heading to the Kemper thinking about doing well, but that just raised my expectations even more. I was like, forget about just making the cut. We're gonna go up there and finish in the Top Twenty-five."

CHAPTER

• 10 •

RICH BEEM ARRIVED in suburban Washington, D.C., on Sunday night, May 23rd, four days in advance of the Kemper Open. In the preceding two weeks he had pushed himself so hard that his right wrist was feeling a bit sore. He wisely chose to take that Monday off, touring not The Tournament Players Club of Avenel but the White House, Capitol Building, CIA headquarters, Smithsonian museums, and a few of the monuments, along the way grabbing a fancy dinner with an old high school buddy, Corey McDaniel, a lobbyist who lived in D.C. It was a relaxing way to start the week, and anyway, he couldn't have played a practice round without his caddie. During their matchmaking phone call the previous Friday, Beem had said to Steve Duplantis, "Okay, I'll see you Monday then." Duplantis replied that Monday was out. How about Tuesday? "I didn't feel like I had to impress him, because it was just a one-week job, you know?" says Duplantis. He arrived in town late Monday night, with Sierra and his freshly minted nanny, Shannon Pennington, in tow.

Beem wasn't too put off by the blowoff, figuring that Duplantis had paid enough dues not to have to juggle his schedule for a rookie. Beem had no way of knowing that Duplantis's belated arrival would be the first of many incidents that would color their working relationship. "I was very naïve," says Beem. "I didn't know Steve's reputation whatsoever. I had heard rumors, but every time it was something different, so I just kind of dismissed them. What I *was* certain about was his experience, and his knowledge. He had been through the wars with Furyk, and I knew that could only help me."

On Tuesday player and caddie convened at TPC of Avenel for their first round together. In 1999 the PGA Tour visited nine

TPCs, which are owned and operated by the Tour with the express purpose of hosting its tournaments. Most players would rank Avenel among the three or four best, behind TPC at Sawgrass, home of The Players Championship, and TPC at Sugarloaf, site of the BellSouth Classic, and on par with TPC of Scottsdale. Avenel is a par-71 of 7,005 yards that snakes through the rolling Maryland countryside, alongside the meandering Rock Run Creek, which comes into play on ten holes. The key to Avenel is hitting its narrow, twisty fairways and maintaining the proper pace on its grainy greens, which in 1999 were rolling faster than usual, due to a mini-heat wave that had left them parched and a bit crusty. It was, in other words, a perfect course for Beem, and in his first romp around the grounds he continued his strong play of the previous two weeks, making seven birdies. Duplantis was duly impressed. Stepping off the 18th green, he said to Beem, "I can't fucking believe you've only made twenty-four grand this year." The next day, with Avenel off-limits because of the Wednesday pro-am, Beem and Duplantis were a guest of McDaniel's at Bellhaven Country Club, a short, sporty layout in Alexandria, Virginia. Again Beem went on a birdie binge, shooting a 67 to come within two strokes of the course record, and Duplantis spent much of the day whispering sweet nothings in his ear. "I could see Rich had a lot of talent, but also that his confidence wasn't really there," says Duplantis. "I felt like that was where I could really help him, so I went out of my way to try and make him feel positive about his game."

There were other developments boosting Beem's self-esteem. The week prior to the Kemper he had signed with Intrepid Sports, a fledgling agency out of San Diego that was desperate to sign somebody, anybody to its roster of players. If Intrepid wasn't the big time exactly, at least now Beem had some professional advocates. Prior to signing with Intrepid Beem had negotiated a couple microdeals on his own, notably an agreement to wear clothes by the mall staple Structure. Beem was able to finagle only a paltry $10,000 for his services. Nevertheless, he was pleased as punch, because at least now he would be able to display a logo over his heart. Wearing a plain shirt is the professional golf equivalent of a scarlet letter A, branding its wearer as an outcast, or, at the very least, a player of depressingly low marquee value.

The first shipment of Structure shirts and pants finally arrived at Beem's apartment in El Paso on Monday of the Kemper week, while he was seeing the sites in D.C. Amy Onick FedEx'd them to Potomac, where they arrived on the eve of the tournament.

For Thursday's first round Beem wore a khaki pants/navy shirt ensemble, and his game looked sharp, too, at least on the first couple of holes. Going off on the back nine in the morning, Beem birdied his first hole, the short, devilish par-4 10th, then followed with a routine par on 11. At the long par-4 12th Beem drove perfectly but then caught his approach heavy and left it twenty yards short. He chipped on and then missed a ten-footer to make bogey. Discouraging, but no big deal. After a par at the tricky par-5 13th, Beem stepped to the tee of 14, a 301-yard par-4 with the creek running the length of the right side of the hole. Attempting a cautious layup off the tee, Beem blew a 4-iron way right into the hazard, a loose swing that spooked him to the core. "All of a sudden the thoughts started creeping back into my head: Not another round like this, not another wasted tournament," Beem said following the round. "I was really embarrassed. I wanted so badly to play well for Steve." When Beem got to his ball he was delighted to find that it had hung up in the long grass, rather than tumbling into the creek, and was therefore still playable. He hacked it out short of the green, and from there, "Steve got me a great yardage," Beem said. He played a low, hard slider of a sand wedge to six feet and made that left-to-right curler for a crucial par, and, said Beem, "That got me going. I got strong after that." On the next hole, the long par-4 15th, he stuck his approach to a foot for a gimme birdie. After a routine par at 16, Beem nearly holed his tee shot at Avenel's signature hole, the par-3 17th, catching a piece of the cup and stopping his ball two feet away for another birdie. On the foreboding par-4 18th, which begins with a blind drive and then demands a pinpoint approach from an elevated fairway, Beem played two "awesome" shots, and then drained a fifteen-footer for back-to-back birdies. Beem was now three under par on the round and creeping up the leaderboard. "That's when Steve started talking to me," he says.

"The thing that was interesting about that week was, in that situation, I think most caddies would try to shelter their guy," says Duplantis. "I went the other way. For whatever reason—and

I know this sounds crazy, but I swear to God it's the truth—I could tell on Thursday that Rich was gonna be around on the weekend, so I wanted to prepare him, to try and take the shock away." When Beem made the turn he was tied with Corey Pavin for second place in the early going. Duplantis said, "Hey look, you're tied with a U.S. Open champ." When they encountered their first TV cameras Duplantis said, "Hey look, Rich, I bet you're on TV right now. Your mom's probably watching at home." When the crowds began to build, Duplantis said, "Look at all these people. I want you to pretend that every one of them is here to see you play. Get used to that feeling, because you belong."

Beem responded to the challenge. After parring number 1 he played three textbook shots on the 622-yard par-5 2nd, and then rolled in a fifteen-footer for birdie, to move to four under par. The third hole—a downhill 239-yard par-3—turned out to be crucial. Again Beem uncorked a monstrous push, this time some thirty yards off-line. It was so far right, "I didn't even know there was a hazard down there," he said. "I was kind of wondering if it was out of bounds where I hit it." After some serious bushwacking Duplantis found the ball, which wasn't exactly good news. The lie was horrendous. Beem gouged a chip out to the edge of the green, still forty feet above the hole. Now slightly rattled, he rolled the putt eight feet by. Eight-footers for bogey usually come with one-way tickets to the Buy.com Tour, but Beem knocked his in, and then all heaven broke loose. Routine par on number 4. Smooth twelve-footer for birdie on 5. Then came number 6, the archetype of the risk-reward par-5.

The hole doglegs gently around Rock Run Creek, which runs the length of the right side before crossing the fairway just in front of the green. The presence of the creek forces the issue of whether or not to lay up. Beem ripped a drive up the left side, leaving himself in perfect position to attack the green. He had 207 yards to carry the water, 215 to the pin. Standing in the fairway, with a wishy-washy Beem agonizing over the decision, Duplantis finally turned to his man and growled, "Now's not the time to start playing like a pussy." Beem grabbed a 4-iron, which normally would not be enough club. "I was running so hot I just decided to gas the four," he said. Beem covered the flag, stopping his ball eight feet short. He missed the eagle putt but it was, in his estimation, a "solid, solid birdie."

Beem underclubbed again on his approach to the 461-yard 7th, but this time he came up well short of the green. An adroit chip left him a tap-in par. When Beem got to the 8th hole he found himself staring at a large leaderboard, which his name was sitting atop, clear by two strokes. "That's where you belong," Duplantis said. Beem drove perfectly on the long par-four 8th, but while strolling to his ball he began to feel the butterflies for the first time. He rushed his approach shot, missing the green to the right, then flubbed his chip. Beem was still off the green, with three feet of collar to contend with, plus another twenty feet of green. "I was just so determined to make that putt," he said. "I just willed it in." It was another unlikely par save, and it kept him at five under. The 9th hole at Avenel is the Angelina Jolie of par-3s—gorgeous, and nothing but trouble. It is steeply downhill, and usually downwind, with the creek again fronting the green. For the first round it was playing 184 yards to the hole, and Beem had no idea what club to hit. Duplantis argued for a 9-iron, which Beem would normally hit 145 yards, tops, on level ground. After much discussion Beem took the advice, and then breathed a tremendous sigh of relief when his tee shot settled safely to the middle of green. Two putts later he had his par, a 66, and the first-round lead, a shot ahead of a solid group of veterans, Pavin, Bill Glasson, and Brian Watts. Shaking hands on the final green, Duplantis told Beem, "That was no fluke."

Indeed it wasn't. Everything that Beem had worked on in the preceding two weeks came together. His long game was sharp, his wedge play dynamic, and his "new" old putting stroke held up magnificently. Beem's course management had also been excellent—he waited patiently for the easier holes to attack for birdie, and when it was prudent, he merely played for par.

Beem floated to the scorer's tent adjacent to the green to sign his scorecard, and when he stepped from the tent he was shocked to encounter a horde of TV camera crews and radio interviewers, waving their oversized phallic microphones. "I didn't understand," he recalls. "I was like, do you even know who I am? Do you care?" Yes, and yes. The first question came from a cheeky radio guy.

"Who are you?" he asked, with the understatement typical of sports radio talent.

"Rich Beem," came the response. "Who are you?"

"I threw a little Bart Simpson at them," says Beem now, with a laugh. Beem held forth for the better part of fifteen minutes, supplying an excess of sound bytes. "He handled it perfect, like a PR genius," says Duplantis, who stuck around for the show. "He was honest, genuine, and just really enjoying all the attention."

Eventually an officious volunteer, waving a walkie-talkie, broke in and informed Beem that his presence was requested in the media center, where he was to face an inquisition by the print reporters. What followed, says Beem, "was one of the neatest things that's ever happened to me."

Beem was led to the interview area, which at the Kemper was a temporary tent adjacent to the clubhouse, plushly carpeted, with some seventy-five folding chairs and a makeshift Astro Turfed stage. Atop the stage were two oversized velour chairs, where Beem took a seat opposite Lee Patterson, a courtly PGA Tour official who was presiding over the proceedings. Understanding that Beem was new to the game, Patterson handed him a microphone and subtly explained the process. "Maybe just a couple thoughts about your round today," he said, "then we ask questions."

Beem's first utterance, recorded for posterity by an on-site stenographer, was, "This is different. I'm used to sitting around and saying bad things about my round." This brought a chorus of chuckles from the three dozen or so reporters on hand, and Beem was off and running. Asked to share a little personal information, he said, "You know, I am a pretty boring guy. My hobby, my passion is my stereo. What I am out here trying to do is make enough money so I can dump more of it into my truck. I wrote on my PGA Tour bio that I ski and fish. I don't think I've been skiing in about fifteen years and I haven't picked up a fishing pole in twenty. I just had to make up something." It was great schtick, and the reporters spooned it up. Beem was pressed for more details on his truck's sound system, which, given the circumstances, was a deliciously offbeat topic. "I've got a kicker, subwoofers, sound stream amplifiers, tweeters, mids, sixes . . . it's kind of fun to pull up to the low riders in El Paso that are playing all the jams and put in Van Halen, crank it up, and blow them away."

With little prodding he gave a condensed version of his highly unlikely road to the Tour: the minitour grind, the bad old days at Magnolia Hi-Fi, his broken engagement, the El Paso Country Club apprenticeship, his Sun Section winning streak, and finally the march through Q School. Beem stopped the narrative only to drop a couple of bon mots.

On how to get to El Paso: "Turn left to nowhere. Go twenty miles."

On how he would sleep as the overnight leader: "Probably on my left side."

In all Beem spent more than half an hour cracking wise, and the transcript of his press conference ran a full six pages, single spaced. Given that the average PGA Tour player has the personality of roadkill, it was a startling performance, and it left the reporters shaking their heads in collective wonder. (The next day Thomas Boswell, the crusty old *Washington Post* scribe, would devote his entire column to Beem, calling him in one breathless passage "young, bumptious, honest, funny, generous, green as grass, and in miles over his head.")

After leaving the tent Beem spent a couple minutes signing autographs, and then he finally made it to the clubhouse. He was stunned to discover that the number of voice mail messages on his cell phone was already into double digits. The news of Beem's first-round heroics had rippled seismically across the landscape, from El Paso and Las Cruces to Sioux Falls to Seattle to Ontario, and dozens of points in between.

At Southwest Engineers, where Beem's mother, Diana, works as an accountant, the phone began ringing off the hook early in Rich's round. "Whenever Rich is playing my daughter Tina keeps track of him on the Internet and gives me updates," says Diana. "If he's not playing well she'll call maybe two or three times in a day, but if he's having a good round it gets a little more frequent. I think on that day she was calling every five minutes or so." Still, says Diana, "We never imagined it was anything more than one good round. It was just like, oh, isn't this cute."

Up in Sioux Falls, South Dakota, Corey Thie was working in the pro shop at Westward Ho Country Club (bartending in Seattle was but a pleasant memory). In the three years since they had roomed together Thie had lost track of Beem, but that wasn't the case with everybody at the club. Says Thie, "Jeff Brecht, the head pro, comes up to me and says, 'Hey, guess what, Rich is leading the Kemper.' I said, 'Leading the Kemper? What the hell is he doing *at* the Kemper?' I didn't even know he was on the Tour." Thie, however, couldn't wait to share the news. He picked up the phone and called his aunt Tanya, Beem's onetime fiancée, who by now was married and working as a freight broker for the family trucking business in Minneapolis. "I told her to log onto pgatour.com," says Corey. "She didn't know what was going on but I walked her through the site until she got to the scores. When she saw Rich's name she just dropped the phone and started screaming, 'Ohmygawd! Ohmygawd!' At that point pretty much the whole family started following it on the Internet."

That same afternoon Stephen Duplantis had gone to North Halton Country Club, in Brampton, Ontario, for a friendly game, and the grillroom exploded when he walked in. "Steve has always been something of a local hero around here," Stephen says of his son, "and after what happened with Furyk there was a certain amount of concern about his future. After all those weeks went by without him picking up a regular bag people stopped asking, so not many folks around here knew he was going to be working with Rich. Well, after that first round, everybody seemed to know about it. Word travels fast."

Were it not for the busy schedule of a laser surgeon, Beem might not have had anyone with whom to celebrate the first round lead. The day before the Kemper Beem had finally gotten in touch with Dr. Ronald Whitten, a hard-core PGA Tour fan who does cutting-edge eye surgery. In 1998 he had corrected Maryland native Fred Funk's vision two days before the Kemper Open started, and when Funk nearly won the tournament Whitten, and his procedure, received a ton of publicity. Soon dozens of players were flocking to his practice, and in exchange for signed merchandise and free gear, any and all Tour players could have the surgery done gratis. Whitten told Beem he could squeeze him in the Wednesday following Kemper (and after some pleading by Duplantis, Beem called back and got his caddie an appointment, as well). This meant Beem had to postpone his plans with Onick, who he was supposed to meet in San Diego after leaving Potomac. Wednesday night, on the eve of the tournament, Beem called Onick in El Paso to cancel their trip to the San Diego Zoo, their deep-sea fishing expedition, and a week of quality time together. Onick was so miffed that Beem immediately went into the damage control mode, offering to fly her into D.C. the next day so he could make amends. Onick's flight landed Thursday afternoon, around the same time Beem was holding forth in the press tent.

Beem was so exhausted from the day's proceedings that instead of a big night out on the town, as promised, he took Onick to a glorified burger joint "behind the Red Lobster and a bowling alley," a greasy spoon that had only one real appeal—it was within walking distance from the hotel. Duplantis and his crew tagged along. Beem delighted in mingling with Pennington, and anybody else in the restaurant who happened to be within earshot. Duplantis couldn't help but be amused at his enthusiasm. "On a scale of one to ten in giddiness Rich was an eleven," he says. "I was maybe a two or three. I had just been there so many times before. If it had been Furyk leading a tournament after one round? Nothing. It wouldn't even register on the scale."

When Beem and Onick finally reached their hotel room, he was ready to celebrate. Beem turned off all the lights, pulled back the covers . . . and tuned into ESPN. "I had to see myself on Sportscenter," he says. "Hey, man, you gotta do it."

FRIDAY MORNING the headline splashed across the *Las Cruces Sun-News* read "Former Aggie Beem Jumps Out on Top; Pavin Close Behind." The paper ran a decent-sized wire account of the action. The *El Paso Times*, which had done a good job of keeping tabs on Beem throughout the season, missed the story entirely. Back in Potomac, however, Beem was being given the star treatment. In addition to Boswell's rave, he received prominent placement in the game stories in both the *Post* and the *Baltimore Sun*, and he was pictured in *USA Today*. "I'll be honest with you, I read all the articles," says Beem. "Even Sunday morning, when I probably shouldn't have. It was just too much fun to see all of that." The only disappointment was how his new Structure shirt reproduced. "It was a weird shade of blue to begin with, and in *USA*

Today it came out looking purple," says Beem. "Here I am, in a national newspaper for the first time, and I look like fucking Barney."

With his typically unlucky draw, Beem's second round tee time wasn't until 1:40 in the afternoon, which left a long, tortuous wait. Because of the late starting time, and all the hoopla he had generated in the press, a sizeable crowd was waiting on the first tee, hoping to figure out for themselves just who in the world is Rich Beem. "Until Kemper I was deathly afraid of crowds," says Beem. "I remember the Hawaiian Open, we had fifty people watching, and that made me nervous. At other events, playing to the eighteenth hole, where there would always be a good crowd waiting, I would get very, very uncomfortable. Until Kemper I would look around the crowd and see faces, and that was distracting. At Kemper I didn't see anybody. I guess I had reached a different level of concentration."

Beem wasn't the only one with his game face on. Duplantis was determined to make sure Beem stayed focused despite the escalating distractions. "If Rich came back with a seventy-six on Friday, what he did on the first day would have been just another lucky round by a rookie," says Duplantis. "I was on him from the first hole on Friday to be intense and make every swing count."

Which is exactly what Beem did, at least for a while. He drove perfectly to open the round, then nuked a 7-iron from 168 yards to fifteen feet. He snuck the putt in for a stress-reducing birdie. On the 4th hole the wind shifted on Beem just as he was striking his shot, and it barely reached the front of the expansive green, leaving him an uphill fifty-foot putt. Just trying to lag it close, Beem poured the putt into the cup for a shocking birdie. On the next hole, from ninety-nine yards out, he spun a wedge to two inches for a gimme birdie, pushing him to 8-under par on the tournament and, for the moment, a commanding three-stroke lead. That's when things got interesting. On the par-5 6th, where the day before Beem had boldly reached the green, he again drove impeccably and whipped out his 4-iron. Beem thought he had hit another perfect shot, but sixty yards shy of the green it clipped an overhanging branch and fell straight down, into the long grass of the hazard. Unable to ground his club and get a feel for the thickness of the turf, Beem caught his recovery fat, and it trickled toward the stream in front of the green, stopping just a few paces shy. This left an exceedingly delicate shot, which he failed to pull off. He two-putted from twenty-five feet above the hole for a scrambling bogey. In the gallery Amy Onick was nonplussed. "He's got the strongest focus of anyone I know, sometimes irritatingly," she told an Associated Press reporter who was walking with her. "He's not going to let this bother him." That turned out to be the worst prediction since "Dewey Defeats Truman."

At the 461-yard par-4 7th Beem again drove accurately, but was indecisive about what club to hit to the green. Duplantis argued for a 7-iron, but Beem went with a 6, hoping to stuff a shot next to the flag, which was positioned back right. He should have gone with the 7-iron. Beem overshot the green, and left his ball hanging on the lip of a cavernous bunker. He was forced to stand in the sand to play his third shot, with the ball approximately chest high, and sunken into the gnarled grass of the bunker's lip. He slashed that weird recovery shot twenty-five feet above the hole, and then proceeded to three-putt for a momentum killing double bogey. Across the golf course harried volunteers began pulling his name from the top of the manually operated leaderboards.

"A lot of guys make double bogey out here," Duplantis said as they were walking off the green. "The big boys always come back with a birdie."

On the long par-4 8th Beem cranked another drive, and then from 165 yards downwind played an 8-iron that was, he said in his postround press conference, "eatin' fiber all the way."

Eatin' fiber?

"The flagsticks are made out of fiberglass," Beem said. "At least I think they are."

Beem's ball ended up five feet from the hole. He made the putt for a crucial birdie, and an instant promotion to the rank of Big Boy. "The theme of the week was that every time he hit a rough patch he came back strong," says Duplantis. Beem further righted the ship with four straight pars, which brought him to the tricky par-5 13th. He was going to lay up off the tee with a 3-wood and play it as a three-shot hole, but Duplantis said, "You've been hitting the driver perfect all day. Just step up and hit it again."

"Let's do it," said Beem.

He smoked yet another flawless drive—on the day Beem would hit 14 of 14 fairways—which left him with 228 yards to clear the water, 235 to the pin. Beem followed with a good 3-wood to the front of the green, then two-putted for birdie. On the short par-4 14th he hit a cautious 4-iron off the tee, then put a wedge to six feet for another birdie. He was now leading the tournament again, and, nearing the clubhouse, his gallery was bigger than ever. Beem began surfing on a tidal wave of enthusiasm. "I get a little emotional out there," he said after the round. "I do that even when I make a ten-footer against the guys back home. I enjoy showing emotion on the golf course. When I hit a bad shot I might toss a club. But when I do something good, I will get excited, I will pump my fist. I think that is very healthy for me and my game." Beem might have gotten a little too swept up in the excitement, because he made a sloppy bogey at 16, dropping him to two under on his round. The good news was that meant he didn't have to hit first on the nasty downhill par-3 17th. Playing partner Chris Smith had the honors; watching him helped Beem decide on a 7-iron, and he put it pin-high, twenty-five feet from the cup. When Beem banged the putt in he pumped his fist so hard "I gave myself a little head rush," he said. Beem followed with another twenty-five-footer for birdie on 18, which put an exclamation point on his 67 and gave him a healthy three-shot lead over the low-wattage trio of Bradley Hughes, Tommy Armour III, and Dave Stockton Jr. Beem's stellar finishing kick set off a sustained ovation from the sodden, sun-toasted fans who had packed the grass amphitheater behind the 18th green. Beem tipped his cap to the fans, and upon reaching the press tent he did the same to Duplantis.

"Hats off today to my caddie, Steve, for keeping me focused and keeping my head on straight when I could have lost it a little bit," Beem said. "He kept my spirits up more than anything else and we just kept rolling." Beem also said, "For the first time all year I haven't carried a yardage book because I trust Steve so much. Other caddies, it wasn't that I didn't trust them, I just wasn't sure about their numbers. I believe in Steve. So instead of having to pace off yardages I can go to my ball and soak in the shot at hand. It is a lot less work, and an easier way to play golf."

Beem's press conference was slightly more subdued this time around, but it had its moments. An inquiring mind amongst the writers asked Beem if he were to win the tournament would he be buying Onick a "fifty-thousand-dollar rock."

"I am not that . . . no," he stammered. "Not yet. Man, I am . . . I am a couple years from that, I hope."

"A bigger truck, right?"

"Bigger truck, more stuff," was how Beem ended the interview.

After wading through a few more radio interviews and a growing number of autograph seekers, Beem beat some balls at the range and then worked on his putting. It was nearly dark when he finally left the golf course, and he and Onick, Duplantis, Pennington, and Sierra wound up at the same restaurant as the night before. Though Beem professed to be exhausted, he seemed to have plenty of attention to devote to Pennington, with whom he was clearly enamored. "Oh, yeah, I dug her," he says. "It was hard to remain on my best behavior." What with his girlfriend sitting next to him and all.

"Rich was so flirty at dinner," says Pennington. "I was definitely getting vibes from him, but that was okay because it was mutual." (Luckily, for the sake of domestic harmony, no one else at the table seemed to notice Beem and Pennington batting eyes across the table. "That's news to me," says Duplantis.)

Away from suburban Maryland plenty of other folks were feeling overheated as well. Beem's mom had fielded calls at work from old acquaintances in Berlin, family friends in South Carolina, Rich's college buddies around town, her sister in Flagstaff, Arizona ("four times" says Diana), and both of Rich's sisters, who were checking in with switchboard-clogging regularity. "We didn't get a lot of work done around the office that day," says Diana. "I don't think anyone was that surprised with Rich's success the first day. We all knew he was capable of playing like that. But when he hung in there during the second round, it was like, oh my goodness, this is a bit different."

El Paso Country Club was also abuzz. "The only thing anyone could talk about was Rich," says Cameron Doan, the head pro. "It was just a real nice feeling around here, because that kind of success was a long time coming. I can tell you, there were a few toasts made in his honor around the bar."

That night the *Las Cruces Sun-News* was going to the presses with a long version of the wire story under the headline "Beem Keeps Shining." The *El Paso Times* was putting together two stories on the top of the front page of the sports section; one was by the AP, and the other from their local golf writer, Bill Knight, who had gotten ahold of Beem on his cell phone following the second round. Under the headline "Beem: 'It's a Little Nuts Around Here,' " the man of the hour said, "But it's a good kind of nuts." The story ended with Beem talking about Duplantis. "We've talked about staying together," Beem said, "and I'd have to say there's a pretty good chance we will."

BACK IN LAS CRUCES a different sort of drama was playing out at the Memorial Medical Center, as two of Beem's best friends—Max and Dina Schroeder—were awaiting the birth of their first child. Beem had met both while a senior in high school in Las Cruces, and Dina had been Beem's date to the senior prom. They were just friends, but in the absence of proper companions had decided to attend the dance together. Shortly after asking Dina to the dance Beem began dating another girl. However, he honored his commitment to take Dina to the prom, talking another of his dateless buddies into escorting his then-girlfriend.

Said girlfriend and buddy wound up flirting throughout the night, and actually went home together. Beem was so distracted by the unfolding events that he all but ignored Dina. Max, ever the gentleman, danced with Dina and made sure she had a nice time. Five years later they were married, and Rich was the best man. When it came time to give his speech, he dropped to his knees and begged Dina to forgive him for having been such a lousy date all those years ago at the prom.

When Beem found out that Dina was going to have a boy, he badgered her relentlessly, saying, "You know, Richard is a great name for a young man." Finally, after months of pressure, Dina made a deal with Rich—if he won a tournament on tour before the kid was born, Richard would become the kid's middle name.

Otherwise, the little guy was going in the books as Evan Patrick. This seemed like a pretty good bet for the Schroeders.

Dina's due date turned out to be May 30, which coincided with the final round of the Kemper. On the 27th, the day of the first round, Dina went for a checkup, and it was discovered that she had begun dilating. When Max arrived at the hospital the first thing he said was, "Guess what, Rich is leading the Kemper Open!"

The Schroeders left a message for Rich on his cell phone Thursday afternoon, and when he returned the call that night he was quick to remind Dina of their deal. On Friday morning Dina's water broke, and she went into labor that evening. Evan was born in the wee hours of Saturday morning. "The hospital people were pressuring me for a middle name, so they could complete all the paperwork," says Dina. "Honestly, I really preferred Patrick, but a deal's a deal. If I'd had to make up my mind on Saturday I don't know what I would have done." Following the birth Dina developed a minor complication that required her to stay an extra two days in the hospital. That meant Evan wouldn't get a middle name until Sunday night, by which time the Kemper Open would have been decided.

WHEN BEEM AWOKE Saturday morning his mind was going a hundred miles an hour. Thank God for David Wyatt. Following the first round Beem had called his best friend and extracted the promise that if he was still leading the tournament on Friday night then Wyatt would catch a redeye from Seattle, so he could make it to Avenel in time for the third round. Wyatt kept his word, catching a midnight flight that got him into Ronald Reagan Airport Saturday morning. Beem arranged for a tournament volunteer to pick Wyatt up at the airport, and they rendezvoused at the course shortly before noon. Again Beem wasn't teeing off until 1:40, but he killed much of the dreaded waiting by catching up with Wyatt over lunch in the clubhouse. "We had a great time," says Beem. "It was awesome to have David there. Really put me in a good frame of mind."

Duplantis also had some things to keep his mind off of the

impending round. He was scurrying around trying to pack up his daughter and her nanny. Pennington was going to fly back home to Dallas with Sierra, which was fine by Duplantis. Having Pennington along had been a tremendous help already, and the lack of child-care worries was one of the reasons Duplantis was able to devote so much of himself to Beem. Now, with the girls leaving, he would be distraction free for the final two rounds.

Though Beem enjoyed his time with Wyatt, the waiting took its toll. "I was too anxious to get on the golf course," he said later. "I was kind of running out there, and not real comfortable. When I start rushing my swing gets fast and I hit quick hooks." That was what Beem did on the second and third holes, costing him a pair of bogeys. On the fourth tee Beem fixed his swing. "I just made up my mind to relax and hit a good tee shot," he said, and that's what he did.

In an effort to slow Beem down further, Duplantis insisted they walk side-by-side down the fourth fairway, and he may have set a record for the 260-yard stroll. Beem followed with a 6-iron to twenty-five feet, which he holed for a very helpful birdie. "When I made that putt," Beem said, "I knew I was going to be all right."

The tee markers were pushed way up on the next hole, the par-4 5th, shortening the hole from 359 yards to 301. Duplantis wanted an aggressive play, cutting off the dogleg. "I was really putting it on him that round," says Duplantis. "I wanted to challenge him, I wanted to make him rise to the occasion. I knew if we could get to Sunday around the lead we would have a good chance of winning. Saturday was the key day, so I just kept challenging him. It was a risky thing to do, because if he blew it, he could have been shattered."

"On four tee Steve asked me if I had a problem hitting a driver, even though I hit it poorly on the first two holes," said Beem. "I said, 'If you think it's a driver, then I promise you I will put it in play.' " Beem carved a perfect drive, landing it thirty yards short of the green, and got that up-and-down for his second birdie in a row. Walking off the green Duplantis said to him, "See, you just proved to me you can win this thing."

"The most important thing I did that week was make him

believe he could win," says Duplantis. "That's what I did that week—I made him believe."

On number 6, the par-5, Beem creamed another drive, and had only 205 yards to reach the green. Beem wanted to play a 6-iron, but Duplantis was convinced that wasn't enough club. In the course of the discussion he extended his arms as if to give Beem a big hug, only he was trying to demonstrate that there was so much room behind the pin it was better to be long than short. In the end Beem took the advice, playing the 5-iron, and it was "exactly the perfect club." He stuck it to six feet, back of the pin, for eagle. Unfortunately there was a large spike mark in his line. It knocked his putt out of the hole, but after tapping in Beem had another birdie, and he was now under par on his round. He parred in on the rest of the front 9, and then rolled in a twelve-footer for another birdie at the 10th, pushing him to 11 under par and a whopping four-stroke lead.

The Kemper Open is usually one of the better-attended tournaments on tour, but on this sunny Memorial Day Saturday the crowds were even bigger than usual. Beginning on the 10th hole, and continuing throughout the back side, Beem was repeatedly serenaded by the bleating of cell phones in the gallery. It was poignant music, a reminder of how far he had traveled since his days at Magnolia Hi-Fi. Time and again Beem shook off the distraction, but he was so thoroughly in command of the tournament his mind began to wander. "Things entered into my head a little bit—kind of personal stuff more than anything else," he said. Beem held off the demons on number 11, producing a par, but all the week's mojo caught up to him at the long, watery 12th, which not so coincidentally was when the CBS telecast kicked in.

After a painfully cheesy introduction, featuring footage of the sights around Washington and the tournament's marquee players hamming it up for the camera, the Tiffany Network's estimable announcing duo of Jim Nantz and Ken Venturi welcomed viewers and offered a windy hype job about Beem. Venturi, the 1964 U.S. Open champ, is in his fourth decade announcing golf for CBS, making him the dean of all network sports announcers. He often speaks in such exotic constructions it is not clear if he's addressing the viewers or reciting poetry. In the intro he offered this haiku to Beem:

This kid is for real.
This kid can play, and he's hit
Some wonderful golf shots.

From Venturi the telecast cut to the 12th tee, where a national audience saw Beem pound a perfect drive. There was an extra spring in his step as he marched down the fairway, the sprawling camera crew trailing in his wake. On his long walk to the ball Beem couldn't help but think about the boys back at El Paso Country Club, whooping it up in the grillroom, his dad and the rest of the family watching at home in Las Cruces, and the other assorted millions who would be scrutinizing his every twitch. Beem arrived at his ball and went through all the traditional waggles, but he was rushing again, and he never really committed to the shot. Trying to cut an 8-iron from 160 yards, he uncorked that old trouble shot, a block, dead right, and the second he hit it he slammed his club down and turned away in anguish. It was clearly a bad shot; given the creek fronting the green, the only question was how bad. Beem's ball hit squarely on the steep bank in front of the green, but instead of pitching forward onto the putting surface it kicked right, tumbling into Rock Run Creek. As national debuts go, this was not encouraging.

Beem slunk toward the green, tail between his legs. His ball was visible in the creek, though clearly unplayable. At this point Beem did a funny thing. With the cameras still rolling, he pulled out his wedge and attempted to retrieve his ball, like some kind of penny-pinching weekend hacker. For the better part of a minute Beem fished around in the creek, finally inspiring his playing partner, the salty Australian Bradley Hughes, to say, "On tour they give those to you for free, you know." With his ball slowly bobbing toward Virginia, Beem finally gave up. The whole episode was bizarre, and totally endearing, and the gallery cheered throughout his misadventure. Then, in what seemed like a shameless attempt to milk more airtime, Beem called for a rules official to help him with his routine penalty drop. In all, ten minutes elapsed before Beem finally played his par chip, which he ran a knee-knocking eight feet by the hole. He never came close to making the putt, resulting in a brutal double bogey that trimmed his lead from three strokes to one.

In the group ahead of Beem was Tommy Armour III, the thirty-nine-year-old grandson of the legendary "Silver Scot" who, in his glory years from 1927 to '31, won a U.S. Open, British Open, and a PGA Championship. With only one victory in his eleven years on tour, TA3 has never quite lived up to his grandfather's legacy, but he is a scrappy, experienced competitor and in 1999 he was playing some of the best golf of his career. (Three months prior to the Kemper, Armour had reached a playoff at the Tucson Open before losing to Gabriel Hjerstedt.) With Beem standing in the fairway Armour knocked in a birdie on the par-5 13th green, tying for the lead at -9. Beem followed with a good 5-wood to just off the green, but he failed to get up-and-down and had to settle for a disappointing par. Facing his first real adversity of the week, Beem's putter got a little wobbly over the next four holes. He missed a short birdie putt on 14 and then three-jacked to bogey the 15th hole. On 16 and 17 Beem hit solid iron shots only to lip out two more good birdie chances. By the time Beem reached the 18th tee he was one stroke back of Armour and looking like he was on the ropes.

In one of his many little triumphs of the week, Beem nutted up and hit an ideal drive on 18. Then, from 160 yards, playing to a green that was downhill and downwind, he hit an 8-iron of such purity that as soon as it left the clubface Duplantis said, "You are the man, Beemer." It stopped six feet from the hole, and Beem poured that putt in for a 71 that tied him with Armour at -9. They would play together in Sunday's final twosome. After making the putt at 18 Beem followed with two Tiger-esque uppercuts, and the gallery roared its approval. On the telly Nantz said, "You can tell who the crowd is rooting for."

No one was more tuned in to the action than Corey McDaniel, Beem's D.C. friend who had hosted him early in the week. That Friday night, after feverishly following the second round on the Internet at work, McDaniel proposed to his girlfriend at the Pizza Hut where they had met years earlier. Early the next morning the betrothed flew to California, ostensibly for the wedding of a friend, but they were so glued to the tube they missed most of the service. "We had wandered into a sports bar Saturday afternoon to get an update on how Rich was doing and then we simply couldn't leave," says McDaniel.

After his round Beem was interviewed live on national TV by CBS funnyman David Feherty. Beem couldn't swallow an oversized grin throughout the interview, but otherwise he was cool and collected. Asked what he was going to do that evening, Beem said, "Have dinner, drink a few beers, watch a movie or something, fall asleep, and do it all over tomorrow."

Turning to smirk at the camera, Feherty said, "My kind of guy.

"You said earlier in the week," Feherty continued, "that your goal was to earn enough money to upgrade the stereo in your car. Are we aiming a little higher now?"

Said Beem, "Yeah, actually, if we have a real good day tomorrow we're gonna go ahead and buy a new car and then upgrade the system in *that* one."

Clearly Beem was getting comfortable in his new role as media darling. When he took his now familiar seat in the interview room's cushy velour chair, he began mouthing platitudes like a seasoned vet.

"I can't control what anybody else does," Beem said. "I can only control what I do. I am going to try to go out there tomorrow, hit fairways and greens and make some putts. If Tommy chooses to lay up on the par-fives and be conservative, that is his game. If I have even a marginal chance of going for it, I might just go for it. I don't have a whole lot to lose here, and I am loving it."

Beem, as is his wont, got a little sidetracked during the Q&A, going on a long soliloquy about how much he valued his friendship with David Wyatt, who happened to be sitting in the back of the press tent. It did not go unremarked upon that during the third press conference of his life Beem took time out to talk about somebody else. Beem also offered expert analysis on the cell phones that had disrupted play. "A couple of them were Motorolas for sure," he said, drawing on his eight months of hawking cells at Magnolia Hi-Fi. "I think a couple of them were Nokias. They have these different rings you can program, while Motorolas just ring." The final question of the day was the most obvious one: Have you thought about what it would mean to win the tournament. "I am trying to keep that out of my mind," Beem said. "Obviously it's my dream, but I just want to go out tomorrow and play the best golf I possibly can, and keep my composure and just do myself proud. If it works out and I am able to sit in here tomorrow night with a big ol' crystal trophy, even better. But I am just going to go out and do the same things I have done the last few days."

As if it were that easy. Golf is a choke game. The ball is completely still, the crowd utterly silent, and nobody is playing defense. There are those who think all of these factors make golf less of a test than other sports, but the thinking fan knows just the opposite is true. Alone between the ropes, a player's fate, particularly on Sunday afternoon, is determined by his courage and his will at least as much as by his talent. This is what makes tournament golf such compelling theater.

In 1999 only one other rookie had led a Tour event heading into the final round—Eric Booker at the Honda Classic. On Sunday Booker blew up with a 77, which had been the unofficial over-under in the press room. Bill Glasson, lurking two shots back of Beem and Armour at the Kemper, offered an interesting perspective. Glasson has long been one of the most fearsome competitors in golf, a maniacal weightlifter and owner of the most intense visage in the sport. Brandel Chamblee once said of Glasson, "He's an intimidating fellow. If this were a thousand years ago and the Tour were a tribe, he would be our leader. He could single-handedly scare the hell out of any enemy." And yet Glasson, too, was once a jittery youngster trying to break through at the Kemper Open. In 1985 he was a winless twenty-five-year-old when he found himself in contention on Sunday, and with a series of long putts down the stretch Glasson stole the victory. Fourteen years later, on the eve of the final round, he relived the experience: "I wasn't trying to win my first tournament, I was trying not to have a heart attack before I finished the seventy-second hole," Glasson said. "Winning had nothing to do with it. It wasn't even in the equation. I turned to say something to my caddie on the seventeenth hole and nothing came out. I mean, it wasn't a matter of winning. It was a matter of just trying to finish without bleeding to death."

SUNDAY MORNING Beem awoke with a start. It was not yet 7:00 A.M., but he couldn't force himself to sleep any longer. Lying there in the dark the enormity of it all finally hit him. "I honestly felt like I was going to throw up," he says. "I thought I was going to blow chunks all over Amy and the bed. I'm dead serious—that's how I felt." Beem managed to quiet his nerves, and thinking that a little breakfast might settle him down, he woke Wyatt, who was crashed on a second double bed in Rich and Amy's hotel room. Wyatt suggested a nearby Starbucks, for selfish reasons—as a Seattleite he is utterly discombobulated without a couple cups of joe in the morning. Beem nursed an orange juice and nibbled on a blueberry muffin, but that morning's *Washington Post* hardly helped quiet his nerves. There was another valentine by Thomas Boswell on the front page of the sports section. "Rich Beem is what sports used to be about and, sometimes, still is," was how Boswell began his column. "He is tied for the lead of the Kemper Open after three rounds, a minor fact that could go a long way toward transforming the rest of his life . . ."

Beem obviously needed something a little stronger than OJ to coat his stomach. "I said to David, 'I got to buy some Pepto Bismol or I won't survive,' " Beem would later tell reporters. "I didn't take it until I got to the golf course. Hid it in my pocket so nobody would see. I carried it into the locker room and went to the bathroom, still hiding it. I went into a stall, so nobody would see exactly how nervous I was, and took a couple of big chugs. That definitely calmed me a little bit."

"He's got a weak stomach," says Wyatt. "You can pretty much count on Rich for a constitutional within twenty minutes of finishing every meal. You can set your watch by it. It's like he lost part of his stomach in Nam or something."

Others were dealing with the stress in different ways. Beem's mother, Diana, had boycotted the Saturday telecast entirely, choosing instead to run errands around town. "I was just a mess," she says. "I couldn't stand it, so I figured I might as well get out of the house." She was forcing herself to watch on Sunday, but in the hours leading up to the three o'clock (Eastern) telecast she fluttered around the house, losing herself in busy work. "Mopping, dusting, ironing, you name it," she says with a laugh. "The house has never been so clean."

Up in Brampton the phone was ringing off the hook at the home of Duplantis's mother. "The number of phone calls was amazing," says Sandy Cantin. "People were calling to tell me they were setting their VCRs, and friends from all over, really, just wanted to check in to let me know they would be watching."

The phone was also ringing at Magnolia Hi-Fi, outside Seattle. "When the first reporter called, we thought it was a joke," says Bobby McCory, a longtime employee who had worked alongside Beem. "But then we got used to it." Over a dozen TVs, mostly big screens, would be devoted to the telecast.

At El Paso Country Club the expansive grillroom was filling up fast. By the start of the telecast every seat would be taken, a mob scene 150 people strong. "It was definitely a happening," says Greg Johns. "The pope could have been on the other channel and we wouldn't have had any idea. There was a lot of electricity in that room." Eventually camera crews from the local affiliates of all three major television networks would come to the club to record the events of the day.

A similar scene was playing out at Westward Ho Country Club, up in Sioux Falls. The crowd there would eventually reach nearly one hundred, and the local TV stations also showed up to film the party.

Thankfully, Beem had insulated himself from the cresting hysteria. In something of an upset, he turned off his cell phone so he could enjoy a little quiet. He had arrived at the course far earlier than the previous two days, and after doing those Pepto shots he set about righting the rest of his person. Beem's legs had been jelly ever since he crawled out of bed, and in an effort to build some strength he stopped by the fitness trailer and did twenty minutes on the stationary bike, in addition to another half hour of exercises. Not that he really needed the workout. "I was just trying to waste time," he says. From there he wandered into the clubhouse to have lunch with David and Amy. Well, at least *they* had lunch. "I just sat there and watched," says Beem. "I wanted no part of any of that."

By the time Beem reached the driving range it was eerily deserted, as virtually all the other players were already on the course. "My swing felt good," he says. "It felt like it had every other day that week, which was a relief, obviously." CBS court jester Gary McCord came over to do a quick interview, and a couple of random players wandered by to mouth encouragement.

But mostly it was just Beem, a pile of gleaming practice balls, and a pressure that was as thick and palpable as the humid summer air.

Noticeably absent was Steve Duplantis. That morning he had decided to do some laundry at his hotel, one of those extended stay complexes that function more like apartments than a traditional hotel. On his way down to the laundry room to pick up the final load, Duplantis locked himself out of his room. At this point it was a little after 11:00 A.M. Duplantis walked down to the front desk to borrow a spare room key, and was shocked to discover that on Sundays it was not staffed until noon, which is when he was due at the golf course. "That was just typical of my luck," says Duplantis. "Any hotel in the world, you lock yourself out of your room, they let you back in within five minutes. I mean, I couldn't believe what was happening. It was un-fucking-believable. It had been a dream week. Things were going so well I knew there was no way I could fuck it up, and then this happens." With a heavy heart, Duplantis called Beem to let him know what had transpired, and that he would be late arriving at the course.

"I took his story at face value," says Beem. "It wasn't that big a deal to me. Obviously I had other things to focus on at the time. He wasn't all that late, and it's not like it affected our day at all."

It was at the range, following his belated arrival, that Duplantis gave Beem the best pep talk since Blutarsky's riff about the Germans bombing Pearl Harbor. Duplantis was worried how Beem would respond to the subtle gamesmanship that was sure to emanate from his playing partner, Tommy Armour III. In a sport in which failing to say "nice shot" can be construed as poor sportsmanship, there have always been a few players who delighted in giving the needle. A classic example came on the 72nd hole at the 1966 U.S. Open, as Arnold Palmer was in the midst of the worst collapse in Open history (Palmer would ultimately succumb in a playoff to Billy Casper, a devout Mormon and father of eleven who was nonetheless one of the sport's all-time greatest trash talkers). After leaving his thirty-footer a nerve-jangling four feet short, Palmer asked Casper if he would be stepping in his line if he putted out. "Go ahead, Arnold," Casper said cooly. "You're hot." Armour is no Billy Casper, but he is one of the

Tour's cooler cats, or so he thinks. Away from the course his tastes run to pimpish floor-length black leather coats and between the ropes he has an aloof air about him. In interviews following Saturday's round Armour had discussed Beem in dismissive tones, and later that evening at the driving range he went out of his way to convey his feelings directly to Beem. It was just the two of them at the range, and, according to Duplantis, Armour spent much of the time barking into his cell phone, bragging to whoever would listen about how he was going to go out and win the tournament the next day. "He was trying to get into Rich's head," says Duplantis. "He was talking so loud it was obvious he wanted us to hear. A couple of times he even referred to Rich as 'some rookie.' He didn't even call him by his name. Totally disrespectful, but that was the point.

"So on Sunday I got in Beemer's face and told him, 'Tommy is gonna be a prick out there. He doesn't respect you, and he thinks you're weak. Well, fuck him. Who the fuck does this fuckin' guy think he is? You don't need his approval. The only friend you need out there is me. We're gonna wipe that shitty little grin off his fuckin' face. We've been shoving it up his ass all week, and we're gonna do it again today.'

"I know Tommy," Duplantis continues. "I knew he wasn't gonna talk to Rich, and that he would have this look of disdain on his face all day. I just wanted to prepare Rich for what was coming. You know how Rich is, he always wants to be friends with everybody. I didn't want him out there going, 'Gee, I don't think Tommy likes me. Why doesn't Tommy like me? What can I do to make Tommy like me?' Fuck Tommy. This was business."

After warming up Beem moseyed to the practice putting green. "I didn't make a lot of putts, but I felt pretty comfortable," he says. "My hands weren't shaking, if that's what you're wondering." At last the moment of truth arrived. When Beem was announced for the final tee time the crowd roared its approval. There was no doubt who the masses were rooting for, and the outpouring of support helped to further settle him down. Taking his practice swings Beem realized he was less nervous than he had been the day before on the first tee or, for that matter, the morning of the last round at the final stage of Q School. "One thing I learned during Kemper is that you can only get so nervous, and that's it," Beem says. "There is not an infinite nervousness. I'm not gonna lie, I was feeling it big time on Sunday. But I had felt that way before and I had pulled it out when I had to, so that helped the nerves." On the first drive of the rest of his life, Beem smashed one down the middle.

He followed with a cautious approach to the fat side of the first green, leaving himself a forty-footer for birdie. Beem was just trying to lag it close, but the ball kept tracking . . . tracking . . . tracking toward the hole before falling in the side door for a stunning birdie. In contrast to the manic fist-pumping of the previous days, Beem showed virtually no outward emotion. It was only the first hole, but already he had found a grim determination. Duplantis, on the other hand, had raised a fist in triumph after the putt fell, and he pounded Beem on the back as they walked off the green. "Sunday I wanted it so bad," says Duplantis. "I could taste it. I could feel it. My hands were sweaty long before we ever got to the first hole. I knew Rich had the talent to hit the shots, and I was determined not to let him make any mistakes."

A routine par on the second hole brought Beem to the number 3, the epic downhill par-3 that was playing 247 yards on Sunday. Beem had missed the green in all three previous rounds, which led Duplantis to say, "I think you are good enough to hit this green once this week. Why don't you show me." Beem smote a 3-wood to fifteen feet, then calmly rolled in the birdie putt. This brought his first fist pump of the day and pushed his lead to two strokes over Armour III, who looked like he had gotten a whiff of something foul.

When Armour bogeyed four, the lead was stretched to three strokes, and then on the 5th hole Beem played a delicate wedge to fifteen feet. At the exact moment Beem was standing over the putt the CBS telecast kicked in. Without so much as an opening thought they cut to Beem putting on the 5th. "What a story we have developing here," Jim Nantz intoned. "Rich Beem, a rookie who had lived out of his car earlier this year [a myth that CBS propagated throughout the day] is your leader here in the final round." Beem clobbered his putt. "The ball was going Mach eight," he said later. "If it didn't hit the hole it might have rolled off the green." It did hit the hole, falling in for his third birdie in five holes. He was now 12 under for the tournament, and a whopping four strokes in the lead.

After showing the putt CBS faded into their prerecorded opening, which was pure Velveeta even by the standards of a network golf telecast. "For one week one young man has lived the American Dream," Nantz said in a voice-over, as a montage of Beem filled the screen—holing putts, pumping fists, and generally emoting enough to shame Al Pacino, all set to the strains of throbbing Muzak. From there CBS cut to highlights of Beem's birdies on 1 and 3, and then went to a live shot of Nantz and Venturi, in their familiar aerie in the tower above the 18th green.

"How long can the kid hold on?" Nantz asked. "It's not every week where you have a story like this, a guy coming from oblivion to take over a tournament."

"He's on a mission," agreed Venturi.

By now Beem had driven on the par-5 6th hole, and CBS cut to him in midfairway. Though he had only 223 yards to the flag, he opted to lay up, a sure sign that the lead was already toying with his mind. It was the first time all week that Beem had turned conservative, and in the galley Amy Onick said, "Larry (Beem) must have just fainted on his couch."

"Nah," said David Wyatt, who was turned out in Beem's lucky blue shirt and lucky Chicago Cubs hat, "he's probably so mad he crushed out his cigarette on the living room carpet."

Back in Las Cruces, sequestered in his living room with his daughter Susie, Larry was already beginning to field phone calls from reporters. "That wasn't Rich," Larry grumbled about the layup. "That was his caddie. I know it wasn't Rich." Larry had allowed a reporter from the *Las Cruces Sun-News*, Sam Aselstine, to watch the telecast with him. In a subsequent interview, Aselstine says, "You know how Larry is—real gruff, right? He spent most of the time making unprintable jokes and speculating how Rich was going to spend the winner's check. He was trying to downplay how nervous he was, but it was pretty obvious he was feeling it. He was chain-smoking up a storm. He wouldn't even finish one cigarette before he had lit another."

After a commercial break the telecast resumed with Rich Beem standing over an eighty-three-yard wedge shot on the sixth hole. He struck it purely but the ball took a big hop on the firm green and landed in the long grass just behind the putting surface. As player and caddie strode to the green together, Duplantis got his first props of the afternoon. Said McCord, "He's got a Tour caddie on his bag, Steve Duplantis, who used to caddie for Jim Furyk, and he's really, really helping Beem out right now." As Beem arrived at the sixth green the crowd went wild. "He's getting a fabulous reception every time he walks on a green," said Feherty, who was following the final group on foot. Beem got up and down for his par, not without the usual emoting. "He's not one of those guys who come out here by the hundred who don't say anything or give you any expression," said McCord. "This kid is fun to watch." As Beem idled on the 7th tee, Nantz invoked, for the first time, the name Roy McAvoy, the fictitious hero of *Tin Cup.* With the marquee players all having dropped out of sight—including Furyk, Vijay Singh, Hal Sutton, Justin Leonard, Mark O'Meara, and Lee Janzen—CBS had clearly decided to turn the telecast into the Rich Beem Show, and they were working every angle. Beem was not immune to what was going on. "The cameras were everywhere," he says, "and I was loving it. I felt so comfortable with that. I can't tell you why, but I did." Between shots, off camera, he was even kibitzing with the agreeable Feherty.

Beem played the long 7th hole flawlessly, with a big drive, crisp 5-iron to twenty feet, and smooth lag putt for an easy par. He was clearly on his game, and so, too, was Duplantis, who was determined to prevent his boss's mind from wandering. "After seven I said, 'From now on, all we think about is winning,' " says Duplantis. " 'All the exemptions, the money, the bullshit, we'll talk about that after the round while having a beer.' Beemer just nodded. There was no backing off in him."

On the 8th hole Beem hooked his drive into a bunker, and the lie was so bad he was forced to lay up by blasting back out to the fairway, where he wound up just barely ahead of Armour's drive. Armour produced a solid approach to twelve feet, and suddenly Beem was faced with his first real test of the day. If he made bogey, and Armour holed his birdie putt, the lead would be cut in half. Beem followed with the kind of shot that did his old man proud—a tricky little wedge that landed long and left of the pin but spun back fiercely to two and a half feet. Armour made his putt to move to -9, but Beem got his par, and the lead remained at three. "That was a really big momentum keeper for me," Beem said later.

Both Beem and Armour followed with routine pars at the par-3 9th. The hole was notable for an exchange between McCord and Feherty. Of Duplantis, Feherty said, "He's one of the best caddies in the business, and he's got an interesting story, too. He's a single parent, and he travels the Tour with a three-and-a-half-year-old daughter, little Sierra, and that's no mean feat."

"Caddying has got to be easy after that," said McCord.

Thus the story line had been set as the action moved to the final nine. Beem was the overachieving longshot, the scrappy dreamer playing his heart out, while Duplantis was the world-weary caddie leading the way. Though both were virtual unknowns four days earlier, Beem and Duplantis were quickly endearing themselves to a nation of golf fans. The back nine promised an excess of melodrama.

Beem produced fairway-and-green pars on 10 and 11, picking up another stroke on Armour, who was listing badly. With the lead back to four strokes Beem eschewed a 3-wood on the dangerous 12th hole and instead pulled a driver, which brought more trouble into play and left him far less margin for error. When Beem split the fairway, Feherty was moved to say, "I'll tell ya, he's got some lead in his pencil." The flag on the 12th hole was front right, only a few paces from Rock Run Creek. This was virtually the same pin position as in the third round, when Beem had been suckered into a double bogey. If ever there was a time for Beem to throttle his natural aggressiveness, this was it. From 173 yards, downhill and downwind, he chose to go with an 8-iron. The plan was to fade a safe shot into the left center of the green, but Beem's brain is hard-wired to fire at flags, and this was no exception. The ball took off well to the right of the intended line and then began drifting toward the pin and the creek that framed it. With both Beem and Duplantis shouting invective, the ball landed with a thud less than a pace from the edge of the green, and then kicked into the first cut of rough—safe, but just barely. ("It wasn't up by more than a couple of inches," Beem said later.)

"You almost gave me a heart attack," Duplantis said, back in the fairway.

"I'm sorry," Beem said, sheepishly. "I promise I was aiming left."

Beem got his par, to stay at -12 and keep his lead at four strokes. Armour bogeyed the 12th, falling to -7, but by now a trio of pursuers had moved into a tie for second place at -8: Bill Glasson, playing in the second to last group; Bradley Hughes, a couple of holes ahead; and a charging Sutton, who was suddenly six under on his round through the 17th.

Bogeyless on the day, Beem should have been looking invincible, but that wasn't the case. The approach shot on 12 was not only a mental error but also the product of a tired swing. By now it was well past four in the afternoon, and all he had eaten since 7:00 A.M. was half a muffin. Idling on the 13th tee, the weight of the entire week seemed to finally hit Beem. He plopped down on a bench next to the tee and then turned to a group of reporters kneeling nearby. "I'm wiped out, man," he said. "I'm sucking wind."

When it came time to hit on the tricky par-5 Beem said to Duplantis, "Get me through this, Steve. You've been in this position more than I have." They agreed to play it safe with a 3-wood, but again Beem pushed the shot right, this time into the rough, and a flier lie. With the long grass resting against the back of the ball, the grooves on Beem's club would be unable to impart the normal amount of backspin. This, in turn, would have the effect of making the ball fly farther. How far it was impossible to say, as fliers bedevil even the best of players. Beem had about 165 yards downhill to the edge of Rock Run Creek, if he played to the right edge of the fairway. The farther left he went the closer the creek crept in on the fairway. Beem decided to hit a three-quarters 8-iron, though Feherty had said on TV that the shot was no more than a 9-iron or pitching wedge. As soon as Beem struck the shot he knew he was in trouble. Instead of an easy swing as planned, he had taken a good rip at the ball. "The adrenaline got me, big time," he says. So, too, did the lie. The ball rocketed off the clubface, and then began drifting left, toward the creek. It splashed into the murky water with a sickening finality.

It was a shocking mistake.

Armour, rising to the occasion for the first time, followed by almost holing his second shot for an albatross. With tapping in for eagle but a formality, Armour was on the verge of moving back to -9 (moments later Hughes would chip in to also go to nine under). Beem was ashen as he arrived at the edge of the creek. He quickly took his penalty drop and then followed with a meek pitch that left him a big-breaking twenty-five-footer for par. He missed that to drop to -11, slicing the four-stroke lead in half. (Up ahead Glasson had birdied to also move to -9.) For the first time all day the pursuers were nipping at Beem's heels.

At this point Duplantis all but took over the tournament. Leaving the 13th green he made his best read of the day; seeing how spent his man was, he made Beem eat a Nutri-Grain bar, and when they reached the tee he draped an arm on Beem's shoulders and gave him a long pep talk. "It was pretty obvious Rich was dragging," says Duplantis. "I think he was just mentally exhausted, just drained emotionally. At that point I decided to get in his face so much he'd have to pay attention." The short par-4 14th was a welcome break in the middle of the exacting back nine, allowing Beem to tee off with a 5-iron. "Just swing the club," Duplantis said. "That's all you gotta do." Beem found the fairway, and then, following another long chat with Duplantis, knocked a wedge to fifteen feet. He missed the birdie putt but came away with a par to stop the bleeding. On the 15th tee Duplantis continued to harangue Beem, so much so that CBS announcer Bobby Clampett was moved to say, "There is some heavy coaching going on right now." Looking as if he had found his second wind, Beem split the fairway, and from two hundred yards out he made maybe his best swing of the back nine, leaving a 5-iron in the perfect spot, on the front of the green, below the hole. From twenty feet he just missed the birdie putt, but pars were now Beem's best friend, as no one else was making birdies, either. With three holes to play Beem still had a two-stroke lead.

On the 16th tee Duplantis waved the yardage guide in Beem's face with such vigor that McCord said, "This is some serious, serious coaching. That's what you gotta do—take him by the scruff of his neck and say, 'Hit it over here.' " McCord fell silent, but after observing Duplantis's continued instructions, McCord added, "There he is, Yoda and his pupil."

Beem again produced a clutch tee ball at 16, finding the fairway on a tricky driving hole. "For a while there, on the early part of the back nine, the club felt heavy," he says. "It was work swinging it. Starting on fourteen or fifteen I got comfortable again." Nevertheless, Beem's fuel gauge was now resting on E. "Walking up the hill after my tee shot, my legs were just about out," he said. "I was so tired physically, and so tired mentally, from not trying to think about everything."

While discussing the play from 136 yards out, Duplantis pointed his finger at Beem, and then slapped him on the shoulder as a parting gesture. Said Feherty, "He's saying, 'Make a good swing or I'll slap you silly and call you Betty.' " This curious remark brought an awkward silence from the rest of the CBS broadcast team, and as Beem's 9-iron began descending toward the center of the green, Feherty added, "He won't call him Betty after that one." From twenty feet away Beem lagged to less than two, and as he was crossing the green to mark his ball, Duplantis followed him step for step, pointing and lecturing at him the whole way to take his time and follow his routine. "He won't let him get away," McCord said with a chuckle. "Look at that, he's still pointing at him! Steve, his faithful little servant." Beem nailed his short par putt to remain at -11. Armour, meanwhile, slashed his way to a double bogey, to drop from contention. By now Hughes's charge had stalled, too, as he missed putt after putt on the back nine, finishing at -9. While Beem was assessing his options on 17, the watery par-3, Glasson was up ahead playing the 18th, trying to make a birdie and post at -10, which would ratchet up the pressure on Beem.

With water short and right, Beem obviously needed to favor the left side of the 17th green, as well as play long to take the creek out of the equation. At 178 yards, steeply downhill, the yardage was a perfect 7-iron for Beem. "It's just a seven," Duplantis said. "Make a good swing. It's just a seven." Beem spent a long time on the tee box, trying to visualize the shot in his mind. At one point he went into some weird gyrations, windmilling his arms in an attempt to relieve the tension. Finally Beem settled over his ball, looking as intensely focused as he had all week. At that exact moment Glasson was missing a twenty-footer for birdie at the last hole, a bit of news that rippled through the gallery thanks to a plethora of pocket TVs and transistor radios. Beem's tee shot at 17, then, would all but decide the tournament. If he kept it dry, he would likely take a two-shot lead to the waterless 18th.

As soon as Beem struck his shot at 17 he looked anxious, as did Duplantis, who sprinted from the side of the tee box to stand by his man. Back in the grillroom at El Paso Country Club the atmosphere was tight. "When Rich got to the seventeenth tee," says Cameron Doan, "the room was pretty rowdy, everyone kinda shouting encouragement. When he hit his shot at seventeen, it got real quiet. That hole is so downhill it seemed like the ball was in the air forever, and I remember they showed him on TV, and he looked a little worried. And then they cut to the ball. It almost hit the hole, and then ran like twelve feet past. When Rich's ball landed safely the room exploded. I mean *exploded.* I remember yelling, to no one in particular, 'I can't fucking believe he went for that pin!' Typical Rich." On the tee Beem shook his head lightly, rolled his eyes, and then floated down the hill toward the green.

With a cautious roll Beem missed his birdie putt but left just a tap-in for par. So to 18 he went, needing only a bogey for the victory. "Come on, kid, don't throw up all over yourself," Larry Beem barked at his TV.

On the 18th tee Beem fished a special ball out of his bag, one he was hoping would get a little TV airtime. He had doctored it the night before with a Sharpie, writing the letters *E* and *S* in block print. It was a message for Max and Dina Schroeder back at the hospital in Las Cruces. The *E* was for Evan, the *S* for Schroeder. Beem had left the middle initial blank. If he could hold on to his lead it would become an *R*, for Richard.

Avenel's 18th is an exceptionally tough driving hole, though you wouldn't know it by the way Beem had played it in the first three rounds—birdie-birdie-birdie. There is out of bounds far to the left, which is generally not a problem (Corey Pavin, however, had jacked his drive O.B. the day before, to fall from contention). The real trouble is to the right. "All I wanted to do was keep it out of the right bunker," says Beem. "On the other hand, when I get excited I tend to pull it left. So I swung as smooth as I could, and naturally pulled it left anyway. I never realized how thick the rough was over there. It was brutal." Beem's drive had sailed 264 yards but settled in a horrific lie. The ball was so buried it wasn't even visible in the long grass. Beem had 180 yards to the green. He conferred briefly with Duplantis, but as soon as he saw the lie he knew what he wanted to do. Instead of trying to muscle a risky shot all the way to the green, he would play short, into the neck, which still gave him a chip and two putts to burn. It was a smart decision, and well executed. With his 5-iron Beem took a heroic swing, and he muscled his ball just short and left of the green. "I thought that was one of the best shots I hit all week," he says.

Victory was now looking certain, and as Beem strode to the final green, the tributes had already begun. "What a storybook this is," Venturi said. "Unbelievable."

"I've sat by your side a long time," Nantz replied, "and I don't think I've ever seen you so nervous. Even at the Masters I haven't seen your hands so clammy."

"I think the last time I was this excited was when I saw John Daly win the PGA," said Venturi.

A third of the way down the fairway, Beem looked into one of the cameras that was shadowing him and said with a grin, "Hello El Paso Country Club."

"That brought the house down," says Doan.

Back in Flower Mound, Texas, Paul Stankowski was jolted awake in his easy chair by a ringing telephone. (It was Stankowski's victory three years earlier that had inspired Beem to take up golf again after his eight-month hiatus in Seattle.) Stankowski had missed the cut at the Kemper and returned home. He knew Beem was playing well, but like a lot of pros, he makes a point of ignoring the Tour while at home. That Sunday Stankowski had fallen asleep watching a baseball game on TV. The phone call was from an old El Paso friend, who wanted to know if he was watching the Kemper.

"Why would I be?" Stankowski asked.

Briefed on the ongoing developments, Stankowski tuned in to CBS just as Beem was strolling up the 18th fairway. Stankowski immediately dialed the El Paso Country Club, where he has been an honorary member since graduating from the University of Texas-El Paso. He wanted to share the experience with someone, anyone, and he knew the EPCC would be in a tizzy. Stankowski was transferred to the grillroom, where the phone was answered but then, amidst the anarchy, simply dropped on the bar, allowing Stankowski to listen in on the scene. "Rich was walking up eighteen, and they were cheering every step," says Stankowski. "It was incredible to listen to. God, I'm getting goose bumps right now just thinking about it. I was on hold forever, but I didn't mind, because it was the perfect soundtrack."

As Beem reached the green the thousands of fans lining the grass amphitheater rose as one to salute him. "This is something he will never forget," Venturi said, back on the telecast. "Look at him, he's teary-eyed." Beem was indeed a bit caught up in the moment, but as soon as he got to his ball he regained his focus. The chip he was facing was hardly a gimme.

The pin had been set in its traditional Sunday spot, back left, on the crown of the green's second tier. Beem had to carry his ball over the corner of a cavernous bunker, across a deep swale, and up the steeply pitched green to get to the hole.

"He's sucking wind right now," Larry said. "Just don't chili-dip it, boy."

Beem damn near did. He caught his chip heavy enough that it barely cleared the lip of the bunker, and then it landed only an inch or two beyond the gnarly rough. "I've been getting so much shit about that," Beem says. "I promise you, it cleared the bunker by more than it looked like on TV." Whatever, the longer grass of the fringe killed the speed of the chip, and Beem's ball ran out of gas a good twenty feet short of the hole. He was now facing a tough sidehill putt, and a three-jack loomed as a very real possibility. Duplantis rushed over to Beem to slow him down and make sure he gathered himself before the putt. On the tube Nantz hailed him for "one of the greatest caddying performances you'll ever see." Beem took a deep breath and then stepped up to his putt. He made a credible stroke, but he missed the putt on the low side. It peeled right of the hole and stopped a full two feet away. It was a putt he had to make to avoid a playoff. Duplantis walked Beem up to the ball and again insisted he mark and go through his full routine. Beem hurriedly crouched to get a look at the line, performed a perfunctory practice stroke, and then addressed his ball.

"Slow down, slow down," Larry cried.

Across town Beem's mother, Diana, turned away from the TV and put her hands over her eyes. "I know that's redundant," she says, "but I was just so afraid. I know it was only two feet but it looked like twenty to me."

"It wasn't a tough putt," says Beem. "I'd had two-footers all day, and this was exactly what you'd like, straight in, slightly uphill. I didn't stop to think about it, because I didn't want to. I just told myself, This is a piece of cake, just step up and knock it in."

Which is exactly what he did.

When the putt dropped Beem put both arms above his head in triumph. "From oblivion to ecstasy," Nantz intoned. Beem stumbled around the green for a few beats, dazed, and then he spied Wyatt and Onick, who had elbowed their way to the front row of spectators behind the green. Beem had been so focused throughout the day that this was the first time he noticed them in the gallery. CBS's Peter Kostis made a move toward Beem to do the traditional champion's interview, but Beem blew right by him and sprinted toward the ropes. He threw his arms around Wyatt for a long, sloppy, teary hug, and then did the same with Onick.

On the other side of the green Duplantis was wiping away tears of his own. He had wandered in the direction of the scorer's tent, where the reporters had gathered, and instantly he was swallowed whole. "For me, personally, the best moment was walking off the eighteenth green and just being surrounded by that semicircle of reporters," he says. "You were there, Golf Channel, ESPN, everybody. It just felt unbelievable to be recognized like that." Up in Brampton, Duplantis's mom was sobbing softly on her couch. "What was so gratifying was hearing Steve get so much of the credit," says Sandy. "I have never heard a caddie have his name mentioned that much on TV. Ever. I just knew how much the victory meant to Steve, considering everything he had been through."

Kostis finally corralled Beem, who made no attempt to disguise the emotion of the moment. Hoarse and breathless, Beem said, "This is a dream come true. Mom, Dad, I did it. El Paso Country Club, I did it. To all my sponsors, thank you. I'm just so excited."

"What a kid. What a win. What a story. What a ride," Larry Beem was saying back in Las Cruces. "It's a real Cinderella story."

Signing off from the booth, Nantz said, "He's got some game. We're gonna be hearing from him for years and years."

"What a day," said Venturi. "I am proud to be a part of this."

"One of the most improbable rides to victory you will ever see, Rich Beem has beat 'em all at the Kemper Open," Nantz said, closing the telecast.

AFTER SIGNING HIS SCORECARD, which made the victory official, Beem dug out his cell phone and placed two calls while still standing amongst the melee around the 18th green. The first was to his father. It was short but sweet. "He wanted to make sure I was watching," says Larry, chuckling at the thought. "All he really had time to say was, 'Dad, I did it.' I think that was all he wanted to say anyway." Beem's second call was to the El Paso Country Club. He told the boys to start a tab, on him. (Later that night he would call Max and Dina Schroeder in the hospital so he could coo at Evan Richard, while parties on both ends of the telephone enjoyed a good cry.)

Beem was then escorted to the middle of the green for the champion's presentation. In a series of stultifying speeches various tournament officials saluted his effort, and then the microphone was turned over to Beem. He thanked the fans for their unwavering support, paid tribute to Duplantis, and summed up with a few self-deprecating remarks. Beem was then presented with a gorgeous crystal trophy and the $450,000 winner's check, which had been discreetly placed in an envelope. Beem tore open the envelope with relish, then mouthed "wow" when he saw the check's cartoon-sized numbers. The cash and crystal weren't the only souvenirs he had to show for his day. Prior to the round Wyatt had slipped Beem a little good luck charm, which he carried in his bag throughout the day. It was a pilfered employee ID card from Magnolia Hi-Fi, a reminder of an old life that now seemed very far away.

CHAPTER

• 11 •

BEFORE RICH BEEM had even left the grounds of TPC of Avenel it was apparent that he was driving into uncharted territory. Following all the interviews, autographs, and presentations, he was handed the keys to a shiny new Buick, a courtesy car to be used while he was hanging out in the Washington area awaiting eye surgery. Stenciled on the driver door was the message CONGRATULATIONS CHAMP. A nice gesture, to be sure, but the car held a deeper significance. This was the first little taste of the endless perks and privileges that would come with his victory.

From the Avenel grounds Beem, Wyatt, and Onick returned to their Best Western for much-needed showers and a change of clothes, and then they rendezvoused with Duplantis at a nearby Mexican restaurant. The four of them were cooling their heels in the bar when highlights of the Kemper flickered across the television. "Turn it up, we're on Sportscenter!" they began screaming. Says Beem, "To tell you the truth, I didn't actually believe it had all happened until I saw it on ESPN. That made it real."

Beem ate enough dinner to make up for the entire day of fasting, but that hardly gave him the energy to hit the town, as he so desperately wanted to do. The spirit was willing but not the flesh. "I barely made it to midnight," he says. "I have never felt so completely exhausted in my life. I didn't fall asleep, I went into a coma."

Late the next morning Beem placed a call to the PGA Tour headquarters in Ponte Vedra Beach, Florida. Duplantis had mentioned in passing that he thought the victory earned them automatic entry into the British Open, and Beem was eager to follow up. Duplantis's hunch had been correct, but it turned out that

that Monday, May 31st, was the final day to register for the Open Championship. With the headquarters for the Royal and Ancient Golf Club of St. Andrews located in St. Andrews, Scotland, all those time zones away, there was not a moment to lose. The rest of the morning dissolved into a blur of forms and faxes.

Early that afternoon Beem put Onick on a plane for San Diego, as scheduled. She was not happy to be leaving, to say the least (and not just because first class was full and Beem wasn't able to upgrade her, as he had promised to do during his champion's press conference). "The whole thing with Amy had been a strain from the time she arrived," says Wyatt. "Her flight into Washington cost like a thousand bucks, and that was money that Rich didn't have at the time. She also just didn't get what a gift the eye surgery was. That procedure usually costs in the neighborhood of five thousand dollars. Again, when Rich agreed to do it, saving that kind of money was a big deal."

"Amy wanted to stay and celebrate," says Beem, "but it was better that she left. It was for her own protection."

It is instructive to note that Beem preferred to whoop it up with Wyatt rather than his girlfriend of well over a year. "People have always misunderstood mine and David's relationship," says Beem, "and that goes all the way back to Tanya in Seattle. We're so close that sometimes other people feel left out."

Eavesdropping, Wyatt says, "I would just like to state for the record that I have never taken it up the ass." He was, however, servicing Beem in other ways. With Beem's cell phone continuing to blow up in the hours and days after the victory, Wyatt became a de facto secretary, screening all incoming calls. This was the first small step in his evolution from best friend to road manager/agent, duties he would increasingly shoulder as the year went on.

After dropping Onick at the airport, Wyatt and Beem commenced the revelry, with Duplantis as a wingman. The boys had already picked up a couple of toothsome tour guides—a pair of best friends, both named Jennifer, who would come to be known simply as the Two Jens. They had been hanging around Avenel Sunday evening, hoping to get Beem's autograph. "Stevie sized up the situation in a hurry, and started giving them the sweet tongue," says Wyatt. "He was hot for one of them, this trashy aspiring debutante—exactly Stevie's type. I liked the other Jen, who was a little more down to earth. Anyway, these girls knew the town, and they wanted to show it to us." That Beem, aglow from his triumph on the links, would have no female companionship seems something of an upset, but says Wyatt, "He was still committed to Amy. Believe me, he wouldn't have had any problem hooking up. I really saw it at the Kemper, just the cornucopia of willingness that was out there. You can spot these girls a mile away—perfectly coiffed, and just so eager to meet a player, especially one that had just won half a million dollars."

On Monday night this fivesome of celebrants journeyed to 1120, D.C.'s club of the moment. It was the kind of place with a velvet rope, $8 drinks, and a crowd full of overdressed twentysomethings all telling lies to one another. "We pulled up to this fancy club, and there was a huge line, and one of the Jens popped out to ask if we could get in," says Wyatt. "The answer was no way. Then they mentioned that we were with Rich Beem, and the guys at the door must have been golf fans, because the doors just swung open."

The next day Beem and Wyatt paid a visit to a Porsche dealership in Rockville, Maryland. Beem had always dreamed of owning a Porsche, and, "If the sales guys had been golfers I probably would have bought one that day," he says. "I had the fever, big time. The guys at the dealership were a little stiff, though, and that kind of slowed me down."

"He was too scared to step up to the plate," says Wyatt. "It wasn't real to him. It was too new. The fact that he could actually buy one of these cars didn't compute." Beem, drawing upon his experience as a salesman, still managed to talk his way into a test drive, and he and Wyatt rolled off the lot in a $90,000 Carrera, unchaperoned. "I went a little nuts," Beem says. "I was doing one hundred thirty miles an hour on the freeway, and David and I were screaming at the top of our lungs. I brought the car back a half hour later, and the tires were just melting. They were not amused."

That night Beem, Wyatt, Duplantis, and Corey McDaniel (who was now back from the wedding in L.A.) went barhopping in Georgetown, and they wound up, inexorably, at a strip joint named Joanna's. The establishment's owner immediately recognized the freshly minted Kemper Open champion, and made a big deal of coming over to shake hands and offer a free round of drinks. The warm welcome did not go unnoticed by the talent, who swarmed to Beem and his friends like bees on honey. "We got the star treatment," says McDaniel. "Especially Rich, obviously. He was throwing around a fair amount of cash, just having a great time. You could tell he was loving all the attention."

It was a setting in which Duplantis felt at home, and that night much was revealed. For the first time he talked about his soon-to-be-ex-wife in any kind of detail, as well as some of his history with his nanny, Shannon Pennington. Beem also got an up-close look at Duplantis's interactions with the opposite sex. "Some of the things he said were truly shocking, even to me," says Beem. "It was pretty clear he's a little dysfunctional when it comes to women."

They partied at Joanna's until 3:00 A.M.

The next day—Wednesday—Beem, Wyatt, and Duplantis took a VIP tour of the White House, which McDaniel had set up through his politico connections. They didn't get to meet the First Golfer, but it was a fun outing nonetheless. At some point that afternoon Beem decided he wanted to see a tape of the Kemper's final round. Wyatt got on the horn and talked the local CBS affiliate into setting up a private screening. Duplantis tagged along for this stroll down memory's fairway, so Beem and his caddie and Wyatt went to the station's headquarters, where they had been given a conference room all to themselves. They ordered in Domino's, popped the top on a couple of Cokes, and let the tape roll. "It was strange to see it all play out," says Beem. "It was like an intense out-of-body experience, because I really didn't remember a lot of the stuff that had happened. The film brought it all back. Watching that chip on eighteen, my palms were sweaty, and my heart was racing."

That night Beem threw himself one more victory celebration, renting out a back room at Buffalo Billiards, a DuPont Circle hotspot. All the usual suspects turned out—Wyatt and Duplantis of course, the Two Jens, McDaniel and his brand new fiancée, and "a bunch of people I had never met," says Beem, who all turned out to be friends of the Two Jens. The party had its own bartender, and a half dozen pool tables at its disposal.

Thursday brought the long-awaited trip to the eye surgeon. "Of course I was worried," Beem says. "You don't see many blind golfers on the PGA Tour." The procedure was remarkable only for how ordinary it was—it took less than five minutes, and was so painless Beem likens the entire experience to dropping off dry cleaning. Thursday also brought the first round of the Memorial tournament. "Getting my eyes done was a great thing, and the time we spent in D.C. was a blast, but looking back a big part of me wishes I had gone to the Memorial and played," says Beem. "When I get hot I tend to stay hot, and who knows what could have happened there? I think about that sometimes."

Friday afternoon, following a checkup with the surgeon, the grand D.C./Potomac adventure finally came to an end. Duplantis headed for home, outside of Tampa, while Beem jumped a plane bound for San Diego.

INTREPID SPORTS was birthed in 1998 when a small management company, Triangle Sports, was renamed and brought under the umbrella of Pinnacle Enterprises, an event management company that caters to corporate America. Intrepid's golf division has grown in fits and starts ever since, with the total operation now up to six employees. Prior to signing Beem, the client list included only four players anyone had ever heard of: Keith Fergus, a three-time winner in the early '80s who was still clawing to remain on tour; Mark Lye, the winner of the 1983 Bank of Boston Classic, who more or less gave up the game in the late '90s to work as the Golf Channel's lead analyst; Pete Jordan, a six-year vet who had never done better than 110th on the money list; and Jill McGill, the 1993 U.S. Amateur champ who was finally beginning to show some promise on the LPGA tour. Needless to say, Beem's victory meant as much for the careers of his agents as for him personally. "It was like winning the lottery," says Intrepid's Adam Lincoln. Though Beem went to San Diego ostensibly to hang out with Onick, he was compelled to mix some business with pleasure.

On Saturday he journeyed to the Intrepid offices, in La Jolla, to meet and greet all the new faces at the agency. There was much to be discussed. Beem's victory would bring a windfall that went far beyond the $450,000 winner's check. For starters, he was now due bonuses built into his endorsement contracts. Both Callaway and Titleist had victory clauses worth $50,000 each, and with his higher profile Beem now had the leverage to cut better deals for the remainder of 1999 and beyond. The company that manufactures the shafts in Beem's clubs, AJ Tech, also chipped in with a $30,000 bonus, no strings attached. Beem didn't have to appear in any ads, wear any logos, or make any appearances. "They just do it to create loyalty and goodwill," says Beem. "Obviously it works. Any company that is going to give me that kind of money and not expect anything in return is the kind of people I want to be associated with."

There was another bonus to be had, as well. Kemper Insurance Companies, the title sponsor of the Kemper Open, was so charmed by Beem—his performance, personality, and his unlikely story—that it was offering an endorsement contract which was reported by one newspaper to be worth $100,000, although that figure was actually subject to negotiation. Also reported, correctly, was that the contract was to contain a proviso that should Beem win one of the year's three remaining major championships, or the following season's Masters, he would get a $200,000 bonus, just because. Beem was unaware of the potential bonanza until he read about it in the paper the day after his victory. When he mentioned it to his people at Intrepid, they were clueless, as well.

Finalizing the Kemper deal, then became priority number one. Also on the to-do list was lining up some lucrative Monday corporate outings. Wherever the PGA Tour blows into town it is common for the prominent local companies to throw pro-ams or clinics for their clients and/or employees. They pay handsomely for the services of the visiting professionals, and the higher a player's Q rating, the more dough he can command, obviously. Prior to the Kemper Beem had played in a dozen of these pro-ams, all arranged through that particular week's tournament. The appearance fees ranged from $750 to $1,500. After his star turn on CBS, Beem was expecting his fee to double or triple, at least. For a young, mostly unproven player this extra income can be important. Not so long ago this kind of barnstorming was how most pro golfers paid their mortgage. Dave Stockton, winner of eleven Tour events across the 1960s and '70s, including a pair of PGA Championships, has often lamented that his career résumé would be far more impressive had he not devoted so much energy to playing up to forty Monday pro-ams a year. (Considering how much cash he scooped up on the side, maybe Stockton shouldn't complain.) With the explosion of the PGA Tour's purses at the end of the '90s the top players rarely waste their time anymore in the back-slapping world of corporate pro-ams. Then again, every player has his price; following his epic win at the '97 Masters Tiger Woods committed to three annual appearances at an event in Pennsylvania, for what was reported to be in excess of $1.5 million. Beem couldn't dream of commanding even 1 percent of that payday, but he was still hoping his agents would be able to line his pockets a bit.

Though there were obviously few suitors prior to his victory, Beem was pleased to be hitched to Intrepid. "My perspective was always that it would be better to be the big fish in a little agency, than vice versa," he says. In the weeks following his victory Beem was wooed by all the larger, more established agencies—International Management Group and Cornerstone among them—but he rebuffed their advances. IMG was the most tempting to Beem, simply because of its omnipotence in the golf world. Founded by Mark McCormack in the early 1960s, IMG swiftly rose to power behind the "Big Three," McCormack's slick packaging of clients Jack Nicklaus, Arnold Palmer, and Gary Player. Presently the company represents more than one hundred top golfers, including Woods, David Duval, Karrie Webb, Annika Sorenstam, and, not least, Palmer. IMG is so ruthlessly effective at scoring extra money for its players—through endorsements, pro-ams, and overseas appearance fees—the company name has become a verb. To be IMG'd means to be driven to the edge of burnout in pursuit of the filthy lucre that exists outside the PGA Tour. Following his historic victories at the Masters and British Open, Mark O'Meara spent the 1998 off-season globetrotting so he could play in a dizzying number of meaningless tournaments, all for the sake of inflated appearance fees. Not surprisingly, he was exhausted and apathetic throughout much of '99, failing to win a tournament on tour for the first time since 1994, and freefalling to forty-fifth on the money list, his second-worst showing since 1983.

Despite these kind of cautionary tales, Duplantis felt Beem made a mistake by not defecting to an agency with more juice. "From everything I've heard the guys at Intrepid are fucking clowns," he says. "They're going to school on Rich, and that's gonna wind up costing him a lot of money."

Though cash was not falling from the sky for Duplantis, as it was for his boss, the victory did have its financial rewards. At the range prior to the Kemper's final round, Duplantis was approached by a representative of Norelco. They offered their standard deal to any caddie whose player is in contention, and thus likely to be featured on national TV. For every second Duplantis's Norelco visor was visible on the telecast the company would pay him $50. After his unprecedented amount of airtime, Duplantis received a check for a whopping $10,300. This more than made up for the income he lost when he was fired by Furyk. Caddies to the big-name players often get deals from the companies their player endorses. In 1996 Duplantis received about $150 a week to wear a Callaway visor, and he stayed with the company for two more years, ultimately earning a little more than $10,000 annually. In '99 he signed on for a STRATA visor, which was to pay him $10,000 for the year. In any caddie contract it is a given that the deal's off should they get fired. The week after Duplantis got his pink slip from Furyk a modest check arrived from Top Flite, maker of the STRATA ball, with the minimum buyout per the terms of the contract.

Beyond the Norelco payday the Kemper victory came with a different kind of payoff for Duplantis. After his firing he often heard from his fretful lawyer, Robert Tropp, who would demand updates on the job search. Though it had been nearly two years, Duplantis technically had only temporary custody of his daughter. Tropp knew that Duplantis's healthy income was one of the factors that had tipped the initial custody battle in his client's favor. With a hearing to determine full-time custody looming sometime in the future, it was important to Duplantis's case that he be bountifully employed. During the champion's press conference at the Kemper Open, Beem had said, "Without Steve this week wouldn't have happened. He was absolutely a huge part of me winning. I can't say enough about the guy. He is awesome." Beem also repeated what he had said the day before: "The job is his for as long as he wants it." The morning after the victory Duplantis rang Tropp's office and said, casually, "Hey Robert, I got myself a loop last week." He also got 10 percent of the winner's check, good for $45,000. It didn't take long for him to part with a big chunk of it.

After four days at home, Duplantis arrived in Memphis on Monday, June 7th for that week's tournament, the FedEx-St. Jude Classic. Upon hitting town he immediately went shopping for a new Rolex. He selected a 1999 Presidential, which retailed for a cool $19,000. "But I got a great deal," he says. "I only paid twelve-three." This from a guy who a couple of weeks earlier was worried about not being able to make his mortgage payments. "It's the only thing I've ever treated myself to," Duplantis says. "After pissing away so much money on lawyers and women, I just figured, if I'm going to go down, I'm going down with a nice watch."

The new timepiece wasn't the only thing boosting Duplantis's self-esteem. He had heard from his family up north that there had been long stories about his role in the victory in both of Canada's national newspapers, the *Globe & Mail* and the *National Post*. More significantly, upon arriving in Memphis he received plenty of slaps on the back from the other players and caddies. "I got nothing more than the usual congrats that week," he says, "but I could tell I had earned respect from a lot of people. It was unspoken." One person who Duplantis never did hear from in the wake of the victory was Jim Furyk. "That was disappointing," he says. "That hurt." Still, Duplantis was careful not to bad-mouth his ex-boss, a restraint he displayed even in the heady moments after the victory. On Sunday afternoon at the Kemper, standing on the edge of the 18th green, his eyes moist and voice thick with emotion, Duplantis had made only a passing allusion to Furyk, saying, "It's redemption for me, for sure. Hopefully the people who have been bad-mouthing me the last couple of weeks will see I'm still a pretty good caddie."

Though he was secretly thrilled by all the fawning he received in the wake of the Kemper, Duplantis tried to keep a low profile. There is no upside to being a celebrity caddie, a point driven home by the very public firing of Fluff Cowan a couple of months earlier. As a caddie, "The more you put yourself in the public eye, the more aggravation you get," Duplantis says. "All of a sudden I was the man again. I was on the high horse and could have taken potshots at Jim or anybody else, but I didn't. It just wasn't worth it. After I got fired I knew everybody was . . . not so much expecting me to fall flat on my face, but not to ever have that kind of success again. The victory was satisfaction enough."

In a weird way, however, the events of the Kemper vindicated Furyk. Beem was quick to dismiss Duplantis's maddening tardiness prior to the final round. "We still won, so it just kind of got swept under the rug," he says. Others were harsher in their judgment. "Like I said, word travels fast on tour," says Furyk. "When I heard about Steve being late, I was so mad at him. I just couldn't believe that he hadn't learned his lesson. If he was late once I knew it would happen again, and I knew he and Rich would eventually have problems because of it. I didn't say anything to Steve, but I was really upset knowing that he was already throwing away such a good opportunity."

BEEM FLED San Diego Sunday at noon, after barely thirty-six hours in town. "The vibe with Amy wasn't very healthy," is all he says.

At least Beem had something to cheer him up upon his arrival in Memphis—another sparkling new courtesy car. Every PGA Tour event provides such rides to its players, but they are generally reserved for those who finished in the Top 100 of the previous year's money list. Before arriving in Memphis, Beem rang the tournament office and asked if he could have a car for the week.

"Where did you finish on last year's money list?" he was asked.

"I didn't play the Tour last year," he said.

"Well, then, I'm afraid there won't be any cars available."

"Would it help if I mentioned that I won the Kemper Open last week?"

"Hold a moment, please. Let me speak with someone here in the office."

Pause.

"Mr. Beem, there will be a car waiting for you at the airport."

So it went for the rest of the season.

Two days after arriving in Memphis Beem had his near miss at U.S. Open qualifying, but even that disappointment couldn't take away from the giddy excitement of the week. One of the highlights came on Wednesday night, on the eve of the tournament, when he had a jam session with John Daly, the vastly talented, deeply troubled alcoholic who makes his home in Memphis. Beem and Daly had played a couple of practice rounds together at the San Diego Invitational and hit it off immediately, a couple of kindred spirits who had little in common with the country club brats who populate the Tour. Since San Diego they had kept in touch sporadically, and Beem was blown away that Daly had taken the time to email congratulations the day after his win. It was ironic that they were becoming buddies, because since the Kemper it had become fashionable to compare their respective first victories. Daly's had been the 1991 PGA Championship, when, as the ninth alternate, he sneaked into the field and then overpowered a very long, very strong course, Crooked Stick Country Club, and a sterling international field. The atmosphere at a major is far more intense than a tournament like the Kemper Open; there are suffocating numbers of fans and reporters on hand, the course conditions are nastier and more exacting, and the pressure to perform—to make history—can be overwhelming. That Daly would have his coming out in such circumstances was remarkable, but despite the mythology surrounding the '91 PGA, Beem's victory, in context, may have been a more stunning achievement. Daly had been an All-American at the University of Arkansas, and in 1990 he won not only on the Nike Tour but also twice in Africa. He was a proven, if erratic, commodity. Beem had none of these credentials.

Anyway, Beem was one of a half dozen or so buddies Daly had over to his manse the evening before the tournament began. "It was cool to see how the other half lives," says Beem. "I spent an hour and a half just looking at all his memorabilia. He had the coolest shit you could ever imagine." This included replicas of the Claret Jug and Wannamaker Trophy (which come with winning the British Open and PGA Championship respectively), signed memorabilia and photos from a galaxy of stars of every genre, and, what Beem dug the most, a collection of two dozen guitars, gifts from two or three generations of famous ax wielders. Beem was fondling a vintage Fender Stratocaster when he was thunderstruck to discover that it had been signed by Eddie Van Halen, his all-time rock god. Beem mentioned casually to Daly that Van Halen would be a part of his dream foursome, along with Jack Nicholson and Joe Pesci. "Shit, we'll do that next year at L.A.," Daly said. "I got all those guys on speed dial."

This was the kind of thing that made Beem's head spin. He was all of a sudden a somebody in the world of golf, hanging out with his more famous colleagues and only one step removed from their even more famous friends. Another sign of Beem's burgeoning status could be seen in his playing partners during the first two rounds at Memphis. With his victory Beem was elevated to class one in the pairings system, and so he drew a plum tee time alongside Hal Sutton and Scott Simpson. The winner of the 1983 PGA Championship, Sutton was coming off one of his finest seasons. In 1998 he had won two tournaments, including the Tour Championship, and over $1.8 million to finish fifth on the money list. He was only a couple of months away from starring at the Ryder Cup. Simpson, the 1987 U.S. Open champ, had also won in '98, in San Diego, the seventh victory of his career. "I was messing around in my bag on the first tee on Thursday," says Beem, "and I overheard these two fans. They were looking at the pairings sheet, and this guys says, 'I know who Hal Sutton is, I know who Scott Simpson is, but who the hell is Rich Beem?' I just kind of laughed to myself, but I knew a lot of people were thinking the same thing. It made me determined to play well."

And play well he did, shooting 68-69-69-68 to finish tied for twenty-fifth, and earn $17,147.73. It was the first time in his Tour career that Beem had put together four straight rounds in the 60s. "The only difference was confidence," he says. "Just knowing I could hit the shots, knowing I belonged."

Duplantis's week was not quite the same kind of unqualified

success. In Memphis, as in Potomac, he and Pennington were crammed into the same hotel room along with Sierra. Sharing a Cubicle by Marriott with an ex, as well as a business arrangement, would be dicey under any circumstances, but the previous week's victory had only added further strain to the situation. "As soon as we got to Memphis Shannon started up with this whole trip about, 'If it wasn't for me you wouldn't have made all that money, so I should get some, too,' " says Duplantis. "This was after she had already insisted that I get her a cell phone, so we could quote-unquote keep in touch when we were apart. It was like all of a sudden I was a human ATM."

The week following Memphis brought the U.S. Open, which, after Beem's near miss at qualifying, would mean a dark week for player and caddie. "The deal from the very beginning was Steve was going to pay me six hundred dollars a week, regardless of whether or not he was working a tournament that week," says Pennington. "For me to make a commitment to him, I needed some kind of stability, some kind of steady income. All of a sudden he didn't want to pay for that off week, so we had a huge argument." This was Monday afternoon in the parking lot of TPC of Southwind (rain had delayed the final round a day). The tenor of the discourse was far from civil.

"I think Steve's ex-wife destroyed him, at least as far as dealing with other women," says Pennington. "I really saw it this second time around. He had so much anger. When we had our fight, he was such a jerk. He really degraded me and made me feel like dirt. I was in tears before we even left the tournament. He was yelling at me, 'You are such a loser. You can't keep a job, you don't know how to handle money,' all this stuff. He's always been so judgmental about other people's lives, especially mine, which is a joke, because he should look in the mirror."

From Memphis Pennington drove home to Dallas, and she and Duplantis severed their ties forever. (Duplantis wasted no time in canceling her cell phone service. With a cackle, he says, "That felt good.") Duplantis returned to Tampa with Sierra for his week off. Once again he was in the precarious position of having a full-time caddying job, but no help with his daughter.

•

FOLLOWING MEMPHIS BEEM, too, returned home, to El Paso. He met with his accountant, had a few celebratory meals with his family, played a couple of casual rounds around El Paso Country Club, and did a few interviews for local media outlets. It was, by design, a mellow week. "We really needed to slow the train down," he says. "You know, I don't think anyone can be fully prepared for how much your life changes when you win your first Tour event, but some guys are better equipped than others. You look at Tiger, or Phil Mickelson, guys like that, they have their whole entourages in place before they ever step foot on tour. They've got armies of agents, financial advisors, gurus, etc., etc. They've got pros on their side. Me, I had a bunch of good ol' boys from back home. I was so ill prepared for all of it."

One thing Beem did have, which few other players could ever hope to experience, was the support of an entire community. He was given a hero's welcome at the El Paso Country Club upon his return. The only disappointment came when he went to settle the bar tab, which had begun with his phone call in the moments after his victory. The tab was a mere $30. "I was upset," he says. "I was hoping it would be a thousand dollars. I really was, because it would have been money well-spent. But what happened, I was told, was everybody was so pumped up from watching the telecast they all ran out to play as soon as it was over. They had a couple of fifteen-somes go out, wacky stuff like that."

The enthusiasm was still surging on Tuesday night, two days after Memphis, when the El Paso/Las Cruces golfing aristocracy turned out to fete Beem at the El Paso Country Club, where less than a year earlier he had been a lowly shop hand. The setup was similar to the victory party thrown for J. P. Hayes in 1998, the party that inspired Beem to finally roll the dice at Q School. There was a big-screen TV showing an endless loop of highlights from the Kemper, a large bar (of course), an oversized buffet, and hundreds of chairs. Beem reckons some three hundred people turned out for the party. Bill Eschenbrenner and Hayes both said a few words about Beem, and then the man of the hour got on the microphone. Beem opened with a joke, saying of his disastrous layup on the 13th hole during the final round at Kemper, "At least I hit it in the middle of the hazard, and didn't just dribble it in." Then he turned serious.

"Rich said something that brought tears to my eyes," says Greg Johns, one of his sponsors. "He said, 'Last year when you all threw this party for J.P. I was right over there in the pro shop, trying to hurry up and finish my vacuuming so I could come out here and celebrate, too. I remember thinking that someday I'd really like to have something like this for me. Not in my wildest dreams did I dream it would happen this year.' Of course, that brought the house down."

The party lasted until the wee hours of the morning. At one point a handful of the stragglers became entangled in a cutthroat match on the practice putting green, which was illuminated by floodlights. It was Beem, one of his college buddies, and Eschenbrenner versus Hayes and a collection of five EPCC members. For forty-five minutes the teams were putting an uphill thirty-footer, but nobody could sink the putt. "Realize, there had been a few cocktails consumed," says Eschenbrenner, by way of an explanation. The venue was finally changed to a much easier twenty-footer. Hayes banged in the putt straightaway, leaving Beem's team to try and salvage a halve. Eschenbrenner and Beem's buddy both missed, placing the match's fortunes in Beem's hands. "We're looking at losing three or four hundred dollars apiece," says Eschenbrenner. "This ain't a happy deal." Midway through the putt-a-thon Beem had borrowed a putter from one of his opponents, and as he was preparing for the crucial putt, the putter's owner demanded it back. It was the lowest form of gamesmanship, and sparked a mock-serious melee. Finally, Beem was allowed to continue using the borrowed blade. Naturally, he banged in his putt like a champion. Beem then wheeled and heaved the putter into the pond that guards the 18th green. It goes without saying that the entire crew eventually wound up in the water, as well.

"It was a sloppy night," says Beem, a bit redundantly.

BACK IN TAMPA, Duplantis's homecoming was hardly a festive affair, though Sollange Lewis did come down from the Bronx for a visit. Shortly after arriving home Duplantis was informed that his wife had begun a new offensive in their ongoing divorce proceedings. He spent much of the week on the phone, including numerous calls to Vicki. On that Friday morning Lewis returned home to New York, taking Sierra with her. The following week's tournament was in Westchester County, just outside the city, so she was merely getting a head start on her nanny duties. Vicki arrived in Tampa a few hours after Sollange had split town.

"I've been down that road so many times," says Duplantis. "We've gotten back together probably seven or eight times since we first split up. She will use whatever leverage she can to get back into my life, but none of that ever explains why I take her back. The only explanation, if there is one, is that when you love someone you do things that don't always make sense. And Vicki is the only girl I have ever loved."

Over the weekend Duplantis called Beem in El Paso to catch up.

"He says, 'Guess what, I'm happily married again,' " says Beem. "I said, 'What are you talking about? You bad-mouth her every chance you get.' "

" 'Oh no, I love her.'

"I said, 'Let me guess, she's sitting right there next to you.'

" 'Yes she is.' "

On Monday Steve and Vicki flew to New York, stopping at Lewis's to pick up Sierra. "Sollange wasn't home when we got there," says Steve. "That was probably a good thing. Knowing Vicki, it wouldn't have gone well if she had been around."

The family enjoyed a nice week together, with Steve and Vicki stealing away a couple of times to visit Manhattan, including a trip to the theater to see the acclaimed play *Art.* ("It was shit," he says. "I think you had to be a yuppie to get the jokes.")

"Were we going to stay together?" says Steve. "Who knows? I guess I was willing to stick it out and see."

ON MONDAY of Westchester week Beem harvested the first fruits of his alliance with Intrepid Sports. His agents had lined up a pro-am that would pay him $5,000 to play a round with three back-slapping amateurs at venerable Winged Foot Country Club, in Mamaroneck, New York, site of four U.S. Opens and, more recently, the 1997 PGA Championship. Refreshed from his week at home, Beem brought his A-game to Winged Foot, going out in thirty and posting a 65. When Beem finished his round he was told that he had won a $25,000 bonus, which had been set aside for the pro who shot the lowest round. Welcome to New York.

With the pro-am over by the early afternoon, Beem spent the rest of the day tromping around Manhattan, having been asked to film a segment for the weekly ESPN show *Inside the PGA Tour.* Tailed by a camera crew, he provided a running commentary on the sights in midtown (sample: peering down upon the hubbub of Grand Central Station, he said, "I haven't seen this many people since the Phoenix Open."). Beem was a natural in front of the camera—relaxed and funny and telegenic in a blue denim shirt. The day's only setback came when he tried to crash the MTV studios in Times Square, and was unceremoniously rebuffed.

Beem's affinity for Winged Foot was understandable, but on Tuesday he made a curious decision. Instead of playing a practice round at Westchester Country Club and getting his first peek at an old-school course full of blind shots, confounding doglegs, and rollercoaster greens he chose to have a casual day playing Winged Foot's east course with Gus and his father, with whom Beem was staying in Connecticut. "I wasn't too worried," says Beem. "I figured Steve knew Westchester well enough." Following the round Beem wound up sharing a drink and a table with Jack Salerno, a big swinging dick at Bear Stearns in Chicago. He slid Beem his card and told him to keep in touch, especially with both the upcoming Western Open and PGA Championship being played outside Chicago. Taking advantage of the long summer days, Beem did sneak over to Westchester to play nine holes before hunger drove him from the course.

Beem continued his cash grab on Wednesday, playing in yet another pro-am, this one arranged through the Buick, though it wasn't on the tournament course. Beem had agreed to the outing before his victory, so he received only $1,500.

Paired with Vijay Singh, the reigning PGA Championship titleholder, during the first round of the tournament proper, Beem opened with a disappointing 73, including a 40 on the nine holes of Westchester CC he hadn't bothered to play. "Sure, I was kicking myself a little bit at the time," he says. Especially when he came back with rounds of 71-68-71, to move up to twenty-eighth place, and take home $16,267.86. Looking back on his opening nine, Beem says, "If I play in even par I'm right there in the hunt on Sunday." In fact, subtract those hypothetical four strokes from Beem's overall score and he finishes tied for fifth, only three behind the eventual winner Duffy Waldorf. "You know what, I had a great week, and I don't regret a thing," he says. "I mean, hey, I won thirty grand by Monday afternoon, how can it not be great? I tell you what, I'm gonna spend the week exactly the same way next year."

In the three weeks since his victory Beem had put together two good tournaments, sandwiched around a dream evening in his adopted hometown. "I didn't feel like all of sudden I had the PGA Tour licked by any means, but I was feeling good," he says. "Things were going well."

Duplantis, his domestic and professional situation stable for the first time in years, adds, "It was smooth sailing for all of us."

CHAPTER

• 12 •

There are only two professional American tournaments that date back to the nineteenth century—the U.S. Open and the Western Open, the latter of which Rich Beem traveled to from Westchester. The first Western was played in 1899 and won by Willie Smith, who also took that year's U.S. Open. For much of its history the Western held an importance on par with any of the major championships, as it was played at such elite courses at Medinah, Olympia Fields, Oakland Hills, and Canterbury and won by legends like Willie Anderson (four times, from 1902 to '09), Walter Hagen (four times, including back to back in 1926 and '27), Ralph Guldahl (three years in a row from 1936 to '38), and Sam Snead and Ben Hogan, who each won the tournament twice in the years 1946 to '50. Larry Beem had grown up following the Western Open, and he made it clear he wanted to watch his son play in it. With the exception of one practice round in Tucson, this was to be Larry's first journey to the PGA Tour.

The weeks after the Kemper were a strange time for Larry. To be sure, he was proud of his son and elated with his success, but at some point all the attention became a little much. Three weeks after the Kemper the *El Paso Times* had run a long story on the front page of its sports section under the headline "Respect Grows for Golfing Father, Son." In the story Rich said of his father, "He's been my only coach and I still listen to him quite a bit."

Privately Larry says, "What a load of horseshit. Why he feels the need to peddle that fabrication is beyond me. Is it his way of being condescending toward me?"

The conflicted feelings Larry has always had about golf were only made more complicated by his son's success. "I don't e vicariously through Rich in any way, shape, or form," Larry says. "I'm not Earl Woods—I have no interest in promoting myself through my son. It's not like, wow, I'm sure glad he did it because I couldn't. It never has been that, because I don't care enough. Basically tournament golf is just a way to make a living. It's not anything that special—it's still a game, a silly-ass game. Take away the money and it's just a bunch of kids wasting their time."

For his part, Rich knew that having Larry at the Western would change the feeling of the week. "It made me want to try harder," he says. "Doesn't every kid try harder when his dad's watching?"

Duplantis also had traveling companions in Chicago, as once again he brought Vicki and Sierra along. On that Tuesday night the Duplantises and the Beems went out for dinner in Lemont, Illinois, in suburban Chicago, the site of the tournament. It was the first time Rich had met Vicki. Her hair was bleached platinum for the occasion, and she was spilling out of a skintight outfit. "I just about had a heart attack when I saw her," says Beem. "I wanted to hit Steve. I couldn't believe that was the woman he had married."

On Wednesday Rich, Larry, and Steve traveled to Butler National Golf Club, as guests of Jack Salerno, whom Rich had met the week before at Winged Foot. Butler National, the site of the Western Open from 1974 to '90, is one of the top tracks in the Midwest. The strength of a golf course can often be measured by who has won there, and in the first thirteen Westerns at Butler National, Tom Watson prevailed three times, and Tom Weiskopf, Hale Irwin, Tom Kite, Larry Nelson, and Al Geiberger also chalked up Ws.

Beem thrived on the challenge of the course. "Rich was very loose, having a good time, but it was obvious he was playing very well," says Salerno. "I was telling him how to play the holes, and if I said, 'Aim for that tree,' he would say, 'Which branch?' " By the time he reached the eighteenth hole Beem had made ten birdies against no bogeys. Walking down the last fairway, Salerno told Larry Beem, "If Rich makes a par here, he shoots the course record."

"Don't tell him that," said Larry. "Just let him play."

Beem missed the 18th green with his approach and then followed with an indifferent chip, to twelve feet. As he was loitering on the green none other than Michael Jordan arrived at the adjacent 10th tee, which sent Beem into spasms of excitement. Says Salerno, "Rich says to me, 'Jack, finish my putt for me, I gotta go get Jordan's autograph' I say, 'Rich, I guarantee we'll get Jordan's autograph. You gotta make this putt.' "

It was a tough roll, downhill, with a foot and a half of break. Beem, still oblivious to what was hanging in the balance, drilled it center cut.

"As soon as the ball left the putter he was running over to Jordan," says Salerno. "When he came back over I told him about the course record. He couldn't believe it, but I'm pretty sure he was more excited about meeting Jordan." (Because it did not come during tournament competition, Beem's round is not officially recognized by Butler National as the course record—that distinction goes to Bob Gilder, with a 63 at the 1982 Western Open. However, Beem's scorecard is on file in the pro shop. "Put it this way, it may not be the course record, but it is the lowest round ever shot here," says a Butler National spokesman, in eloquent doublespeak.) Following his quasi-historic round Beem and his father caught a Cubs matinee, with tickets, and a limo, courtesy of Salerno. As a way of saying thanks for all the hospitality, Beem later presented Salerno with the driver he used to shoot his 62, signed, with a nice inscription. It now hangs in the office of the senior managing director of Bear Stearns.

Beem had little to be thankful for after the first round at the Western, because he opened with a 75. "The day before at Butler National actually hurt him," says Duplantis. "He couldn't hit any shots that measured up to expectations. Frustration was a problem." It was Beem's first truly bad round since Friday in New Orleans, a span of nearly two months. He was philosophical about it. "I didn't like the course," he says of Cog Hill No. 2. "It was set up for the long hitters, where you have to hit power fades off a lot of tees. That's not my game."

The next day Beem shot a 72 to miss the cut. He had followed his game plan at Cog Hill to no avail. "I played defensively," he says. "After Kemper maybe I should have said, 'Fuck it, I got my card, so now let's let it rip.' But you don't get instant respect with just one win, and I wanted to put together a good second half, make cuts, contend a couple of times more. I didn't want to play with reckless abandon."

The poor showing was not a big deal for one simple reason. "Our bodies were in Chicago," says Duplantis, "but our minds were on Scotland."

CARNOUSTIE GOLF CLUB, in Angus, Scotland, has long been known as Carnasty. There are many people in golf who think Carnoustie is the toughest course in the world; everybody else is certain of it. Carnoustie is as much fun as eighteen punches in the nose. It is a relentless, artless, joyless track, made memorable only by the toughest three finishing holes in golf, a brutish par-3 and a pair of unnavigable par-4s which are crisscrossed repeatedly by the Barry Burn. Lacking the history of St. Andrews, the beauty of Royal Troon, or the towering dunesland of Royal Birkdale, Carnoustie has never been fully embraced as part of the Open Championship rota, as prior to 1999 it had hosted only five Open Championships. But what a five they were, the victors' pedigrees confirming that only the very best players can survive a tussle with Carnasty: Tommy Armour in 1931, Henry Cotton in '37, Ben Hogan in '53, Gary Player in '68, and Tom Watson in '75.

Though Carnoustie sits on the edge of the Firth of Tay, the water is never in play, and after the second hole it is all but invisible. Carnoustie is a bleak, flat landscape and the place has always emanated a foreboding atmosphere, owing in large part to the austerity of the clubhouse, a square concrete eyesore that looked to be a Soviet-era bomb shelter that had somehow been belched to the surface. For the 1999 Open Championship a new clubhouse debuted, but Carnoustie was more fearsome than ever, thanks to the work of a renegade head greenskeeper, John Philp, who seemed determined to single-handedly humiliate the world's best golfers. Acting without the blessing of the R & A, Philp had moved back a series of tees, lengthening an already long course, and then reduced the widths of several fairways to an anorexic twelve yards. Framing the ridiculously narrow landing areas was knee-high heather. For his efforts Philp would eventually be dubbed "the Mad Scientist of Carnoustie" by *Golf Week*.

This was the course awaiting Beem.

He had insisted that Larry come along for the adventure, kicking down over $8,000 for two business-class tickets. After six days at home following the Western Open, the Beems boarded a redeye to Glasgow, where they rendezvoused with Duplantis on Saturday morning, five days before the start of the tournament. Duplantis had convinced Beem to follow a favorite itinerary of Furyk's: make the short drive from the airport to the town of Ayr, to recover from jetlag at the luxurious, full-service Turnberry Hotel, and get acclimated to linksland golf on its renowned Ailsa course, which has hosted three Open Championships, including the 1977 shootout between Jack Nicklaus and Tom Watson, the greatest *mano à mano* in the sport's history. Beem was all for it.

Just as with other weeks, caddies must pay their own way to the British Open, but recognizing the extra cost, it is common for a player to pick up some of his man's other expenses. Beem had offered to pay for the expensive rental van and all of the pricey gas as long as Duplantis did the driving. Beem was petrified at the thought of having to drive on the wrong side of the road. Duplantis, with three previous Open Championships under his belt, enthusiastically agreed to the deal.

After checking in at the hotel Rich, Larry, and Steve teed it up at the Ailsa, which is known as "the Pebble Beach of Scotland," because like Pebble, the first ten holes hug the coast, making for spectacular shotmaking and sweeping vistas. This was only Larry's second sojourn to the ancestral home of golf, and for both father and son it was a moving experience to stroll the linksland together. "It was neat I was able to make that happen," says Rich. "I think *pride* is probably a good word to describe it."

That night Rich and Steve decided to head to a pub in town and tip a pint or two. Or three or four. "We only had a few," Beem insists, "but over there a few go a lot farther." By the time they stumbled out into the night both were blotto. "I was really intoxicated, Rich was only regularly intoxicated," says Duplantis, "so he said he would drive."

"I took one for the team," says Beem.

Beem and Duplantis sat in their rental van for nearly an hour in an attempt to sober up. By now it was past 2:00 A.M., and time to go home. Beem pulled out of the pub's parking lot and the second he hit the surface street, "there were blue lights everywhere," says Duplantis.

A couple of Ayr's finest had seen them leave the pub and had been lying in wait the whole time. "They said they knew we were drunk by our erratic walking pattern," says Duplantis, with a smirk. Beem was taken to the police station and charged with driving under the influence of alcohol. Duplantis went along, but because of his condition they wouldn't release Beem in his custody. Beem wouldn't even consider waking his father, so after two hours they were finally able to talk an employee of the Turnberry Hotel into picking them up.

Beem made it clear that under no circumstances was Larry to be told.

The next day, Sunday, Duplantis did all the driving on the four-hour journey to Carnoustie. That afternoon Beem played his first practice round on the fearsome links. He toured it again on Monday, but then his preparation was rudely interrupted. Beem had to return to Ayr on Tuesday for a court hearing. He talked an Odyssey rep into serving as his chauffeur and Duplantis into being his baby-sitter. Larry was still oblivious to what had happened, so Rich cooked up a story about having to play in a corporate outing, and Steve, ever the obedient caddie, drove Larry down to the Kingdom of Fife, on the north side of the Firth of Forth, to take him around Crail's Balcomie Links, the seventh-oldest course in the world.

Beem spent eight hours in the car to go through a three-minute hearing. He was fined £450 and ordered not to drive in Scotland for eighteen months. ("A blessing," he says of the latter.) As he was leaving the courthouse a Scottish reporter approached him and asked, "Are you the Rich Beem who is playing in the Open Championship?" Beem blew by him without saying a word, but the next morning *The Scotsman* newspaper reported Beem's transgression for all the world to see. Except Larry, that is. He still hadn't gotten a whiff of the story as he arrived at Carnoustie with Rich and Steve for a Wednesday practice round.

They were at the practice range when the cat nearly got out of the bag. Rich had stepped away from his hitting station for a moment when Nick Price walked by, where Duplantis and Larry where loitering.

"How much did you boys drink, anyway?" Price asked.

"I shit a brick," says Duplantis. "I walked right over to Nicky and said, 'Dude, you gotta keep it down—his dad doesn't know a thing.' " When Rich returned Duplantis told him, sotto voce, what had happened. Beem was already spooked because he thought he had noticed a couple of reporters circling. Still, he didn't breathe a word of what had happened to Larry. It was not until Thursday, five days after the incident, that Rich came clean.

"He was embarrassed, I guess," says Larry. "Of course, I'm left to guess about a lot of things.

"He's not an alcoholic, but he's definitely got a drinking problem," Larry adds. "It's a habit he can't break. At one time he needed it to escape. I don't think it's as important now, but it still interferes, obviously."

After facing Larry, Rich spoke to a small group of American reporters. With a little time to reflect, he says, "I'll say this—it was unfortunate. I'm very sorry about it, very embarrassed. Some things happened that were out of my control. It won't deter me from going back. In fact, it makes me more determined to go over there and do well in the future."

Amazingly, the DUI wasn't the only crisis of the week. Duplantis spent most of the Open Championship trying to put out a fire back in Tampa, where Vicki was staying with Sierra at the family home. Duplantis had left his wife a large amount of cash to cover a week and a half's worth of expenses, but Vicki had gone through the money well before the tournament even started. Her behavior, according to Duplantis, was alarmingly erratic and they had a series of trans-Atlantic rows. "Duplantis is more hosed-up than anybody I've ever met at that age," says Larry. "His profession is about order and his life is so disorderly. All he was doing was adding turbulence. At Carnoustie he spent the entire time screaming into the phone. I had to get out of bed and tell him to shut the fuck up a couple of times." Duplantis and the Beems were all sharing a smallish house, and so Rich couldn't avoid overhearing his caddie's rantings. "I was shocked at what I was listening to," he says. "Every other word was, 'You stupid bitch.' I honestly could not believe my ears."

Needless to say, none of this was ideal preparation for one's first major championship. On Thursday, paired with 1969 champion Tony Jacklin, Beem went out in high winds and shot an 80, which sounds abysmal until you find out the average score that day was 78.31. Sergio Garcia, playing in his first major as a professional, shot 89 and afterward was reduced to weeping in his mother's arms.

"The whole setup over there was one big jerkoff," says Larry, with typical pitch. "Any tradition that tournament has was buried under two feet of overfertilized grass." Nevertheless, "I thought Rich was a little bit intimidated by the whole thing," Larry continues. "He backed off when he should have attacked, which was the only way to handle a course like that."

On Friday, "I fought like hell," says Beem. "I didn't care about making the cut. All I wanted was to break eighty." Though the breeze had slackened, Beem wound up shooting an 81, missing the cut by seven shots and becoming one of fifty-seven players who failed to break 80 over the first two rounds, including defending champion Mark O'Meara and five-time winner Tom Watson. "That course was set up for failure," Beem says. "It was totally defensive golf. Hit-and-hope golf." If that sounds like sour grapes, consider that Gary Player called Carnoustie's setup "the toughest course I have seen in forty-five years of championship golf," adding that, "they went over the brink of reason." It turned out that a 6 over par 290 was what it took to reach a three-way playoff, the highest winning score in a British Open since 1947.

With so much carnage Beem had little trouble shrugging off his score, and even with his disasters on and off the course he tried to focus instead on some of the high points of his first major. "Despite everything, it was an amazing experience," he says. "Every kid should get to play in the British Open once, with his dad at their side." Larry had walked inside the ropes with Rich during the practice rounds and shadowed him on the range. At one point during the week Rich was hitting balls in the middle of a group of five players, sandwiched by two generations of legends. Down the line it went Faldo, Woods, Beem, O'Meara, Jose

Maria Olazabal. "My dad was just back there shaking his head and laughing," he says. "It was such an incredible sight." One of Beem's practice rounds had been with Vijay Singh, at the time the reigning PGA Championship title holder. Singh may be the purest ballstriker in golf, and yet after the round, at the range, he asked Larry to check out a couple things in his swing.

"Vijay was telling me that when he wants to hit the ball hard he can get a little too quick," says Larry. "He asked me, 'Did you see that out there at all today?' I told him about a couple of times when it might have happened. He says, 'Come over here and watch this swing.' So he hits a homerun, just knocks the crap out of a driver. 'That was not quick,' I say. 'That was hard.' "

Says Rich, "That was awesome for my dad."

Of course, all these good feelings went up in smoke upon Beem's return to El Paso. Though none of the local papers had the temerity to run items about Beem's scrape with the law, it's impossible to keep a secret in El Paso's tight-knit golf community. Further, a couple of days after Beem returned home *GolfWeek* hit the newsstands with an account of his escapade. If Beem's drinking had in the past always been shrugged off just as good clean fun or boys being boys, this time around public opinion was far more sour. "I thought Rich really tarnished everything that he had accomplished," says John Butterworth, Beem's friend, accountant, and one of his sponsors. "After the incident was made public I had people call me from all over the country. Their reaction was the same that I had, the same that all of us back at the club had: What a waste. What the hell was he thinking?"

Says Beem, "The whole incident was a quick, painful education about life in the public eye. I'm not just some guy from El Paso anymore. I'm Rich Beem of the PGA Tour, winner of the Kemper Open, and that changes things a little bit."

THOUGH DUPLANTIS largely escaped censure for his part in the drunk driving misadventure he, too, received a chilly reception upon returning home. Vicki was waiting for him as he stepped off his plane at the Tampa airport. She handed him Sierra and the keys to his Wagoneer and then bolted. "She said maybe two words to me and then took off," Duplantis says. He chased her through the airport, trying to figure out what the heck was going on. It turned out Vicki had already checked her bags onto a flight heading for the Dallas-Fort Worth airport. She disappeared onto the plane. After collecting his own baggage Duplantis tried to buy a ticket for himself and Sierra on the same flight. They couldn't squeeze aboard, but Duplantis decided to wait around the airport for the next flight out.

"I needed to find out what was happening," he says. "I thought we were back together and then this happens."

By the time Duplantis made it to Fort Worth, and to Vicki's parents' house, she was nowhere to be found. He spent the next five days in Fort Worth, trying to locate her, to no avail. "She just vanished," Duplantis says. "She never once came home."

Finally, Duplantis returned to Tampa, along with Sierra. "That was the last time," he says. "After that, I was done trying."

TWO WEEKS AFTER the British Open Beem found out that Kemper Insurance was revoking its endorsement offer because of his episode at the British Open. Beem was upset with himself, of course, but he had plenty of anger left over for his agents. In the six weeks between his victory and the British the sharpies at Intrepid had somehow failed to close the deal with Kemper Insurance. To be sure, his conduct was inexcusable, but Beem felt that if his agents had done their job he should have cashed the endorsement check long before he ever got into trouble.

"The story we were told," says David Wyatt, "was that every time they tried to contact the people at Kemper they couldn't get through. Either the lines were busy, or they got voice mail, or whatever. How fuckin' stupid is that?"

Greg Romine, the president of Intrepid Sports, vigorously disputes the assertion. "Why wouldn't we pursue it?" says Romine. "That's how we make our money, too. We were extremely interested in the deal and we pursued it actively. We had numerous conversations with Kemper Insurance, and this included a series of offers and counteroffers." Rifling through his files on the deal, Romine says, "We sent them our final proposal on—let's see here—July seventh." That was two days before Beem left for Scotland.

According to Romine, the mulityear deal was all but done, with only the logo placement left to be determined, and a little legal jargon to be ironed out. There were two options regarding the logo. The first was on the left crest of his shirt. A secondary placement comprised the left side of Beem's hat and both sleeves. (Much like slaughtered cows, a Tour player's person is carved up and sold at different prices, depending how choice the cut is. Visibility is the key, and shirt collars, hat brims, and the left breast are considered the prime real estate, because these areas can be seen in even the most tightly framed TV shots and newspaper and magazine photos.) In addition to having Beem wear its logo, Kemper was also going to pay to use his name and likeness for advertising purposes, and for a handful of personal appearances each year. It was a hefty commitment. Romine characterizes the deal as "very, very lucrative."

The day after the British Open ended Romine phoned his contact at Kemper Insurance. "He told me that the terms of the deal had gone to the executive committee, and the paperwork would be done imminently," says Romine. "At that point I said, 'Joe, I gotta be upfront with you, there was an incident at the British Open.' I told him what had happened. He said, 'That's interesting, because one of our board members had heard a rumor about that.' He said that he would have to get back to me the next day."

Which he did.

"It was absolutely a no-go," says Romine. "There was the sense that it would be irresponsible for an insurance company, which does significant business in the automotive sector, to be promoting through a person who had so publicly broken one of the cardinal rules of the road, which is you don't drink and drive.

"It was just a gross misstep by Rich. Just incredibly unfortunate timing, and incredibly costly, for us as well as him."

AFTER ALL OF THIS hullabaloo Beem was relieved to get back to work at the Buick Open in Flint, Michigan. He played well in his first practice round at Warwick Hills Country Club and was determined to post a good finish after two straight missed cuts. That Tuesday night Onick arrived from El Paso. The summer was running out and this would be one of her final opportunities to travel with Beem.

Since the Kemper, things had not been going well between them. "Rich would bring it up every once in a while," says Duplantis. "I think he was realizing Amy was not the woman he wanted to marry and if that was the case, why bother, you know? She didn't seem cut out for the lifestyle or like she really enjoyed it." That night Beem and Onick went out to dinner and had one of those conversations that seem to generate their own momentum.

"Amy basically asked Rich a lot of questions and he was honest about his feelings," says Wyatt. "As the evening went on it became obvious to both of them that they were going in different directions."

"Amy didn't understand Rich's world of social turmoil, she didn't understand the plastic world of golf," says Larry Beem. "She couldn't understand how he could make more money wearing a certain hat than she made busting her ass all year teaching school. It's not a surprise things didn't last between them; it's a surprise things lasted as long as they did."

Wednesday morning, frozen out by the pro-ams at Warwick Hills, Beem and Duplantis were supposed to play the excellent Tournament Players Club of Michigan, in nearby Dearborn. Duplantis got a call from Beem that morning, canceling the round. "He was putting Amy on a plane back to El Paso," says Duplantis. "They had had the big breakup. Rich was a little shocked by what happened. It wasn't like he had planned it. He wasn't counting down the days till freedom or anything like that. It just sorta happened."

Beem and Duplantis met that afternoon at the Warwick Hills range. "He was working the phones pretty hard," says Duplantis. "I mean here he is, Rich Beem, the most famous man in El Paso, and Amy's on her way home to drag his name through the mud. Rich was trying to spread his side of the story, do some damage control."

After hitting balls for twenty minutes, Beem shook his head and said, "I can't do this right now." He returned to his hotel room and the phone.

The next day brought the opening round and Beem actually ground out a decent score, a 70. On Friday, however, he sleepwalked through a 79, including an ignominious triple bogey on the 15th hole. Beem had been paired with J. L. Lewis, and on 15, a straightforward par-4, both found the fairway. Lewis was away and played his approach to the green. Beem knocked his shot on the putting surface, as well. When it came time to putt both players realized they had each played the other's ball. They had to march back to the fairway, holding up the play behind them, take a drop, eat the penalty stoke, and replay their approaches from their previous spots.

"Walking back to the fairway, J.L. kept saying, 'Guys, I'm so sorry,' " says Duplantis. "I was like, 'Dude, all four of us fucked up—you, your caddie, Rich, and me. We were all equally responsible.' " Even without the triple, Beem still would have missed his third straight cut, but it was an embarrassing way to end a lost week.

"I didn't have my head in the ball game," says Beem. "I was trying to figure out where I was going. Amy was a huge part of my life for eighteen months and it was tough. I wasn't thinking about golf that week, I was just trying to figure things out emotionally."

The embarrassment of the British, the disappointment involving Kemper Insurance, and now the breakup. "It was a pretty shitty time," says Beem.

CHAPTER

• 13 •

PER THE TERMS OF THE SPLIT, Beem was compelled to spend four straight weeks on the road, beginning with the Buick Open, to give Onick a chance to move out of their apartment back in El Paso. So from Flint he traveled straight to Medinah Country Club, outside Chicago, for the eighty-first PGA Championship. It was to be his first major on American soil and the beginning of the end of his professional relationship with Duplantis.

Well before the Kemper, Beem had committed to play in a Monday pro-am, an outing that was so meaningless he can't even recall the name of the company that sponsored it. With Monday taken up Beem decided he wanted to sneak in a practice round at Medinah on Sunday. After missing the cut in Flint, Duplantis was looking forward to a weekend in New York visiting his daughter and Sollange Lewis, but to accommodate Beem's Sunday practice round, he cancelled the trip and flew straight to Chicago.

"I was pissed off, because I had to get there early just so Rich could play in that stupid fucking pro-am," says Duplantis. "First of all, no serious player would ever play in a corporate pro-am the week of a major. That's just ridiculous. You get beat up at majors and you need to save your energy and maximize your preparation time. And then to do it for one thousand five hundred dollars . . . I mean, I can't even comprehend what he was thinking."

Duplantis didn't hide his disdain. On Sunday Beem teed it up with his old mentor J. P. Hayes. Walking alongside them was Bill Eschenbrenner, the old-school El Paso Country Club pro who had flown in to try to help Beem stop his game's downward spiral. "On the third tee box Steve gets a phone call on his cell," says Beem, "and he didn't get off the phone until after we had hit our second shots from the middle of the fourth fairway. I mean, J.P. and Esch are two guys I look up to, and I was personally embarrassed. I just said to Steve, 'Any chance we can turn that thing off?' "

On Monday, while Beem was at his pro-am, Duplantis, having gotten over himself, decided to walk Medinah and do some additional scouting. When he arrived at the first tee Jim Furyk was getting ready to head out. "Jim's a smart guy," says Duplantis. "If anybody is gonna figure out how to play a course, it's him, so I decided to tag along." They had already broken the ice with some small talk at Westchester, so the vibe was relatively mellow. At one point Fluff had to steal away to a Porta Potti, so he handed Duplantis the bag. "I strolled up to Jim, real casual, and handed him his club, and he looked at me like, what the hell do you think you're doing?" Duplantis says with a laugh.

On Tuesday Beem and Duplantis encountered Furyk again. They were on the first tee, about to play a round with Nick Price and Olin Browne, when Furyk asked if he could join. "I could tell it was kind of a big deal to Rich," says Duplantis. During their chat at Westchester, Furyk had never once congratulated Duplantis on winning the Kemper. Afterward, Duplantis mentioned this odd fact to Beem, who said that he, too, had bumped into Furyk, in the locker room, and again Furyk had failed to offer even a perfunctory congrats. Three weeks later, at the British Open, Duplantis asked Furyk on several occasions to play a practice round with Beem, so the rookie could observe, and hopefully learn from his methodical preparations. It never happened. So, back at the PGA, Beem attacked Medinah as if he was defending the honor of his caddie. "Rich wanted to prove something that day," says Duplantis. "You know how he is, always wanting to do something nice for everybody. I know he wanted to play better than Jim, more for me than himself." Prior to the round Eschenbrenner had given Beem a little tune-up and something clicked on the golf course, because Beem began crushing the ball. "He was shitting all over those guys," says Duplantis, "even Nick Price, who is one of the greatest drivers of the ball in golf history. There were a couple of times when Rich outdrove Furyk by fifty yards. It was incredible." Duplantis began to get excited about their prospects in the tournament.

On Wednesday, however, Beem played only seven holes before lighting out for a Cubs game, making the road trip along with David Wyatt, who had come in for the week. (Just as Beem's victory dramatically changed the course of his future, Wyatt had secured a contract a month before the Kemper that provided him with the freedom to travel and attend to Beem's affairs. Wyatt, as it happens, quit Magnolia Hi-Fi back in 1996 only a couple of weeks after Beem had, and with the same analytical skills he once used to pick burglar alarms he was now working for Microsoft, debugging its Internet Explorer.) Only seven holes of practice, the day before a major? "I was gonna play nine holes, but it was kinda slow out there," says Beem.

"At that point I was a little frustrated, because I didn't think Rich was as prepared as he could have been," says Duplantis. "I mean, this was a major. It was supposed to be a big deal." Duplantis wasn't the only one scratching his head.

"Here we are at the PGA Championship, supposedly grinding it out, and Rich was sneaking off to go see the Cubs play," says Eschenbrenner. "It drove me nuts."

On Thursday Beem fought hard for a 72. Medinah, after a series of alterations to the august layout, had been stretched to 7,401 yards, making it the longest course in major championship history. Heavy rains Wednesday night and Thursday morning made it play even longer, and the rough, already long and gnarly, was a wrist-breaking snarl now that it was wet. Though this was Medinah's first PGA Championship, it has hosted three previous U.S. Opens and is typical of a national championship course—oppressive, where every shot is fraught with problems large and small. Little wonder that Beem felt encouraged by his 72. "If even par isn't good enough around here, I'm in the wrong business," he said following his round, while hitting balls at the range. Throughout his second round, however, Beem struggled to control his swing and was forced to repeatedly play out of trouble. The rains reappeared, with a vengeance, and most of Beem's back nine was playing in a driving shower that he calls "the worst conditions I have ever seen." Coming down the stretch he knew he was on the bubble to make the cut, especially after blowing a layup tee shot on 15 into the rough and making bogey. At the 16th hole he pushed another drive into the trees and was forced to pitch out well short of the green, into a deep swale.

"If you're good enough to win the Kemper, you're good enough to get this up-and-down," Duplantis said, with an edge.

Beem played a credible wedge shot, but on the devilishly sloped green his ball skittered fifteen feet past the hole. He drilled the par putt and then executed two textbook pars on 17 and 18 to close out a 73, earning his playing privileges on the weekend by a lone stroke. "Making the cut was huge," he said afterward. "That was the goal. I feel like right now the majors are for the major players—Tiger, Duval, Els, Leonard, Mickelson, guys like that. They're so much more settled than I am, so they can concentrate on them. They can set their schedules around them, set their whole year around them. I hope to be there some day, but right now I'm not."

Beem went backward on the weekend, struggling to rounds of 78-76, to finish tied for seventieth and take home $6,550. Only one player in the field—Fred Funk—took more strokes than Beem's 299. Duplantis saw no great moral victory in making the cut. "It was a disappointing week," he says. "Rich fucked around too much. In those conditions you have to know exactly what you are doing on every shot, and you have to hit it solid every time or you're going to get your ass kicked. That's what happened."

FROM CHICAGO BEEM traveled to Castle Rock, Colorado, outside of Denver, for The International. He was feeling lousy, and not just because of his weekend struggles at the PGA. Beem was fighting bronchitis and strep throat and had called his doctor back in El Paso to have some antibiotics prescribed. He didn't feel up to a practice round on Monday, and eighteen holes on Tuesday all but wiped him out, as did a stressful situation with a caddie known far and wide as Reefer. Beem had bumped into Reef in April at the Houston Open, when he was still without a regular caddie. They agreed to work together at The International, an arrangement Beem had long since forgotten about. Duplantis had no idea of what was brewing until he arrived in Castle Rock and went to pick up his parking pass and was told, sorry, another caddie had already registered for Beem's bag. "Just one more example of one caddie trying to fuck over another," Duplantis says. When he placed a hasty phone call to Beem, the reaction was typical. What should I do, Beem wondered plaintively. Under Duplantis's counsel, Beem explained to Reefer that things had changed dramatically since they spoke three months earlier, and that he was committed to Duplantis. To smooth over any hard feelings, Beem cut Reefer a check for a week's stipend, $600. That little controversy scuttled, Beem spent the whole of Wednesday in bed. However, there would be no more rest for the weary.

Beem's mother, stepfather, aunt, and uncle all came in for the tournament on Thursday, as had long-since been planned. Just as at the Buick Open two weeks earlier—when he stayed in Detroit with friends, rather than in a more conveniently located hotel in the burbs—Beem had an additional entourage at The International. A half dozen of his college buddies had wound up living in the Denver area and they, too, turned out for the tournament.

"My memory of that week is that wherever Rich was there were always so many people around him," says Diana Pompeo, Beem's mother. "At one point I finally said, Rich, who *are* all these people?"

"The fucking guy's got friends in every fucking town," says Duplantis. "It's unbelievable. I've never heard of anybody with so many friends. It sets up this conflict; it's like the old Rich versus the new Rich. Does he want to be responsible and treat this like a job or does he want to get shitfaced and stay out all night?"

Beem's health improved considerably by Thursday, but his dedication to practicing remained sickly. "It was the same thing as the week before," says Duplantis. "Instead of hitting balls or working on his putting, it was, 'I gotta get outta here, go do this, that, or the other thing.' I would try to say something to him, but he would get defensive and wouldn't listen. It was at The International when I decided, hey, if he didn't want to hear what I had to say, then I was just gonna carry the bag and keep my mouth shut."

Beem noticed the change in his bagman. "He wasn't the same caddie I had at the Kemper Open," he says. "He didn't have any enthusiasm, any fire. He didn't seem like he was having any fun or like he even wanted to be out there anymore. His idea of a pep talk had become, 'Let's quit screwing around and make a decent check this week.' It had almost gotten awkward to be around each other."

The International is the only tournament on tour that uses the Modified Stableford System for scoring. Instead of recording strokes, a player earns points, 8 for a double eagle, 5 for an eagle, 2 for a birdie, 0 for a par, -1 for a bogey, and -3 for a double bogey or worse. The scoring system is obviously weighted to encourage aggressive play, and The International is a tournament where the birdies come fast and furious. Beem wasn't up to the challenge.

"I hit the ball great on Thursday, I just didn't make any putts," Beem says. "Not one." His score for the day was a homely -3. (Somehow a 75 would've sounded better). On Friday Beem played a bit better, but he was undone by an X on number 9. (Once a player is assured of making double bogey, he has the option of picking up.) He finished with six points on the day, and at +3 overall he missed the cut by six points. Looking back, he says, "I forgot to play golf that week."

With so many friends and family members to entertain, Beem was not in a hurry to leave town. On Saturday he set up shop at a local bar with his crew. Duplantis showed up there, too. At some point during the day Duplantis rang an old friend, Chris Hanrattie, who he had known since the days when he was living with Vicki's parents in Fort Worth. Hanrattie was burned out on being an assistant pro—at a club outside Dallas—and looking to become a Tour caddie. Duplantis was eager to help his buddy get some experience, and in addition to trying to scrounge a loop for Hanrattie, he had actually offered to give up his own bag for a week, a plan that was okay by Beem, who had talked to Hanrattie on the phone a few times. Beem liked him okay, but more importantly, it was a chance to give something back. Beem, too, had once been a lowly assistant pro looking for a fresh start. When Hanrattie was actually going to caddie for Beem had been left unresolved, however.

That Saturday afternoon in Castle Rock, Beem was, says Duplantis, "pounding down drinks at this bar. He made some crack about Furyk and I kinda snapped. I said, 'You know what, if Jim Furyk had putted like shit and missed the cut, I can guarantee you right now he'd be out working on his putting, not drinking triple Jack and Cokes.' That pissed Rich off big time, and I'm glad it did, because if it hadn't that would have meant he didn't have any pride."

Shortly after his little blowup Duplantis went to hit the head, and upon returning to his barstool Beem had some news. He had just gotten off the phone with Hanrattie, who was going to caddie for him at the Texas Open in four weeks.

IF BEEM NEEDED some extra motivation to pull himself out of his summer slide, plenty was available the week following The International, when he traveled to the Reno-Tahoe Open, a tournament being inaugurated in 1999. The RTO was a consolation prize for all the rank-and-file who were not eligible for the glitzy new World Golf Championships-NEC Invitational, which was being played simultaneously at Firestone Country Club in Akron, Ohio. The Invitational was restricted to members of the previous Ryder Cup and Presidents Cup teams, and forty-one of golf's glamour boys were competing for $5 million, with last place being guaranteed $27,000, as there was no cut (in Reno 156 guys were duking it out for $2.75 million, and there was most assuredly a cut). "Sure, all of us in Reno wanted to be where those guys were," says Beem. "That was motivation for all of us."

Beem's motivation in Reno was sabotaged by the calendar—his twenty-ninth birthday fell on that Tuesday, two days before the tournament was to begin. A birthday is a sacred event to Beem, and if it happens to be his own, all the better. "I have always loved celebrating birthdays," he says. "To me it's the best day of the year. I was determined to have a good time." Beem's desire to whoop it up was fueled in part by the memory of birthdays past that had been spent on the road. In both 1994 and '95, when he was haunting the Dakotas Tour, Beem had had the misfortune of spending his b-day all by his lonesome in the dead-end town of Minot, North Dakota. These were some of the lowest moments in his altogether miserable minitour days. One of those years, knowing how down he was, Beem's mom overnighted a care package stuffed with cards from friends and family, a remote control car, a few gag gifts, and some money. "That meant more to me than I could ever tell you," says Beem.

This time around, in Reno, Beem had a homecourt advantage. One of his best friends from college, R. C. Ordish, lived in nearby Carson City, Nevada, and Ordish's pad became ground zero for the festivities. Beem didn't want to miss any of the action by staying in a hotel, even though the fledgling tournament, hoping to build loyalty, supplied a deluxe room gratis. Instead, he crashed at Ordish's. The house was so overflowing with humanity Beem was consigned to the couch. "That was fine by me," says Beem. "I'd done that plenty of times before in my life."

On Tuesday, the day of his birthday, Beem squeezed in a practice round at the Montreaux Golf and Country Club, site of the RTO, and then he journeyed to Royal Oaks Country Club, where Ordish was an assistant pro. Beem gave a two-hour clinic for the club's juniors, which was followed by a surprise birthday bash at the club, attended by some fifty people. The real celebration came later that night. Beem had hired a limo to take him and his buddies into Tahoe and for seven hours, "We were gambling, drinking, and carrying on," Beem says. "It was a great night."

Duplantis had tagged along for the evening and he was dismayed to see how impaired Beem's faculties were. "I couldn't stand it," says Duplantis. "I'm watching Rich's friend, this guy who probably makes fifteen grand a year, play five-hundred-dollar hands of blackjack with Rich's money. He blew through like six thousand dollars in a matter of minutes and Beemer didn't say a word."

("I don't know what Steve is talking about," says Beem, though he admits to losing "a couple grand" playing blackjack.)

On Wednesday Beem hit a few practice balls at the Silver Oaks driving range, but didn't feel up to a practice round. During the next day's first round Beem proved once again that drinking and driving don't mix. He hit the ball miserably throughout the round, and after a spectacularly poor tee ball at the 15th he proceeded to put his foot in the middle of the shaft of his driver, snapping it in two. "It felt good," he says. "It released some of the tension."

"We were playing with a couple of veterans—Willie Wood and Paul Goydos—and it was embarrassing," says Duplantis. "It made Rich look bad."

Three over par as he reached number 18, Beem was forced to hit a 3-wood off the tee of a 616-yard par-5. He followed with his best swing of the day, another 3-wood to fifteen feet for eagle (the ball travels farther in the thin air of Reno). With one putt Beem had the chance to salvage a decent round, but he "three-willied it," as he says, Tour-ese for three-putting. Beem tapped in for a 75, and then, for good measure, broke his putter over his knee.

The next day he was forced to play with a backup putter and driver. "It felt like crap," Beem says of the latter, and in fact he gave it to Ordish following the round. He carded another 75 and was again down the road, his fifth missed cut in six tournaments.

Reno was the breaking point in Beem's relationship with Duplantis. "I'd had enough," says Duplantis. "If he wasn't going to try, why should I? I mean, I'm kicking down five, six hundred dollars of my own money for a plane ticket, I got meals, a hotel, an expensive rental car, plenty of other expenses. He was literally costing me money.

"Rich stopped playing practice rounds, he stopped working at his game, he stopped acting like a professional. In Reno he was sleeping on a couch in a house full of clowns, just miles and miles from the course. He was like, 'Dude it's cool, it's like a frat house here.' Gimme a fuckin' break. How is that gonna prepare you for a golf tournament? I remember one time that week when he was talking to one of his many friends, and he was like, 'Hey, I need to go hit some balls.' His buddy's like, 'Fuck that, let's go drink some beer.' Rich is like, 'Uh, okay.' Before the tournament had even started I knew he was gonna shoot like seventy-six-seventy-six and miss the cut by a mile.

"The Kemper was the best week we ever had, and I'm not even talking about his scores. Rich was grinding during the practice rounds and once the tournament started he'd get to the course early to practice his putting and then he'd hit balls after every round. He was really putting in some good hours. That just stopped completely and it was disappointing." This is not an entirely unfamiliar story. The PGA Tour has seen many young players corrupted by success, the most glaring recent example being Robert Gamez, who won his first official start on tour in 1990, and then two months later electrified the golf world by holing out a 7-iron on the 72nd hole of the Bay Hill Invitational to beat Greg Norman by a stroke. A unanimous Rookie of the Year selection, Gamez proceeded to party his way into oblivion. Winless since '90, he still hangs around the fringe of the Tour (in 1999 he would finish 208th on the money list).

Having seen a number of promising players come and go through the years, Duplantis—a thwarted junior college golfer himself—adds, "When you have talent like that you've got a responsibility. Jim Furyk recognizes that and Rich Beem doesn't." And to whom does Beem have a responsibility? "To himself, and to golf," says Duplantis. "The price of greatness is responsibility."

FOLLOWING THE SECOND ROUND in Reno, Beem informed Duplantis that he had decided to withdraw from the Canadian Open, which was to be played in two weeks. That stung. The Canadian Open is the tournament where Duplantis had fallen in love with golf, and Clarence Rose, as a starry-eyed twelve-year old. It was to be a triumphant homecoming, his first chance to celebrate the success of Kemper with his family. Duplantis was upset at the news and he and Beem left Reno on bad terms. Beem now had three weeks off until his next tournament, the Texas Open. This was to be his trial run with Chris Hanrattie, Duplantis's friend, and now his stand-in.

CHAPTER

• 14 •

THE LAST TIME Rich Beem had a significant break from tournament golf was leading up to the Kemper Open, and he had used those two weeks to get his game and his body in shape. This time around he needed the time to tidy up his life away from golf. When Beem arrived home from Reno his apartment in El Paso was strangely lacking. The furniture was still in place, but all the life had been boxed up and carted away. Amy Onick was gone, as was any evidence that she had ever lived there—her clothes were out of the closets, and all her knickknacks were off the walls. She even took the pots and pans. As soon as Beem set foot in his old apartment he knew he was ready for a change of scenery.

"I had been thinking about moving for a while, but after the breakup with Amy it all fell into place," he says. "It wasn't anything premeditated. It wasn't, 'Okay, I'll dump Amy, move to Scottsdale, and start a new life.' It just sorta happened that way."

After only a couple of days in El Paso Beem flew to the desert to look for a new place to live with a prospective roommate, John Buttemiller, an old college friend who was now in the real estate biz in Scottsdale. Beem had always been fond of the Scottsdale/Phoenix area, having lived there as a kid, and through the years he had returned frequently to visit his maternal grandparents. After five days of pounding the pavement Beem and Buttemiller settled on an expansive two-bedroom condo in the popular Grayhawk development, a quintessential desert community of indistinguishable stucco complexes clustered around a pair of target golf courses, none of it more than a few years old. Grayhawk had a couple of things going for it, besides its affiliation with Phil Mickelson, who is a paid spokesmodel. Beem's condo was just down the road from TPC of Scottsdale, site of the Phoenix Open. As a member of the Tour he could play and practice there anytime he so desired, at no cost. Beem was also close to the Phoenix airport, which offered more options and cheaper flights. But what Beem liked best about his new pad was that it wasn't in El Paso. One of Beem's golfing buddies describes the Sun City as "the littlest big city in the world," and, following the tumultuous events of the summer, Beem was tiring of life in the fishbowl. "One thing I really liked about Scottsdale was that I could be totally, one hundred percent anonymous out there," he says.

Not that Beem wanted to completely cut his ties with the El Paso community. After returning from Scottsdale he served as an honorary sponsor at the country club's member-guest tournament, and he even kicked down enough dough to earn the status as one of the tournament's sponsors. "It's the biggest event of the year and I used to work it from the pro shop," Beem says. "I had always promised myself that if I made the Tour I'd come back and be a sponsor, and it turned out to be a blast." Though Beem was around golf courses during his time off he rarely bothered to actually play much golf. He reckons that during the three weeks leading up to the Texas Open he played eighteen holes only four times. The rest of the time was spent packing and decompressing.

Steve Duplantis, on the other hand, played golf nearly every day during the first two weeks of his time off. After all these years he was still a junkie. He also enjoyed some quality time with his daughter, frolicking in the pool, visiting amusement parks, and screening an endless number of Disney movies. The week before the Texas Open, Duplantis traveled to upstate New York, to the B.C. Open, dropping Sierra off with Sollange Lewis along the way. At the B.C. Open, Duplantis spent much of the week pressing flesh, quietly trying to line up another caddying job (he declines to reveal which players he contacted). "It's a delicate situation," he says. "You don't want to bad-mouth your current player, or backstab another caddie, but at the same time this is a business, and if another, better job might be available you need to let it be known you're available." In the nearly three months since Westchester, Duplantis had earned a grand total of $327.50 above his weekly stipend. "In my situation I can't afford to take an entire summer off," Duplantis says. "I need the checks coming in, because there are bills to pay and mouths to feed. I can't afford to be with a player in a slump."

Duplantis had lined up two jobs at the B.C. Open—one for himself, and one for his buddy Chris Hanrattie, who he wanted to show the ropes before his big week on Beem's bag at the Texas Open. Hanrattie was packing for Guy Boros, the winner of the '96 Greater Vancouver Open and son of Hall of Famer Julius Boros. Guy had fallen into the abyss in the three years since his victory, but it was a great bag for Hanrattie to lose his cherry.

Duplantis was packing for a twenty-eight-year-old rookie named Brian Gay, who to that point in '99 had missed fifteen cuts in twenty-one tournaments, including six of seven leading up to the B.C. Open. What Gay lacked in talent he made up for with inexperience, but Duplantis had taken the job anyway, mostly to get Gay's wife, Kimberly, off his back. "She definitely wears the pants in that family," says Duplantis. Kimberly Gay is a fixture on the PGA Tour as a scout for Darrell Survey, a company that tracks what equipment the pros are using and then sells the info to manufacturers and advertising types. Kimberly's colleagues can be found standing on the first tee of virtually every tournament at every level of golf, feverishly scribbling down the clubs, balls, shoes, gloves, bags, sunglasses, and clothing the players are putting to use. It is one of the few ways a traveling wife can earn a living, short of caddying. Kimberly had fallen for Duplantis early in the year when she caught a broadcast of the GolfChannel's *Golf Talk Live,* on which he was a featured guest. "I liked his attitude and I liked his philosophies on caddying," says Kimberly. "I said to Brian, 'That is who you need on your bag.' "

Says Brian, "I just said, 'Uh, Kim, he's caddying for Jim Furyk, one of the Top Ten players in the world. I'm a rookie. End of discussion.' "

In the early part of the season Gay had used a Nike Tour refugee for a caddie, until one day the looper simply vanished. "I still don't know what happened to him," Gay says. After that, his caddie situation was pretty much week to week. When Kimberly heard about the split with Furyk, she urged her husband to get in contact with Duplantis, but he dragged his feet. "Brian's not a real aggressive person," says Kimberly. "That has never been a problem for me. I spent a couple of weeks trying to get ahold of Steve, without any luck. At that point I was getting pretty pregnant, so I just kind of gave up."

Brian Gay played in the Kemper Open and had an early tee time for the second round. Kimberly got him out the door of the hotel room and then sat down by herself for a belated breakfast. "I opened up the paper and there was this big story about how much Steve Duplantis was helping this unknown rookie," she says. "I just broke down in tears right there. Granted, I was pregnant, and the hormones were racing, but I said to myself, I knew it! I just knew it! I was almost hysterical. I couldn't help but think, Why couldn't that be us? Now it was too late, and I thought we'd never get Steve to work for us now." Sunday evening Brian and Kimberly were at the airport (he had finished fifty-second to earn $5,717) when they caught highlights of the final round. "There was Steve leading Rich around, keeping him composed, keeping him in the moment," says Kimberly. "I started crying again, right in front of Brian. From then on my credibility was pretty high whenever I talked about Steve Duplantis."

In Memphis, two weeks later, Kimberly introduced herself to Duplantis on the first tee, her Darrell Survey clipboard in hand. If anything ever changes, she told him, be sure to give us a call. So that was what Duplantis did in the days leading up to the B.C. Open.

"She gave me this whole speech about how Brian needed an experienced caddie to kick him in the butt, and that if he didn't have a couple of good finishes down the stretch he was gonna lose his card and they couldn't afford that because she had a baby on the way and on and on," says Duplantis. "Man, talk about pressure."

When Duplantis wasn't by Gay's side he spent the better part of the week squiring Hanrattie around, introducing him to all the right people and instructing him on some of the more subtle matters of the trade. For instance, if another player in your group hits out of a bunker, it is good etiquette to clean his ball, freeing that player's caddie to rake the trap without delay. Little things like that. By all accounts Hanrattie acquitted himself nicely at the B.C. Open, though the same can't be said for Boros or Gay—both missed the cut. "I felt a little pressure," says Gay. "I figured Steve was expecting me to play well. He'd caddied for two big-time players. He was used to seeing good golf."

Duplantis and Hanrattie took advantage of the free weekend and drove down to the city to spend Sunday with Sierra and Sollange Lewis. "Nice lady," says Hanrattie. "Tough part of town, though."

That night the vagabond caddie pair flew into Dallas, crashed at Hanrattie's place, and then the next morning drove to San Antonio for the Texas Open. Duplantis was again caddying for Gay. "I knew Brian didn't have Rich's kind of talent, but it was a job," says Duplantis. "I wanted to be out there for Chris in case he needed anything. I wasn't worried about how he would do with Rich, but I wanted to be able to keep an eye on things."

BEEM ARRIVED at the Texas Open Tuesday morning, in order to squeeze in some practice time that afternoon. Hanrattie was already in town, eagerly awaiting Beem's arrival. They had never met before, but the chemistry was good from the beginning. In the two days leading up to the tournament, Beem felt "energized" by Hanrattie. "It was a totally different experience," says Beem. "Chris was early for everything. He would be waiting for me at the range. He would do all the little things, things Steve had stopped doing, like standing on the putting green and kicking balls back to me, or cleaning the grass off my balls on the range. When I hit a good shot in a practice round he was always like, 'Good swing there, champ.' It was small stuff, but I definitely felt taken care of. It put me in a real good frame of mind."

La Cantera Golf Club sprawls across the hill country of San Antonio, and the constant, dizzying elevation changes are the defining feature of the golf course (the 11th tee at La Cantera is the highest point in all of San Antonio). When the wind blows, which is often, it can be a testy track. On a still day La Cantera is easier than a cheerleader on prom night.

Beem caught a mild day on Thursday and, paired with two-time U.S. Open champ Lee Janzen, he proceeded to roll in a fifteen-footer for birdie on the first hole. "It may sound crazy coming from a professional, but the first hole is huge for me," says Beem. "It can affect the entire round." Beem's ballstriking was erratic on the front nine but he scrambled adroitly, making the turn at -1. Then things got a little nutty. On the par-5 10th he blew his second shot, a 3-wood, way to the right, but it pegged a marshal in the leg, preventing the ball from bounding into what he was certain was going to be a horrible position. Beem made the most of the charity, getting up-and-down for a birdie. At 11 he hit it to a foot for another birdie, and then at the 12th, a long, twisty par-4 that is La Cantera's toughest hole, Beem followed with a textbook par. "At that point I started to feel nervous," he says. "I knew I was playing well and didn't want to blow it." At 13 Beem rolled in a fifteen-footer for birdie, pushing him to 4 under on his round. The 14th at La Cantera is a cupcake par-5 of 527 yards, but after a perfect drive Beem pushed his second shot twenty yards to the right of the green into some ankle-high weeds. He followed with a chip that Hanrattie calls "miraculous," then nailed a ten-footer for another birdie. He was now -5. Beem missed the green at 15, a brutal par-4, but he rolled in a devilishly fast eight-footer for par. "The best putt of my week," he says. At the short 16th he laid up smartly with an iron and then wedged to five feet. Another bird. At the par-3 17th, Beem hit it to eight feet and then banged that putt in, as well. He was now 6 under par on the back side, 7 under overall. "When I got to eighteen I was thinking twenty-nine," he says, which would be his score on the back nine if he could birdie the 18th hole. After a good drive Beem tried to kill a 7-iron to the elevated green, but the shot went awry. A poor chip left him a twenty-five-foot putt for par. He holed it for a 65, the low round of his PGA Tour career, and good for the early lead in the tournament.

After signing his scorecard Beem was carted to the media center. He was disappointed in the reception. "I swear to God, two guys showed up for the interview, and they asked a total of two questions and that was it," Beem says, sounding wounded. "It was bizarre." Actually, there was a perfectly good explanation. That Thursday was the day before the Ryder Cup was to commence, in Brookline, Massachusetts. The golf literati were all busy scarfing down free meals at the Country Club. Leading the Texas Open? The week of the Ryder Cup? That was like crossing the Atlantic the day after Lindbergh.

Hanrattie and Duplantis were sharing a hotel room that week (Sierra had stayed with Sollange Lewis), and they rendezvoused for dinner Thursday night. "First thing I said to Steve was, 'I oughtta be a Tour caddie,' " says Hanrattie. "I was pretty excited. It was the best round of golf I had ever seen in person. I mean, Rich didn't miss a putt inside eight feet the entire round. Steve gave me such a hard time. He was like, Settle down, don't get too jacked up. Just because you're a rookie doesn't mean you have to act like it.' I could tell Steve was excited for me, and for Rich, but I could also tell it was a little bittersweet. I know he wanted me to make money as a caddie, but I'm pretty sure he didn't want it coming out of his own pocket."

"I'd be lying if I didn't say I had mixed feelings," says Duplantis. "I was thrilled for Chris, I really was. And believe me, I knew how important it was for Rich to have a good tournament. But ever since we arrived in San Antonio I had been getting questions about what was going on with Rich and I, and it was getting old. Then he goes out and drops a sixty-five. It made me look bad."

Duplantis's mood wasn't brightened by Gay's lackluster 73. Or that at dinner that night with Beem and Hanrattie, "Rich made quite a few comments to Steve about what a good job I was doing," says Hanrattie.

STEPHEN AMES came in with an afternoon 64, so Beem didn't have the pressure of being the leader entering Friday's round. His 70, then, was easy to explain. "I didn't make any putts," he says. "None." Still, he was in fourth place, only two strokes back of Ames. Beem's so-so second round helped to slow his friends' and family members' jailbreak for San Antonio. Thursday evening Beem's cell phone had practically melted, as any number of folks began to make preparations for the short flight into south central Texas. "Nobody was at the Kemper, 'cept Dave and Amy, and everybody else felt a little left out," says Beem. "Ever since Kemper I had been hearing that the next time I was near the lead half of Las Cruces and El Paso was coming out. The fact that we were in Texas made it a no-brainer."

One person who wasted no time in arriving in San Antonio

was David Wyatt, who took the Friday night redeye from Seattle. "Rich dropped a grand on that ticket," says Wyatt, "but a deal's a deal. Anytime he's in the Top Five after the second round I'm on my way." Conspicuously absent from Beem's Saturday gallery was Duplantis. His man Gay had shot a second-round 69 to make the cut by a stroke. "If Brian had missed the cut I'm still not sure I would have watched," says Duplantis. "That might have been a little weird."

Beem played in the second to last pairing on Saturday, along with Ted Tryba, who after six years on tour was suddenly an overnight sensation. At the '99 L.A. Open he had torched Riviera (aka Hogan's Alley) for a course record 61, but that was only a taste of what was to come during an explosive summer. In June, Tryba blew away the field in Memphis to earn his second career victory (his final-round 66 included two eagles), and then at the end of July he dropped a 62 on TPC at River Highlands to propel him to a third-place finish at the Greater Hartford Open. The following week Tryba finished tied for second at the Buick Open, thanks to a 29 on the back nine on Sunday that included seven straight birdies (it was his second 29 of the week).

Back at La Cantera, Beem and Tryba squared off in an old-fashioned Texas gunfight on Saturday's front nine, combining for nine birdies and making the turn tied for the lead, at -12. "I thought I was gonna go to work on the back side," says Beem. "I was playing well and I was confident." The 10th hole at La Cantera is a 541-yard par-5 from an elevated tee, where a par feels like a bogey. After a poor drive, however, Beem failed to birdie the hole. He also settled for a disappointing par on the back side's other eminently birdieable par-5, the 14th. He could do no better than even par for the back nine, finishing with a 68. "Nothing gelled," he says. "I was trying to force it, I was too impatient. I didn't make any horrible mistakes, but I kept putting myself in the wrong position on the doglegs—which you can't do on that course—or leaving putts just short. It was little things, but they hurt me." Still, Beem remained in fourth place, three strokes back of Ames, and one behind both Tryba and Duffy Waldorf.

By Saturday evening Beem's entourage had begun streaming into town and he took a group of a dozen friends and family members out to dinner. This included a woman he had gone to high school with in Berlin who happened to be in San Antonio. After reading Beem's name in the paper, she sought him out at the golf course. "That was random," says Wyatt. This sprawling last supper was just one of the more obvious ways that Beem's approach to the Texas Open differed from the only other time he was in contention at a PGA Tour event. "At Kemper he was so myopic, so unbelievably focused," says Wyatt. "At Texas, Rich was really relaxed and jovial." Among the topics of conversation at dinner were the impending final round and Beem's hopes and expectations. "It wasn't a taboo subject, at all," says Wyatt. "People were asking him a lot of questions."

Cameron Doan, the El Paso Country Club head pro, was not among those who roadtripped to San Antonio, but he would not have approved of the dinner conversation. "Winning a golf tournament is such a delicate thing," Doan says. "It takes a lot of luck and a lot of other factors beyond your control, and you gotta be respectful of that. Most guys don't want to talk about winning, because they don't want to hex themselves. It's almost like the more you talk about it, the more pressure you're placing on yourself."

Beem was not content to pretend like nothing special was happening that week in San Antonio. "Kemper was such a grind," he says. "I was just worn out every day when I left that golf course. I was determined to enjoy it this time around. You don't get that many chances to win out here and I wanted to savor it."

SUNDAY MORNING another dozen or so folks arrived in San Antonio and Beem went to the airport to greet them. He then drove his mom, aunt, and sister Susie to the golf course.

Wyatt did not slip a Magnolia Hi-Fi employee ID card to Beem before the final round, but he was packing some good karma, in the form of Beem's lucky Cubs hat. Beem had been given the lid as a gift in mid-1998, and it happened to look good with one of his favorite shirts, a blue-and-white striped polo. Beem wore the outfit on the final day of one of his Sun Country sectional tournaments and went on to victory. Feeling lucky, he wore the same shirt and hat combo for the final round of the next tournament and won it, as well. The same thing happened two more tournaments in a row. Thus inspired, Beem wore this charmed shirt-and-hat combo on the last day at the final stage of Q School, and the ensuing 66 propelled him to the Tour. After Wyatt wore the hat during the final round of the Kemper, it was widely believed to have the kind of mystical powers usually associated with Shivas Irons or Bagger Vance, not the hapless Cubs.

Anyway, Beem hit the ball crisply at the range prior to the final round, and when he matriculated to the first tee he was heartened to see a throng of some two dozen supporters waiting to cheer him on. He made a point of kibitzing with all of them. He was obviously relaxed and in good spirits. Hanrattie, meanwhile, had so much cotton in his mouth he could have knitted a sweater. "I was a little nervous, I'll admit it," he says. "My feeling was that Rich had been there before and I hadn't. I wanted to help him where I could but really I just wanted to stay out of his way. He had proved he knew how to win."

So, too, had Duplantis, and he gave his buddy a few pointers. "Don't fall in any bunkers," he said, then adding, a little more seriously, "Just remember, everyone is allowed to get carried away but the caddie. You gotta keep your head in the ball game no matter what's going on around you."

Beem was again playing with Tryba in the second to last tee time. It was a good pairing. Tryba is an affable guy with a dry sense of humor and though he plays hard, he eschews the kind of grim game face that can be off-putting or intimidating.

Beem opened Sunday's round by hitting a wedge to eight feet on the par-five 1st and then rolling in the putt, the fourth day in a row he had opened his round with a birdie. He followed with two-putt pars on the 2nd and 3rd holes, and then got up-and-down for a crucial par at 4. On the short par-5 5th, Beem hit a driver and 6-iron to thirty feet, and then just missed the eagle putt. The tap-in birdie moved him to -15, leapfrogging him past Ames, who was spraying balls clear across Texas, and Waldorf, who was chugging along without any distinction. Beem was now in second place, behind only Tryba, who was looking like his flammable self, with a pair of early birdies of his own. "Understand, I'm broke," says Hanrattie. "I'm thinking about the money at this point." Soon enough, however, it looked like everybody was playing for second-place dough.

After an easy par at 6, Beem came to number 7, the so-called roller-coaster hole, because the aiming point from the tee is a distant amusement park. Beem laid up on the short par-4 with a 5-iron, then hit a sand wedge to twelve feet. Tryba was facing a much longer birdie putt, but he rammed it into the cup and Beem in turn missed his. Tryba was now up by 2. At the next hole, a back-breaking par-4, Tryba birdied again to go to -18, while Beem took a sloppy bogey, missing the fairway, missing the green, and then missing a six-footer for par. The bogey dropped him back to -14. He was now on the ropes, and at the 9th it looked like Tryba would deliver the knockout punch, hitting it to six feet, while Beem was facing a twenty-footer for his own birdie. But in one of the key moments of the round, Tryba missed his putt and Beem made his, cutting the deficit to three. Beem was back in the fight.

When Beem and Tryba arrived at the 10th tee there were already two groups waiting to hit. Directly in front of the clubhouse, the 10th tee is always packed with spectators, and to kill time Beem walked over to his cluster of friends and family in the gallery. "He talked quite a lot with everybody," says Hanrattie. "They were really laughing and joking and carrying on. I thought it was maybe a little too much, given the circumstances. But Rich is very much an extrovert, and maybe that's how he was blowing off steam." Hanrattie, despite his feelings, didn't say anything. By his demeanor Beem had made it clear that he didn't expect Hanrattie to do anything but carry the bag and offer yardage numbers. Clearly this was a radical departure from the partnership of player and caddie at Kemper, but Beem now felt confident that he was ready to win on his own.

When it was finally time to hit on number 10, he pounded a big drive and then stuck a precise approach shot to five feet. He made that putt to cut the deficit to two strokes. Beem and Tryba both parred 11, but Waldorf, playing in the final group, was making a run of his own that brought him to -16, tied with Beem for second place.

At 12—La Cantera's number one handicap—Beem split the fairway with a huge drive and then stuck a pitching wedge to two feet. One back (Waldorf, riding a hot putter, birdied 11 to also move to -17). "I was just clawing, clawing, clawing to get a piece of the lead," says Beem. "Ted hadn't made a bogey all day and he had been sitting on the lead for a long time. I felt like I might be able to shake him up if I could get one more stroke." By now Brian Gay had long since finished his final round, a strong 66 that propelled him to a tie for thirty-eighth, the second-best finish of his season, worth $8,000, and a $400 cut for his caddie. Duplantis had returned to the hotel to watch his best friend and his erstwhile boss fight out the finish. (Gay, meanwhile, had jammed to the airport, and he made it home to Orlando just in time. The day after the tournament Kimberly gave birth to a bouncing baby girl, their first child.) Watching the telecast, Duplantis had a bad feeling about the 13th hole. "That's a real tough yardage, and the wind was really picking up when we played through there," he says.

The 13th hole at La Cantera is only 159 yards, but it is a nasty little par-3. From tee to green there is a forty-seven-foot drop, and sitting astride a notch in the foothills, the hole is buffeted by swirling, unpredictable gales. In three previous cracks at 13, Beem had failed to gauge the yardage correctly, twice dumping his ball in the right-front bunker guarding the kidney bean–shaped green. This time he walked clear to the front of the tee box to get a better feel for the breeze. The choice was between an 8- or a 9-iron. On the shortish par-4s of La Cantera, as well as the 13th hole, Beem had frequently been torn between these clubs during the week, and most of the time he tried to muscle up with the 9. The results had been mixed, at best. "We had been facing this decision the whole tournament, and Rich kept coming up short with the nine," says Hanrattie. "That's what had happened at number four on Sunday, where we needed a hell of an up-and-down to save par. So at thirteen I finally said, 'Let's try something different, taking a little off the eight.' " Hanrattie, alas, did not have the kind of clairvoyance that Duplantis enjoyed throughout the Kemper. The 8-iron was too much stick and Beem flew the green and landed in a patch of sinister rough. He played a lovely flop shot to three and a half feet, but then missed the putt, resulting in a momentum-halting bogey. "I have no memory of that putt," Beem says. "I went brain dead. I don't know what happened." Beem was now -16, in fourth place, two back of Tryba, and one shot in arrears of Waldorf and a surging Brent Geiberger. Though hardly household names, all four of these players had already won a tournament in '99. With the U.S. team completing its thrilling Ryder Cup comeback, the Texas Open was sure to be overlooked in the following day's sports section. Still, a second victory for any of these players would turn a good season into a banner year. The final five holes promised to be cutthroat.

Needing to generate some momentum, Beem couldn't have asked for a more tantalizing hole than the 14th, the 527-yard par-5 with a seventy-two-foot drop from tee to fairway. The hole was playing as the second easiest on the course and Beem's opportunity to make up ground was all the more golden after Tryba slashed a banana slice into the trees. Judging by his swing, Beem tried to become the first player in La Cantera history to drive the 14th green, because he overswung with such force his right hand flew off the handle during the follow-through. Of course, this kind of a rip produced a duck hook into the trees. Opportunity lost. Beem punched out and then played a terrific 6-iron to twelve feet, a putt he failed to get to the hole. He took a disappointing par, matching Tryba's score. Waldorf, in the group behind them, would hit the green in two and birdie to tie Tryba for the lead.

At the steeply uphill par-4 15th both Beem and Tryba hit excellent approach shots—Beem to ten feet, Tryba to six. Beem drilled his putt to move to -17, but moments later Tryba topped him with a clutch roll, once again taking the outright lead at -19.

At the short par-4 16th Tryba blew a layup iron off the tee into the right rough, while Beem drove perfectly into the right center of the fairway, leaving nothing but a little sand wedge to the front left flag. The 17th and 18th holes at La Cantera are brutes, meaning this was Beem's last best chance to make up ground. "I had a perfect yardage, a perfect lie, I was just so ready to hit that shot," says Beem. "I was just dying to hit it. I know I'm gonna stuff it in there and make birdie. Teddy's over there in the gunch stalling, walking off yardages, changing clubs, checking the wind over and over. He's absolutely killing me. Finally he hits, but he's twenty feet above the hole and there's no way he's gonna make that putt. So now I know how big my birdie's gonna be. I doubt his ball had even stopped rolling on the green and I'm already over my ball. I'm in such a rush. I just can't wait to make my birdie." Trying to play a little cut, Beem double-crossed himself and hooked his ball clear over the green and down a little hill into a bad lie in the heavy rough. Earlier in the day Mark McGwire had hit his sixtieth home run of the baseball season, inspiring the ESPN announcer to say of Beem, "He just got in the home run race with that one." "I got up and down for a great par, but that was the shot that really hurt me," says Beem.

At the long par-3 17th, Beem ballooned his tee ball into the wind, but he produced a clutch two-putt from forty feet to remain at -17, tied with Geiberger, who was now in the clubhouse with a 67. Tryba, meanwhile, had missed the green long and left, and done well to stop his chip eight feet from the hole. Bogeyless since the 4th hole on Saturday, Tryba gagged the par putt, dropping into a tie with Waldorf at -18. So with one hole to play, Beem was only one shot out of the lead.

Says Hanrattie, "I remember walking off the seventeenth green and Rich said to me, 'Let's finish like a champ.' He was pumped, and so was I."

Back at El Paso Country Club a good crowd had gathered to watch the telecast, though it wasn't the mob scene that had turned out for the final round of the Kemper (no TV cameras bothered to show up, either). Watching intently was Doan, and he didn't like his pupil's anxious demeanor. "I saw the way Rich walked off the seventeenth green—he was going way too fast. It looked like he was getting carried away by the situation. I was really curious to see how he'd play eighteen."

The finishing hole at La Cantera is a long, uphill par-4, doglegging slightly to the left. The premium is on finding the fairway off the tee, not the easiest of tasks given the landing area is pinched on both sides by bunkers. To the right of the bunkers on the outside of the dogleg is a grove of towering oak trees, but they are so far off-line as to not be considered in play.

Standing on the 18th tee, with honors, "I was absolutely thinking birdie," says Beem. He was also thinking about the pull hook he had hit at the 14th hole. "When I get nervous I rush and yank it left," he says. "I just wanted to swing as slow and smooth as I could."

Instead, he overcompensated and fanned his ball off the heel. It took off on a sickly flight far, far to the right and then clanged off one of the trees beyond the right fairway bunker. (A slow motion replay on TV would show that in his eagerness to crush a drive and make birdie Beem had taken his club way past parallel and on the way down his hands never caught up. He struck the ball with an alarmingly open clubface.) Beem slammed his driver into the turf and then skulked after his ball. "When you're fighting for a tournament like that and you know you've just lost it, it's an incredible letdown," he says. "It's like all the adrenaline drains right out of your body. It's like all your strength just disappears." When Beem got to his ball he was shocked to discover it had landed in a creek. "We had no idea the hazard was down there," says Hanrattie. "I talked to Steve afterward and he didn't know there was a creek there, either. It's so far out of play I guess no one has ever gone there."

On the PGA Tour you play to win. When you have no shot at winning, you play for money. Beem quickly switched gears. "I knew there was a big logjam at fifth place," he says. "I knew I needed to make bogey to finish solo fourth and save myself an awful lot of cash." From Beem's point of entry to the hazard he had no shot at the green, on account of one of the oaks. Cursing under his breath, he was about to take his penalty drop when Hanrattie brought up Rule 26-1c (ii), which allows a player to take his drop on the "opposite margin of the water hazard equidistant from the hole." Beem took the advice and from the right edge of the creek—as opposed to the left, his point of entry—he had a clear shot to the front of the green. From a hardpan lie, he smoked an incredible shot, a 212-yard 2-iron to the front of the green. However, the pin was back right, on the crown of a third tier. Beem's putt was to be some 120 feet, across two deep swales. If he could get down in two he would finish with a 69, a four-round total of 16 under par, and all by himself in fourth place. That would be worth $96,000. If he three-putted, which was a distinct possibility, he would fall into a four-way tie for fifth, which would be worth $78,750. The difference between the two dollar figures was more than Beem's entire El Paso Country Club salary the year before. Beem hit his putt and then started walking after it, curious to see where it would end up. The ball just kept rolling and rolling and rolling toward the hole. With the putt still tracking, Beem began to pump his fist, spurring on the crowd, which was already, in his estimation, "going crazy." Beem's ball burned the left edge of the cup, stopping a mere three inches beyond. He got his bogey. "It was neat to hear the crowd like that," he says. "I will never be disgusted about that finish. Never. I proved to myself I can get into contention again, and the way it ended was a thrill."

As Beem signed his scorecard, Hanrattie whipped out his cell and called Duplantis back at the hotel. Says Hanrattie, "The first thing Steve says is, 'Dude, what the fuck happened on the eighteenth tee?' He wanted to know everything. He definitely had his game face on."

Tryba, meanwhile, had blown his approach to 18 over the green, but he made a stirring up-and-down for par. When Waldorf missed a twenty-footer for birdie at the last they went to a sudden-death playoff, which Waldorf won on the first extra hole with a bird. Beem finished a mere two strokes out of the playoff. Looking back on his round, there are a million ways he could have shaved a pair of strokes. "I fell short when I didn't need to," Beem says. "I wanted it so bad, maybe too much so. I didn't control my game like I needed to. I hit the ball just as good as at Kemper, I putted just as good, but I didn't have the same kind of focus. I wasn't in that zone. At Kemper, my level of concentration literally wore me out every day. It was exhausting. Texas, it didn't wear me out. But I'll tell you what, there's nothing disappointing about finishing fourth and cashing a check for a hundred grand. In the grand scheme of things it was absolutely huge, because it proved what happened at the Kemper Open wasn't a fluke."

CHAPTER

• 15 •

THE DAY AFTER the Texas Open ended, before heading to that week's Buick Challenge in Pine Mountain, Georgia, Rich Beem made two phone calls. Neither one was good news for Steve Duplantis. "When I had those three weeks off prior to Texas I had started to think about making a caddie change," says Beem. "After my week there I knew it would be the right decision. My mind was made up." Beem's first call was to Rich Mayo, who he had known since Mayo was playing for the University of Texas-El Paso in the early- to mid-1990s. Mayo's playing career had long since petered out, but for the previous couple of seasons he had been caddying for his old UTEP teammate Paul Stankowski. Beem and Mayo had always been chatty and back in the springtime, at the BellSouth Classic in Atlanta, Mayo had actually caddied for Beem when he had been unable to scrounge up a looper for a pro-am. "It was a different experience," says Beem. "He beat me to the ball every time, had the yardage ready when I arrived, and was just very, very professional."

In the weeks leading up to the Texas Open, Beem and Mayo had had a few general discussions about working together, but now Beem wanted a commitment. Mayo, of course, was torn. He and Stankowski were thick as thieves, but this was business. Stankowski was in the midst of his worst season since his rookie year in 1994. He had cracked the Top 10 only once all year, and was living in the ghetto below the Top 125 on the money list. Failing a late-season rally he was going to lose his card. Mayo agreed to caddie for Beem at the Las Vegas Invitational in mid-October, two weeks after the Buick.

Next Beem called his old boss Cameron Doan. He needed advice on how to break the news to Duplantis. "I wasn't the greatest employee myself," says Beem, "and now all of a sudden I was supposed to be the employer. How do you learn how to do that? It's one of those things you have to go through as a rookie that no one even thinks about, but it's tough. My diplomacy skills weren't up to speed."

So Beem had made the decision to fire Duplantis. The only question was when was he going to work up the nerve and pull the trigger.

A COUPLE HOURS AFTER the Texas Open concluded Duplantis and Hanrattie piled into the latter's Acura and began the all-night drive to Pine Mountain, which is in west central Georgia, just outside of Columbus. Hanrattie drove to the Louisiana border, which they reached 'round midnight. Duplantis then took over, blowing through Mississippi and parts of Alabama. Under a glorious sunrise Hanrattie returned to the driver's seat and they arrived, no worse for the wear, at the Mountain View Course of the Callaway Gardens Resort just after ten in the morning. The first order of business was to find Hanrattie a job for the week. Duplantis began chatting up folks at the range, but nothing was doing.

Around 11:00 A.M. Beem rolled in, and he, Duplantis, and Hanrattie convened for a spirited practice session. "Rich was hitting the ball great, and he seemed pretty energized by finishing fourth," says Duplantis. "He put in a good couple of hours hitting balls and putting. I was thinking that maybe Texas would inspire him to finish the season strong. I was looking forward to a good week."

While at the range Beem took some good-natured ribbing from his colleagues, who, in the incestuous world of the Tour, were well aware that Beem's two strong showings had come after extended rests. Beem's old practice round foil Briny Baird wandered over and said, "What are you doing here this week, champ? You should be taking three weeks off so you can come out and kick all of our butts. You got the formula now."

For his part Duplantis didn't detect that anything was amiss in his relationship with the boss. Hanging out at the range Duplantis heard through the grapevine that one of Stewart Cink's buddies had just qualified on Monday and needed a caddie. His name was Matt Filipowicz (sounds like a moniker a well-disguised Fletch might have used) and he was even greener than Hanrattie, as the Buick Challenge was to be his first Tour event. (Just to clarify, there are four PGA Tour events with Buick in their titles. They are, in order, the Invitational [San Diego], the Classic [Westchester], the Open [at Warwick Hills, outside Detroit], and the Challenge, which once upon a time used to be known as the Southern Open.)

On Tuesday Beem and Duplantis spent four hours together playing a practice round and again Beem said nothing. The following day they were puttering around the driving range when Duplantis began chattering about the 2000 season. He was raving to Beem about all the top tournaments he would now get into and discussing the cities they would visit—where they should stay, where they should eat, and what strip joints they should visit. Finally Beem, as meek as he was, could take it no longer. In a torrent of words he loosed the speech he had been rehearsing in his head for the better part of three days.

"Steve, this is the deal: I've decided that next year I'm going to go in a different direction, with Rich Mayo or somebody else. It's not a reflection of the job you did caddying, I just think we both need a change."

Just like that, it was over.

"It was left unsaid as to why, though I had my reasons all outlined in case he needed them," says Beem. "Steve didn't say much, but I could see he was physically upset. He didn't take the news well."

This Duplantis downplays. "The entire conversation took two minutes," he says. "It wasn't a big deal. It wasn't like with Furyk, when I was just crushed. I'm sure Rich had gotten wind that I was talking to some other guys, poking around. Maybe he was trying to save face by making the decision first. In all honesty it was probably a relief, because things just weren't working out, and it seemed like only a matter of time before something like this happened."

"I know that at the Kemper Open I said the job was Steve's for as long as he wanted it," says Beem. "All I can say to that is, things change. It became like a romance that went bad. It was great in the beginning, and with the success we had it was easy for a while to overlook each other's faults. Then I started playing bad, and he started getting pissed, then I started getting pissed he was getting pissed. It just got a little strained."

"It was disappointing how things turned out, because Rich wasn't able to build on his victory," says Duplantis. "He just seemed to quit trying there for a while. I take the blame for some of that. I wanted to try to motivate him, to get his head back in the ball game, but I couldn't. Everything I said only made things worse. We just couldn't talk and the frustration built and built."

"I'll never speak ill about Steve, because there is no doubt he was a big part of my winning," Beem says. "When he wants to dive in he does an unbelievable job. He is one of the best caddies in the world. When he wants to be."

THE NEXT DAY's first round wasn't as awkward as might be imagined. Both Beem and Duplantis felt relief more than anything else. Unfortunately, Beem was also feeling a mysterious pain in his left foot. It bothered him throughout the round, and he shot an excruciating 76—picking up right where he'd left off with Duplantis. Then next day his foot felt better, but a 73 took all the spring out of his step. Beem missed the cut by a mile (equally discouraging was that his 149 was the same score shot by Hanrattie's starry-eyed first-timer, Filipowicz).

The adventure, however, was not over for Beem and Duplantis. Mayo had decided he couldn't abandon Stankowski just as he was fighting for his livelihood. The trial run for Las Vegas was still on, but he wasn't willing to go to work full-time for Beem until the following season. In addition to Vegas, Beem was planning to play two more PGA Tour events, plus the unofficial mixed-team JCPenney Classic. He promised Duplantis a healthy season-ending check if he would stay on for those tournaments. Beem called it a bonus, while his soon-to-be-ex-caddie considered it a severance package. Either way, Duplantis agreed to the deal.

CHAPTER

• 16 •

"What are we gonna do with this thing?" Rich Beem asked, of no one in particular. In his hands was the spectacular winner's trophy from the Kemper Open, twenty-five pounds of intricately sculpted crystal. In front of him were five hundred miles of interstate. The time had come for Beem to bid adieu to El Paso and move into his new digs in Scottsdale. The only problem was deciding where to wedge the trophy in his already over-stuffed Ford Explorer. All that crystal had arrived months earlier via air mail, in a crate big enough for a family of stowaways. That packaging had long since been discarded, and now all Beem could do was seat belt his most prized possession into the backseat and try to steer clear of potholes.

Five days had passed since Beem missed the cut at the Buick Challenge. He had been making the rounds at home ever since—family dinners, business meetings, golf with the boys, and, not the least, taking delivery of a shiny new hunter green BMW 323i, with a beige drop top. (One of Beem's sponsors had a BMW dealership in El Paso, and he made Beem an offer he couldn't refuse.) Now it was time to get out of town. Beem was milling around a hotel parking lot in Las Cruces, where he had rendezvoused with Max Schroeder, minus his son Evan Richard. Schroeder had volunteered to caravan behind Beem with a U-Haul chock-full o' bric-a-brac. Helping Beem load the Explorer was David Wyatt, already irritable at six in the morning because he hadn't yet gotten his morning fix of latte. (Another buddy, Christian Colbert, had driven Beemer's Beemer out to Scottsdale the night before.) By and by all the mementos of Beem's old life were packed up and this motley crew, along with a slightly squashed observer in the backseat, set sail under a sky of the deepest blue, the presunrise color of the desert.

Beem had not yet left the Las Cruces city limits when his thoughts turned to his soon-to-be new hometown and he grew a little wistful in the telling. He had first fallen in love with the Phoenix area as a kid, visiting his grandparents in Paradise Valley. In fact, Beem had almost moved to Scottsdale from Seattle, following his busted engagement. Before the offer to work at El Paso Country Club came through, he was all set to take a job in the bag room at Desert Mountain Country Club. Ironically enough, Scottsdale was also where Beem attended his first professional golf tournament, the 1990 Phoenix Open. "It was so thrilling," Beem said, gunning his rig onto I-10 West. "I realized then I was nothing like those guys. They were the best in the world. Me? At that point I hadn't even finished in the Top Five of a college tournament. I was probably a good two-handicapper." Left unsaid was how far he had traveled since.

Amidst the silence Beem began futzing with the sound system in his Explorer, the one he had so memorably bragged on during his first brush with reporters at the Kemper Open, four months earlier. He waded through the many choices in his CD changer until the throbbing sounds of his favorite band, Live, flooded the truck's interior. Over the music Beem had a final thought.

"I'm not leaving this place behind," he said, the dim lights of El Paso and Las Cruces now just specks in the rearview mirror, "but this is a new start. No doubt about that."

THE NIGHT BEFORE, Beem had enjoyed one of the most momentous evenings of his young life. Naturally, it came at El Paso Country Club, the site of so much personal history. Beem had called a meeting of his sponsors, to talk shop and say his goodbyes. Nineteen of the thirty-five showed up, impressive given how busy these men are, and that it was a Tuesday night. The meeting was held behind closed doors in a lounge in the EPCC clubhouse. A couple dozen folding chairs had been set up and Beem sat at the front of the room on his throne, an oversized red leather chair, facing the crowd. He was glowing. He had played golf at the club that day—losing $15 despite shooting a 64, the downside of a +5 handicap—and the combination of some sun and a few Jack and Cokes certainly had something to do with Beem's rosy complexion. But so, too, did the fact that the former shop hand was now sitting in front of these pillars of the El Paso community feeling like a winner, maybe for the first time.

Beem had a few things he wanted to say, but he would have to wait his turn. This was the first official meeting of the sponsors since before the Kemper Open, and there was much business to be discussed. Beem's friend John Butterworth—the accountant who kept the books for his fellow partners—opened the meeting by handing out a three-page fact sheet that detailed all of the year's income and expenditures, and the tax ramifications for the general partners. Butterworth began by running down the expenses, item by item. When he came to meals—which by this night in early October had already totaled more than $20,000—he stated the obvious. "That sounds excessive, I know," Butterworth said. "I imagine if Rich hadn't been so successful we would be questioning that. But when you consider how many nights he has to eat out, I don't have a problem with that." There was a little murmuring throughout the room, but no challenges. The rest of the expenses provoked no discussion, so Butterworth cut to the chase: All of the partners were facing a major hit on their personal income taxes.

Butterworth explained the situation: Under the terms of the two-year sponsorship deal, Beem wouldn't get more than his 10 percent of the earnings pot until the end of the 2000 season. Therefore, the partners had to assume the tax burden for the other 90 percent of the 1999 income (less expenses). Including Beem's endorsement and bonus money, the partnership had already collected nearly $800,000, and the expenses, including caddie fees, had crept above $200,000. Using round numbers, that left half a million dollars that was going to be taxed at 39.6 percent. An investor who ponied up $3,000 at the start of the year—or 4 percent of the initial $75,000—would thus be responsible for 4 percent of the $500,000, which was $20,000. "Thirty-nine-point-six percent of twenty thousand dollars is seven thousand nine hundred twenty dollars," said Butterworth, "which is the size of the check that will have to be written to the government at the end of this year." Hearing this, the room stirred. Beem's friend Greg Johns finally spoke up. "Goddamnit, Rich, stop winning so much," he said, inducing a chorus of guffaws.

Butterworth droned on: At the end of 2000 the partnership would be dissolved, and the profits would be paid out. Assuming Beem only broke even as a sophomore, the fictitious partner used in the example would get his initial investment of $3,000 back, plus his share of the $500,000 profit, which comes to $4,950, based on the partnership's preestablished payment schedule. With the tax credit from the 1999 loss being applied in 2000, this investor would have paid, over the two years, a total of $2,507 in taxes. Taking that from the $4,950 profit, the sum of the gain over two years would be $2,443, a 81.4 percent return, considerable even by bull market standards. When Butterworth finally finished, all of the oxygen seemed to have been sucked out of the room. Then a great, unwieldy debate began. Nobody seemed to care about the two-year profit. What was on everybody's mind was having to eat the taxes in the first year. This was Texas, after all. Writing checks to the government is a concept about as popular as Hillary for President. A few ideas were kicked around, and then Butterworth said the magic words. "If we write a check to Rich on December 31 of this year for the balance of the earnings then we can reduce our tax burden subtantially," he said. This created considerable enthusiasm, and it was agreed a vote would be taken at the end of the meeting. For now the discussion ceased. It was Beem's turn to talk.

"By now I think all of you have heard about my move," he said. "It's an exciting deal and I think Scottsdale's a place where I can really improve as a player. There are a lot of great players out there I can test myself against, and TPC course is a tremendous facility. We're talkin' balata practice balls, the works. It's a place where I can hang my hat. But I want all of you to know that I'm not gonna forget about this place. I'm gonna keep the El Paso Country Club logo on my golf bag, and when I'm announced on the first tee at tournaments, it will be 'Rich Beem, playing out of El Paso Country Club.' "

This drew a small, spontaneous smattering of applause. Beem plowed on.

"It's no secret that at one point I was going to come here and ask to be let out of the contract," he said. "I even consulted some lawyers about it. From what I was told I probably could have gotten out of it, too. But I've come to my senses. You guys put me out on tour, and you believed in me, and I'm forever indebted because of that. I feel like EPCC is my friend and I always want it to be that way."

From there Beem segued into a couple of matters of personal finance. He wanted the partners to approve a year-end bonus. Under the terms of the contract, he could only get his hands on 10 percent of the $800,000 or so he had earned. "Last year my salary was fifteen thousand dollars," Beem said. "I know you guys can understand where I'm coming from when I say I would like to be able to put to use some more of the money in the pot. I don't need a lot, and frankly I don't want a lot. Half a million dollars scares the shit out of me. I don't want to make any mistakes. There's no guarantees out here. I mean, I'm confident in my playing ability, but I'm scared to death of the future."

Here Butterworth interjected. "By the way, gentlemen, Rich didn't buy that BMW, he leased it," said the accountant. "The condo that he supposedly bought for half a million dollars actually costs $217,000, and he's renting it with a roommate. So don't believe everything you hear."

Next Beem asked for approval to give Duplantis a $10,000 golden handshake. "I like Steve a lot and I care for his daughter a great deal and I want to do something nice for them," he said. "I'll tell you, if you turn me down then I'm going to write them a check out of my own pocket." A showing of hands approved the bonus/severance, but raising Duplantis's name kicked off a larger discussion about Beem's caddie situation. He was asked why he had fired Duplantis, after their success at Kemper.

"I like Steve, I think he's a good person, he's just going through a lot," Beem said. "He's twenty-six and he doesn't really know where he's heading in life."

Asked about a permanent replacement, Beem said that he was giving Rich Mayo a tryout the following week in Las Vegas. "You all know Rich from around here," Beem said, alluding to Mayo's UTEP days. "You know he's a great player, and he's just as good a caddie. I've seen Rich sit on the range and watch Paul

[Stankowski] hit four buckets of balls. With Stevie, it was a miracle if he stuck around for ten minutes."

After a little more small talk Butterworth stepped in to finalize the revised payment schedule. There was a unanimous showing of hands and it was agreed that the balance of the '99 profits would be paid out to Beem on December 31. Just like that, he picked up half a million dollars in spending money. But Beem was clear to say he wanted to keep the partnership going the following season and everyone in attendance was happy to hear it.

After all the talk about tax credits and meal expenses and year-end bonuses, one pleasantly cantankerous older gentleman spoke up, hoping to end the meeting on a different note. "I don't give a damn about the money," he said. "You can have every penny, for all I care. I didn't get into this to make money off of you and I know nobody else did, either. We just wanted to give you a chance to succeed, and we're tickled to death that you have. You've made all of us here at the club very proud. Rich, I want you to remember one thing: Everybody in this room is one hundred percent for you. Out there, everybody will be one hundred percent for themselves."

"And remember, Rich," said Johns, "some of them have big tits, too."

THERE ARE NO MEMENTOS of Rich Beem's career, collegiate or professional, in his father's office at the New Mexico State University Golf Course, though there is a mouse pad emblazoned with a picture of the Three Stooges, turned out in tacky golf regalia. At Larry Beem's home, on a quiet street above downtown Las Cruces, the only souvenir from his son's rookie year is a SONY OPEN IN HAWAII hat hanging in the bathroom. "All of Rich's other stuff is in a box in the attic," Larry says. "I'm not a guy interested in history, in memorabilia. I live in the present tense." On the other hand, Larry's trophies can be found neatly arranged on a shelf in his garage: the first one he ever won, from something called the 1954 Victoria Junior Low Net, in Riverside, California; the 1957 Fox Hills CC championship; the 1960 New Mexico state amateur; and a half dozen others.

Rich is still two days from pulling out of Las Cruces, but he and Larry have already had their farewell dinner. "He brought David Wyatt along," says Larry, taking a long drag on a Marlboro light. "We couldn't be alone, even for that." Another long drag. "In some ways Rich is a stranger to me. We're father and son, but it's not like in *The Brady Bunch*." The old man is sitting in his backyard, enjoying a balmy Indian summer night. The hour has grown late. The sprinklers have been drowning the lawn for over an hour now, though Larry doesn't seem to have noticed, even as he idly watches the water dance. He takes another drag.

"Rich said something last night I wish I had responded to, but I didn't," he says. "I'd like to be able to say things to him, but I can't. We don't communicate well. Anyway, he said, 'I guess I proved a lot of people wrong.' I wanted to say that he really didn't. He made a lot of people happy. Our lack of belief in him as a player had nothing to do with golf itself, and everything to do with his behavior as a person."

Larry Beem has an insatiable appetite for knowledge. He routinely gorges himself on medical journals, marathon viewings of the History and Discovery Channels, and on various metaphysical tomes. "I'm a big believer in fate," Beem says. "Who's that Indian guy? Chopra? I like what he has to say—you are where you are because that is the only place you can be. That's Rich. This whole year has allowed him to see what he's capable of, and what he needs to improve on, in golf and in life. It's been a bumpy road, but that is the only way he could have gotten to where he is going."

Larry is asked if he is sorry to see his son leaving town.

"He's not leaving, he's just moving," Larry says. "Rich left a long time ago."

THE DRIVE TO SCOTTSDALE stretches on endlessly, mile after mile disappearing into the horizon. Every forty-five minutes or so either Beem or Wyatt insists on stopping for coffee, for gum, to take a leak, or for no reason at all. They are ADD travelers. Fifty miles east of Tucson brings the weirdest pit stop of all, a chintzy souvenir shop/museum that they have been giddily anticipating for the better part of the past one hundred miles. Stretched across the desert have been a series of billboards asking, cryptically, WHAT IS THE THING? Beem and Wyatt know the answer, and insist on visiting a run-down museum that is a shrine to cornball Americana, at the end of which the Thing is revealed to be an obviously fake mummified alien. Spying the Thing, yet again, Beem and Wyatt dissolve into spasms of laughter—amazingly, they're not high—and then, in the gift shop, purchase for a guest a replica of Elvis Presley's Tennessee driver's license, which is their way of denoting membership in the Thing Fan Club.

Once back in the car, Beem gets to waxing on his unusual friendship with Wyatt. "I'd like to put David on the payroll some day," he says. "As it is I fly him around plenty, and when he does work for me I pay him for his time. If I get to a point where I'm earning enough I'd love to have him as a road manager. I'm going to try to keep up my end of the deal and play well so it can happen." Wyatt, who has spent part of the drive opening Beem's mail and organizing his bills and various correspondences, rolls his eyes at the talk.

Full of life from having visited the Thing, Beem suddenly asks, "You wanna hear this system? I mean really *hear* it?" Without waiting for an answer Beem cues The Artist Formerly Known As Prince, one of his and Wyatt's faves, and, for the first time on the drive, cranks his much ballyhooed stereo to full tilt. Arm hair sways to the beat. Lumbar muscles contract every time the bass thumps. Eyelids twitch. Meanwhile, Beem and Wyatt are happier than pigs in slop, madly shouting out lyrics, and using their fingertips and kneecaps as makeshift drum sets. Beem yells one line a little louder than any other: "When the elevator tries to break you down/Go crazy!"

FINALLY, Scottsdale appears in the distance, having sprung wholly formed from the desert floor, or so it seems. After some confusion on the roadways Beem wheels into the expanse of the Grayhawk development, a series of tract neighborhoods as envisioned by Rod Serling, where every duplex is identical to the next, and the winding streets circle around and around into an indecipherable labyrinth.

Beem pulls into his driveway, jumps out of the Explorer, and bursts through the front door, eager to show off his swank new domicile. Much *ooh*ing and *aah*ing ensues. There are towering vaulted ceilings, granite counters, and black glass appliances in the kitchen, carpet throughout that is thicker than U.S. Open rough. (The new BMW is tucked away within the textured walls of the garage.) Beem's bedroom is upstairs, a long walk down a winding hallway. Wandering around the place aimlessly, Wyatt says, "Oh man, you're uptown now. I don't even think we can hang out together anymore."

"I'll still slum occasionally," says Beem.

A sweaty unloading session ensues. At some point the fridge is opened to reveal virtually nothing but cases worth of beer, an army of frosted bottles waiting to be called into battle. The atmosphere in the Beem household is festive. Is there going to be a welcome-to-Scottsdale party?

"You might say that," Beem says, smirking at Wyatt.

Pressed for an explanation, Wyatt says, "There's a girl in town who has been promising us a threesome for a while, and tonight she's gonna deliver."

Really.

"Oh yeah, for sure," says Wyatt. "She's a team player."

"Definitely a team player," says Beem.

CHAPTER

• 17 •

THE LAS VEGAS INVITATIONAL has always been one of Steve Duplantis's favorite tournaments. He loves Vegas—the dice and the vice, the bright lights and the long nights. It didn't hurt that through the years he and Jim Furyk had enjoyed tremendous success at the LVI, nearly winning there as rookies in 1994, and then getting the first victory of their careers the following season. Furyk, of course, won the tournament again in '98. This time around Duplantis wasn't feeling the usual enthusiasm as he arrived in Sin City. Rich Mayo was working for Beem that week. Duplantis didn't have any illusions about getting back together with Beem, but that wasn't what was bugging him. Mayo's presence on the bag would make Duplantis's and Beem's split public. That only meant more questions and more explanations, a routine that had long since grown tiresome.

Then, too, there was the added ignominy that he was still packing for Gay, who at the start of the week was the fifth alternate. When Gay moved up to the top of the wait list Wednesday afternoon Duplantis hopped on a flight. They didn't get into the field until early Thursday morning, when two (undoubtedly hungover) players phoned in their withdrawals. During Beem's week off, when he was getting settled in Scottsdale, Duplantis had decided to strap it on at the Michelob Championships, in Kingsmill, Virginia. He's always had a romantic attachment to the tournament where he got his start, six years earlier. It was a wasted trip. Gay shot 74-73 to miss the cut. "Brian's a good guy, he works hard at the game, but he doesn't have half the talent of a Rich Beem," said Duplantis. "Could I see him coming out of the blue to all of a sudden win a tournament? I'm not so sure." In the span of six months Duplantis had gone from working with one of the best players in the world to an exciting prospect to a clueless rookie. "I'm not gonna lie, it hurts your pride," he says. "The perception of you as a caddie is based in large part on how good your player is. That may not be right, but that's just the way it is."

Over the first three rounds at the LVI—which is one of only two ninety-hole events on tour—Gay shot 68-68-69, which sounds terrific until you find out that the cut was -11, a record low, and Gay made it right on the number. Nevertheless, it was the second time in four tournaments that he had made the cut with Duplantis by his side, compared to only six out of twenty-one with other caddies. Coincidence? "I don't think so," says Duplantis, though his tone is more matter-of-fact than boastful.

On Saturday Gay shot a 74, all but guaranteeing a mediocre finish. With his wife and baby girl back home in Orlando, he resisted Duplantis's entreaties to go out on the town with a small band of revelers. After a couple of beers, Gay turned in early, but not so his caddie. "It was a blast. We got back to the room at like five A.M."

And when was Gay's Sunday tee time?

"Nine-oh-four."

Gay sleepwalked through a final round 73, fading to forty-fourth, worth $7,770.00. When Kimberly Gay had told Duplantis she wanted a veteran caddie to educate her husband about life on tour, this probably wasn't what she had in mind.

BEEM AND MAYO opened respectably at LVI, 70-67, but on Friday the putter went cold and Beem shot a toothless 72, missing another cut. Beem had good chemistry with Mayo and felt like he had done a fine job during the tournament. That wasn't the problem. Per usual, Beem wasn't in a condition to play his best golf. He arrived in town with a touch of bronchitis and was popping antibiotics as if they were Tic-Tacs throughout the tournament. "The grind of the whole season was catching up with me," he says. In an effort to conserve his already diminished energy, "I kept it very low key," Beem says. "I turned down a lot of offers to go out on the town."

Pause.

"Of course, after I missed the cut I set my hair on fire for a couple of days in a row."

On one of the quieter evenings Beem accepted a dinner invitation from one of the manufacturers' reps, who brought along a pair of sisters—one was his girlfriend, the other was destined to become Beem's squeeze. Her name was Sara Waide, and though she lived in Seattle, where she worked in pharmaceutical sales, her appearance was strictly Southern California, what with her blonde hair, blue eyes, and golden tan. Rich and Sara hit it off immediately, and dinner featured the kind of sexual tension not seen since the early years of *Moonlighting*. After a long, pleasant meal Beem retired to his room, alone. He didn't have the energy to pursue anything other than a good night's sleep. But he and Sara would begin burning up the phone lines soon enough.

One person Beem was not particularly eager to chat with while in Las Vegas was Paul Stankowski, Mayo's regular employer. "As far as I was concerned there was nothing to talk about," says Beem. "Paul and I are friends but this is a business, too, and this was a business decision. Happens all the time out here, caddies changing jobs. I was dealing with Rich, and the way I see it it's up to him to deal with Paul." Stankowski, with a stand-in on the bag, continued his season-long poor play, missing the cut by six strokes to sink even deeper down the money list. There were only two more tournaments left on the schedule; barring an inspired rally, he was doomed to Q School.

Beem had no such worries and beginning Friday evening, he and David Wyatt hit the town with a vengeance. They played blackjack all night two days running at their casino of choice, the Hard Rock, which jumps on the weekend with displaced beautiful people from El Lay. "Rich caught an unbelievable run," says Wyatt. "We started out on the twenty-five-dollar tables and at one point wound up in the high-roller area, with Rich playing one thousand dollars a hand. That didn't go so well, but he still left town thirteen thousand dollars ahead. I won five thousand dollars myself."

Though the next tournament was on the other side of the country—the National Car Rental Golf Classic at Disney World, in Orlando—Beem stuck around Las Vegas until Monday night. This was so he could tee it up Monday afternoon at the "Fairway to Heaven," a charity outing organized by VH-1 that brings together pro golfers and rock stars of varying magnitude. Beem's outfit conveyed the seriousness of the event: sandals, a Technicolor Hawaiian shirt, and a bucket hat made of Astro Turf, an homage to Bill Murray. In Beem's group was the drummer Tico Torres, of Bon Jovi fame. Beem and Torres got along famously, with Torres going so far as to take down Beem's address, under the auspice of sending along a set of drums (gratis, of course). "I don't play the drums, but I could learn," Beem said of the offer.

Part of the reason Beem had agreed to play in the "Fairway" was so Wyatt's teenage daughter, Cady, could meet all of her favorite musicians. Wyatt had gained custody in late summer of 1998, and when Cady landed in Seattle it had been more than a year since she had last seen her father. One of the few things they had in common was a music jones. "Going to concerts became a place where we could come together," says David. "It was a safe bond." They rocked out at shows by Pearl Jam, Matchbox 20, Live, Lenny Kravitz, Buckcherry, and The Wallflowers, among others, though Cady broke her dad's heart when she showed no interest in going to see Prince. Over time Beem has become a surrogate uncle to Cady, and he says, "That was a cool deal, getting to show her around and introduce her to people. A year earlier I would have gone to something like that as a fan. To be part of the show was awesome. Despite what a crazy year it had been, I never lost touch with how lucky I was to have those kinds of opportunities."

What made "Heaven" so hellish, however, was that Beem was forced to travel to Orlando Monday night on the redeye, the first one he had ever taken domestically. Somewhere over the Gulf of Mexico he decided that the madness had to stop, and he resolved not to enter the season-ending Southern Farm Bureau Classic, which he had planned to play in two weeks. The Disney, then, was to be the final PGA Tour event of this most eventful rookie year.

DUPLANTIS, TOO, was consigned to a redeye out of Las Vegas, his on Sunday night, and the ride was no more enjoyable. Earlier in the day his old boss Jim Furyk had birdied the 14th, 15th, and

16th holes at TPC of Summerlin to eke out a one-stroke victory, earning his first W with Fluff Cowan on the bag, as well as a cool $450,000. From the Las Vegas airport Duplantis called Furyk's cell phone to offer congratulations, though he had to deliver the message via voice mail.

After the round Duplantis was on Furyk's mind, too, though he was never mentioned by name. In his champion's press conference he sang his caddie's praises in a telling way. (Furyk is so square he's the only person in golf who doesn't call Fluff Fluff.) "The reason Mike and I have a good partnership is because he's a hard worker," Furyk said. "People may think of him as a celebrity but he doesn't act that way. He's very professional in his approach to caddying." For their five days of work in Las Vegas, Fluff eared a commission of $45,000, while Duplantis took home $385. Of missing out on the bonanza that comes with Furyk's bag, Duplantis says, "I wouldn't say it eats me up, but yeah, I think about it. How could you not?"

Duplantis had plenty of time to stew during his odyssey home, as he was not flying directly into Tampa but rather by way of New York City, so he could pick up his daughter. From JFK airport he rented a car and drove to Sollange Lewis's apartment in the Bronx (none of the companies offered an hourly rate, so he had to eat a $70 day rate for the hour and a half roundtrip). Sierra and her dad finally arrived in Tampa late Monday afternoon, a wearying eighteen hours after he had left Las Vegas. Sierra was thrilled to be home, and not just for the obvious reasons. Players and caddies and their families have unlimited access to the Magic Kingdom during the week of the Disney Classic. "It's a major championship for her," says Duplantis. To help Sierra make all the rounds at Disney World, her great-grandmother, Dorothy Bilton, flew in from Canada. Bilton arrived a couple of days early, in order to give the Duplantis household the cleaning she knew it would desperately need. Sure enough, "It looked like a hurricane blew through the living room," she reports.

Duplantis lives in a sprawling development known as Walden Woods. Henry David Thoreau went to Walden to strip himself of material excess, and Duplantis seems to have followed suit. There is no furniture in the entry way or dining room or third bedroom. The walls in the house are naked, except for those in Sierra's room, where she has built a shrine to the Backstreet Boys. In the front rooms the windows are covered not by curtains but an assortment of sheets, hung perilously with packing tape. "My wife put those up," Duplantis says, with a dismissive wave of his hand. "She thought the neighbors were spying on her." Of course, that was three months ago, during their brief reconciliation. No word on why the sheets are still there. As for the lack of furniture, Duplantis says, "There used to be more in here but when Vicki found out Shannon [Pennington] had picked it all out, it wound up either in the pool or in the garage." Other evidence of Vicki scattered around the house includes a pair of 5-inch stilettos on the floor of the closet in the master bedroom.

Though the walls are bare, Duplantis has a ton of memorabilia sitting around his house. Leaning against a wall in the living room, mounted and framed under glass, is a caddie bib signed by all of the participants from the 1997 Ryder Cup. There is another scribbled-upon bib from the 1998 Sun City Million Dollar Challenge in South Africa. Also mounted and framed are the 18th hole flags from the '95 Kapalua Invitational, '96 Hawaiian Open, and the Abierto de Argentina. The flag from the final green is the traditional keepsake for a victorious caddie. "I got the Kemper around here somewhere," Duplantis says. "I gotta get it framed one of these days." Scattered throughout the house are golf clubs. Lots of them. Duplantis estimates he has six sets of irons, and some thirty loose woods. "Jim's equipment contract was up at the end of last year," he says. "A lot of manufacturer's reps were trying to cozy up to me. I got nothing against free gear."

On the floor of the guest bedroom, stashed in a corner, is a mounted scorecard dated 12/17/96, when on a cold, windy day at the renowned Stadium Course at TPC Sawgrass, site of the PGA Tour's flagship event, The Players Championship, Duplantis beat Furyk straight up, 75-77. The winning margin came when Furyk dunked a ball at the island green of par-3 17th and took a double bogey. "Jim was so pissed, but I didn't give a shit, I made him sign the scorecard," says Duplantis. There is also a framed article from the *Globe & Mail,* a long write-up about Duplantis from the 1998 U.S. Open. On the mantel above the fireplace are a few token souvenirs from Duplantis's travels—exotic wood carvings from South Africa and New Zealand, an intricately painted boomerang from Australia, and an unopened bottle of red wine. Stamped across the label: PROVEDOR OFICIAL DE LA RYDER CUP. In the middle of the mantel sits a grainy framed photo. It is of a twelve-year-old Duplantis, at his first pro tournament, the 1985 Canadian Open, posing with his new best friend, Clarence Rose. Picking up the photo to inspect it, Duplantis says wearily, "That was a long, long time ago."

LATER THAT NIGHT—much later—Duplantis wheels his Jeep Cherokee into the parking lot of the Doll House, one of Tampa's many strip joints. "I hope not too many of the girls I know are dancing tonight," he says. "That might be a little embarrassing."

Stepping into the Doll House is like falling through the rabbit hole, only this Wonderland seems to have been dreamed up by a panel of frat boys in the middle of an ESPN bender. A grid of TVs comprises an entire wall, allowing for a migraine-inducing number of sporting events to be shown simultaneously, aided by a powerful satellite system. When not disrobing on stage, the dancers parade around in skintight Tampa Bay Buccaneers jerseys, which seems as much a turn-on as their surgically enhanced figures. Duplantis settles into a chair in his favorite corner and then begins a running dialogue on the biographies of the assembled talent.

"Check out the rack on that waitress. Her boyfriend won't let her strip so she just serves drinks. What a shame."

"That girl over there, in the black G-string? She just upgraded. Very nice."

"See that girl there? [A prominent member of the Buccaneers] is like stalking her."

"You see the blonde in the corner, with the jugs, she . . ."

At some point all of the dancers are called up to the stage to display their wares in a single file line, what is apparently a Doll House ritual. This portion of the programming is set to the unofficial anthem of strip clubs everywhere, Motley Crue's "Girls Girls Girls." With the music cranked to eardrum-shattering levels, Duplantis whips out his phone and dials his buddy Chris Hanrattie back in Texas. Getting an answering machine, he holds the phone in front of him for a minute or more, recording the scene for Hanrattie. "Don't worry, he'll know what it means," Duplantis says.

Throughout his stay at the Doll House Duplantis seems particularly preoccupied with one dancer, a woman with kinky blonde hair and a rhinestone-flecked G-string. Though she aggressively cruises virtually every customer in the building, trying to entice the men into purchasing a private lap dance, Duplantis is pointedly ignored. The second he reaches his Jeep, Duplantis calls Hanrattie again, and this time he picks up. Duplantis apparently has some history with the woman and is fuming from the slight. "Guess who was there?" Duplantis says. "Yep. She fucking gave me the cold shoulder the whole night. What a fucking joke. What is the deal with strippers, anyway? Why are they all fucked in the head?"

The conversation comes to an abrupt close when Duplantis arrives at the next stop on his itinerary, the Mons Venus, an establishment that is famous within a narrow slice of the population. "When I tell people, I'm from Tampa, it never fails, someone brings up Mons Venus," says Duplantis. "It happens all over the country, all over the world. It's crazy. It's happens to me in Japan, in Australia, you name it." The Mons is a tiny, circular place, the interior a garish purple, owing to an excess of neon lighting. The aroma is that of a locker room an hour after the big game. It is obviously not the ambience that has drawn tonight's SRO crowd. What makes the Mons such a horndog mecca is what the dancers discreetly call "full contact lap dances." For $20 a patron can purchase a lap dance where biting is the only prohibited activity. This is contrary to the general strip joint ethos, whereby if you lay so much as a finger on a dancer, said finger, along with various other appendages, are liable to be broken by a gorilla in an ill-fitting tuxedo. Groping is so encouraged at Mons Venus a couple of dancers walk around with antibacterial hand wash.

On this night, however, there is as much action outside the Mons as within. It seems democracy is alive and well in central Florida, thanks to some proposed local legislation that would ban lap dancing. Near the front door a buxom libertarian is taking signatures for a petition that begins, "As an American I believe in the First Amendment and the right of self-expression . . ." Surely this is what the Framers had in mind. On the way out Duplantis signs the petition, unable to resist the remuneration, a calendar featuring naked Mons employees in a series of gymnastic positions. Flipping through the calendar, he mumbles, "Tastefully done, just as you'd expect."

On the marquee in front of Mons Venus, in large, bold lettering, it reads:

ASSHOLE OF THE WEEK:
COUNCIL MEMBER BOB BUCKHORN.

Buckhorn is one of the elected officials spearheading the proposed ban on lap dancing. Reached in his office, Buckhorn says with a chuckle, "That sign just proves my place in heaven is secured." He goes on to say, "Tampa has become the Las Vegas of lap dancing. It's not a reflection of our values or what we're all about as a community. I would really question what kind of a person needs this sort of quote-unquote entertainment. My guess is something is lacking in their own family life, their own relationships. Personally I think it's sad and I feel sorry for the type of man who feels the only way he can interact with women is in this manner."

THE NEXT MORNING, Tuesday, a bleary-eyed Beem arrives from Las Vegas and Duplantis turns up at the Tampa airport to meet him. Beem is quite a sight. There is a gash on his forehead the size of a silver dollar. It is raw and red and leaking so much pus that Beem is occasionally compelled to pat it dry. A wound of a similar size adorns his knee and a large cut on the bridge of his nose is so deep the skin is hanging off in folds. "In case you're wondering, I did it water skiing," Beem says, even though no one had been wondering, at least out loud. Says Duplantis, "I just assumed you got into a bar fight." In fact, Beem sustained the injuries over the weekend in Las Vegas on an excursion to Lake Mead. "I'd never been water skiing before," he says. "It looked like fun." It is, until you eat it at thirty miles an hour. Pressed for details, Beem says, with a certain exasperation, "What's there to tell? I wiped out, the ski smacked me in the head, it looks like shit, it hurts like shit, and I'm not gonna water ski for a while."

The Disney is held on two courses, neither of which Beem has ever laid eyes on, but instead of playing a practice round he goes straight to Duplantis's to catch a few winks. Because Duplantis is still waiting on a friend to bring over a spare mattress for the guest bedroom, Beem is forced to sleep on the floor on three borrowed sofa cushions, laid end to end. By the time he rousts himself it is too late to fight the traffic and the crush of humanity around Disney World, so Beem decides to play a round with Duplantis at one of the two courses within Walden Lakes.

This is Duplantis's home turf and he's fired up for the match. On the first tee it is he who engages in talk of a wager. Beem can't resist a little needling, and he even consents to Duplantis's request for two shots a side, but clearly he's not in a state to play his best golf. "I'm done," he says. "I'm just exhausted, wiped out. I'm living for December 6. That's when the year is officially over. All I'm doing that day is sleeping in and watching *Monday Night Football*. I don't know who's playing, and I don't care." As for his decision not to play in the Farm Bureau Classic, he says, "There is nothing left to play for. No way I could make Masters. No way I could finish in the Top Thirty on the money list. Sure, I could go down there and win and end the season with a bang, but realistically that's not gonna happen. I just want to go home, to feel like I have a life again. I want to put my condo together, see my friends and family, and just relax."

Beem starts his round at Walden Lakes like a man with other things on his mind. He's five over par after five holes, including a drive out of bounds on number 2 and a series of blown short putts on the grainy Bermuda greens. "I'll be lucky to break eighty this week," he moans at one point. After another missed putt he says of the Bermuda grass, "I don't know how you guys play on this shit. I'm never coming to this fucking state again." At the 7th hole Beem three-putts from twelve feet, including a lackadaisical effort on a three-and-a-half-footer for par that touches off a *Rashomon*-like dispute about whether the putt had been conceded prior to Beem's miss.

This brings the action to the 8th hole, a long par-3 over a

lake to a shallow green surrounded by gaping bunkers. Now fired up by the controversy, Beem snorts, "I'll bet you two hundred dollars I hit the green." Duplantis is wise to pass on the wager, as Beem proceeds to cover the flag, stopping his ball twelve feet back of the hole.

Duplantis, who to this point has been playing brilliantly, steps up and uncorks a big hook long and right of green, which seems to have been swallowed up by the surrounding jungle. This looks like the hole on which the match will turn. Duplantis, with his caddie's intuition, somehow manages to find his ball, and he then gouges out a very credible chip shot, running his ball twenty feet past the hole on the sloping green. Beem, once again misreading the grain, blasts his putt four feet by, and while marking his ball he launches into a monologue prompted by the dispute on the previous green. "Okay, I'll actually try on this one, Steve," he says. "Obviously there's no way I was trying on the last one. Shit, I'm a PGA Tour winner," he says, his voice rising in mock indignation. "You think I can't make a four-footer?" Duplantis, ignoring the soliloquy, steps up and rams his long, curling par putt into the hole. Beem picks the ball out of the cup and graciously throws it into the lake. With a smirk he addresses his putt and then, shockingly, never even scares the hole, taking a bogey to lose yet another hole. "Nice fucking green," Beem says, slinking toward the next tee. "Why don't you grow some grass on this thing, Stevie. I thought they abandoned sand greens."

Duplantis continues to pour it on, including a stout birdie at the 12th hole. Though no one claims to know the exact status of the match, Beem is clearly getting buried, which explains why he presses on the 13th tee and why, at this point, all hints of sportsmanship go out the window. As soon as Duplantis strikes his tee shot on the long, doglegged par-4—a drive that is drawing gently toward a fairway bunker—Beem shouts, "Get in the bunker, you whore!"

"Run through it, baby," says Duplantis plaintively.

"Plug."

"Skip."

"Plug."

"Get out of there."

Thoroughly confused, the ball actually does run through the bunker but it plugs in the long grass on the lip, leaving Duplantis a very awkward shot.

"That's even better," Beem chortles. "Great shot, Steve."

And so it goes, until the climactic 18th hole. Emboldened by a birdie at 17—his first of the day—Beem arrives at the final tee and announces, "I'm pressing the world. Every bet." He then pipes a drive right down the middle. So Duplantis steps to the tee, with the heat having now been turned up a couple notches. To this point he is only two over par and has hardly missed a fairway, playing, for the most part, a lovely power fade. The 18th hole at Walden Lakes is a long par-4, dogleg right, with townhouses running the length of the right side. They are, of course, out of bounds. To avoid the trouble all Duplantis has to do is play his dependable left-handed fade, and even if he loses the ball left there is nothing but wide-open real estate out there. So naturally he jerks a shocking hook straight O.B.

"Oh, that's just a shame," says Beem.

In one more turn of the knife, Beem sticks his approach to two feet and taps in for a birdie. With a triple bogey at the last Duplantis shoots a 77, but he doesn't collect a dime. Later he estimates that, with all the presses and side wagers, there had been sixteen bets riding on the 18th hole. Aside from the money, though, did he beat Beem straight up in score? "I didn't go through and add it up," he says. "I'm pretty sure I took him, but it wouldn't have been good for Rich to know that, you know what I mean?"

BEEM'S PREDICTION turned out to be all wrong—he did break 80 at the Disney, though not by much. He shot a lifeless 72–75 to miss the cut by a mile, the fifteenth time in twenty-four tournaments he failed to make it to the weekend. It was not a glorious way to end his rookie year on the PGA Tour, but perhaps it was fitting. "I honestly didn't hit the ball that bad," he says. "I putted pretty good, too. It's just that my focus wasn't there. At all."

CHAPTER

• 18 •

NEITHER RICH BEEM nor Steve Duplantis made the trip to the season-ending Southern Farm Bureau Classic, played the final week of October, but both were affected by the events of the tournament. The Farm Bureau (once upon a time known as the Magnolia State Classic, then the Deposit Guaranty Golf Classic) is another of the tournaments run for the Tour's also-rans, in this case those who failed to make the Top 30 on the money list and were thus excluded from the $5 million Tour Championship, which was being played simultaneously. Despite the indignity of the name, the Southern Farm Bureau Classic was for many players the most important tournament of the season, offering $2 million in prize money, and, more to the point, one last chance at salvation. Paul Stankowski was one of the many who limped into Madison, Mississippi, with his job on the line. Stankowski was a distant 140th on the money list. He needed a Top 5 finish to have a chance at cracking the Top 125. Failing that, he was heading to Q School, and as bad as Stankowski had played down the stretch, making it through six brutal rounds at the Qualifying Tournament was no sure thing. A two-time Tour winner, he thus was staring down the gun barrel of the Buy.com Tour.

So all Stankowski did at the Farm Bureau was turn in one of the gutsiest performances of the year by any Tour player, shooting 10 under par to tie for third place, earning $104,000. The loot shot him all the way to 113th on the final money list, with $362,889, securing his playing privileges for 2000. Rich Mayo was by his side throughout, and he was so dazzled by this exhibition of clutch golf he decided he simply couldn't walk away from Stankowski, not after all they had been through together. He pledged to caddie for his old UTEP teammate in 2000 and beyond.

Brian Gay also played at the Farm Bureau, though he didn't pull off any such miracles. Gay actually withdrew midway through the second round, finishing the year with $74,329, which doomed him to 206th on the money list. "I was five, six over par and gonna miss the cut anyway," he says. "With the Second Stage of Q School the next week, I decided to spare myself the mental beating." Gay had originally wanted Duplantis to caddie for him at the Farm Bureau, as well as the Q School's Second Stage. Not knowing that Beem had pulled out of the tournament, and that Duplantis was thus available, he instead asked Hanrattie to come down to Madison. Despite the poor scores, "We had a good tournament," says Gay. "We got along real well. Chris was new to it, he was really enthusiastic the whole time. With Steve, the better I play the more he gets into it. That's not necessarily the best thing in the world." Gay wound up asking Hanrattie to go to Q School with him. After calling Duplantis to make sure it was cool, Hanrattie accepted.

"I thought it would be a good experience for Chris," says Duplantis. "I wasn't that thrilled about spending a week grinding it out at Q School anyway."

Gay sailed through the Second Stage and, not wanting to change his luck, he asked Hanrattie to accompany him to the Final Stage two weeks later, at the Doral Golf Resort in Miami, even though Duplantis knew the course far better from his multiple trips to the Doral-Ryder Open. At the Final Stage of Q School Gay played the best golf of his life, shooting 68-68-68-67-66-68 to finish tenth and earn his card for 2000, to say nothing of $25,000, the largest check of his career. Not surprisingly, Gay asked Hanrattie to be his full-time caddie for the upcoming season, and he accepted.

Duplantis says he wouldn't have committed to a full year with Gay anyhow, but the fact is, he was never given the option. The new season was less than two months away. Beem didn't have a caddie and Duplantis didn't have a bag.

•

BEEM SPENT the first half of November in Scottsdale, tooling around with the top down in his new BMW and trying to fill up his condo. One of his first purchases was a gorgeous new pool table. As if there were any doubt his new pad would become a shrine to bachelorhood, Beem was also on the verge of putting in a state-of-the-art home theater. In a delicious twist of fate, he was in negotiations to sign an endorsement contract with his old Seattle employer, Magnolia Hi-Fi. In exchange for two years of wearing a logo on his sleeve, and lending his likeness to various forms of advertising, Beem's compensation was to be a hi-tech setup that would turn George Jetson green with envy: a (very) big-screen TV, surround-sound receiver, five speakers, a subwoofer, and a DVD/CD player. "It probably doesn't even make sense for us, since we're a regional store and not national," says Jim Tweten, the Magnolia owner. "But we're doing it just to do it, because it should be a lot of fun. Our relationship with Rich transcends money at this point."

Not completely. There was some disagreement about how high-tech the equipment should be. Tweten was offering a setup valued at around $20,000. Beem wanted a top-of-the-line system worth twice as much. Representing Beem in the negotiations was David Wyatt; their lives were becoming so incestuous Beem's sister Tina had taken to calling them "an old married couple."

"Yeah, and David's the naggy housewife," adds Beem's other sister, Susie.

Wyatt was also working on setting up a website devoted to Beem and his career. ("There are going to be embedded links to all kinds of pornography," he promises.) Wyatt's ever expanding role in his best friend's affairs was reflective of Beem's disenchantment with his agents at Intrepid Sports. His contract with Structure having expired at season's end, he didn't have a clothing deal lined up for 2000, a highly unusual situation for a Tour winner and a source of great irritation, and lost income, to Beem. (Shortly after the turn of the year, Beem would leave Intrepid and sign with Gaylord Sports.)

At least his new club deal was finally completed in early November. He signed on with industry behemoth Callaway through 2002, a three-year deal worth six figures annually. As a bit of a bonus, Callaway gave Beem backpay worth $55,000, since he had shown good faith by wearing their logos as far back as September. The new pact called for Beem to use Callaway clubs as well as don its logo on his shirt and hat, while using a putter and golf bag by Odyssey, which is a division of Callaway. (Beem also reupped his ball, shoe, and glove deal with Titleist, at substantially more than his rookie salary of $15,000.) Within weeks of his new deal, Beem began showing up in Odyssey ads sprinkled throughout the various golf magazines. "It's weird, I will say that," says Beem. "I played basically the same equipment years ago, for free. Now they're paying me, and paying me well, just to keep using it. Sometimes I have to pinch myself."

Beem's windfall led to a certain amount of bemusement. Cameron Doan summed up the prevailing attitude in El Paso when he said, "Rich Beem with three hundred dollars in his pocket is dangerous. Can you imagine him with half a million?" This kind of talk irked Beem to no end. "I hear that shit through the grapevine," Beem says, with some heat, "and it's such a misconception. I've busted my ass for three and a half years to get here. Why am I not allowed to enjoy the success a little bit?"

John Butterworth, Beem's accountant, has apparently been rehearsing the answer to that very question. "He can very easily get in over his head," says Butterworth. "It's like the guy who goes to Vegas and wins ten grand in one pull of the slot machine. The idea is to walk out of the casino with some of it left.

"In my position I see young people in financial distress all the time. I'm constantly dealing with kids in their twenties who came into money—through family, insurance settlements, the lottery, whatever—and they have pissed it away and have absolutely nothing to show for it. Rich is heading down that path. He thinks he's a wealthy man. He's not. He's always talking about buying a Porsche, buying a boat, owning a bar. Why? Why does he need a BMW? A condo? I think a lot of it is peer pressure. I think he's hearing from other players, *Why on earth would you live in El Paso? In an apartment?* He's trying to live like one of the big boys now, but he's not there yet. He better be careful because the vultures are circling."

Some of the financial pressure on Beem is coming not from scheming strangers but rather his own family. Ask Larry Beem what his unmarried daughters—who between them have five kids but no college degrees—do for a living, and he comes up with one word: *struggle.* "Hopefully," says Larry, "Rich will recognize his role. His finances can go a long way toward helping those girls, and they need help, to say the very least. In many ways I'm more proud of them than Rich, just for hanging on."

"The other day Rich asked me what I owed on everything," says Tina Beem. "He wanted the full list. He said he wanted to get me and Susie out of debt and up on our feet again."

In his rookie year Beem won $610,555, good for sixty-seventh on the money list, and a nomination for Rookie of the Year. He had no chance of winning; in a banner year for freshmen, three others finished ahead of Beem on the money list: thirty-four-year-old globetrotting Paraguayan Carlos Franco (eleventh), lefty Canuck Mike Weir (twenty-third), and only the second Native American to win on tour, Notah Begay III (thirty-first). Beem brought in just over $300,000 in additional endorsements, bonuses, appearance fees, and pro-am earnings. "Totally, utterly, completely one hundred percent mind-boggling," he says of his near million-dollar year, but the riches did not come without a price. In mid-November, just as he was beginning to recover from the wear and tear of the season, Beem had to pack up for a pair of meaningless tournaments in Mexico, one in Guadalajara, the other on the outskirts of Mexico City. Beem had committed to play in the events months earlier, unable to turn down a combined $40,000 in appearance fees. He finished in the middle of the pack at both events, not that it matters.

Beem did get some practical value out of the trip, however. He used it as a two-week audition for a potential new caddie, his old college buddy, R. C. Ordish, who had grown tired of the club pro grind in Carson City, Nevada. It goes without saying that Ordish had zero experience as a Tour caddie. "Rich will never commit to having a real pro on his bag, an old hardass that knows the course, knows the Tour, and won't let him get out of line," says Larry Beem. "He keeps looking for a friend in his caddie. His caddie has to be a social companion first, caddie second. Without an accomplice, Rich is lost."

"It's true, I don't want some boring old guy that I would never hang out with," says Rich. "You travel the world with your caddie—it's one of the most important relationships you have." With that in mind, Beem was satisfied enough with Ordish's performance south of the border to offer him the job for the upcoming season. Ordish, at the time living with his parents and not doing much of anything, jumped at the opportunity. The Mexican tournaments took Beem through Thanksgiving. There was now but one tournament left in his year, the JCPenney Classic, an unofficial event played in the first week of December. The Classic was being played in Palm Harbor, Florida, driving distance from Duplantis's house, and they had long since agreed to work together. It was to be their swan song.

DUPLANTIS PASSED THE TIME in November mostly by playing golf and taking in Tampa Bay Lightning hockey games. Both were activities he could share with his daughter. Sierra has always enjoyed running around the wide-open space of a golf course and, especially riding in golf carts. She is also captivated by the sound and fury of the NHL, no doubt picking up on her dad's enthusiasm. Duplantis has been a puckhead almost since birth. He played a credible left wing throughout junior hockey, and growing up his big Christmas present every year was a pair of "golds," the best seats in the house at Maple Leaf Gardens in Toronto. When the Gardens was closed down in favor of a spiffy new facility in February '99, Duplantis was riveted to the telecast of the farewell ceremonies. "No joke, I got a little misty-eyed," he says.

Duplantis's current professional situation was enough to drive him to tears, too. Not long after his firing at the Buick Challenge, Duplantis rang up Clarence Rose, his first boss. Rose was coming off a miserable season during which he had made only four of twenty-two cuts, and earned $36,451, to finish 234th on the money list. Nevertheless, Duplantis asked about caddying for him in the upcoming season. "I told him I'd have to think about it," says Rose. "We've got a serious generation gap." If Duplantis was frustrated with Gay's middling play, why would he want to latch on with Rose, who at forty-three was clearly on the downside of his career? "We talked about that," says Rose. "Steve had a rough, rough time of it this year. He had as wild a year as a caddie could have, I reckon. He said he just wanted to get back to having fun again, just get back to caddying without all the other stuff." Rose, however, turned out not to be a viable option. Burned out from two decades as a touring pro, he decided to take the year off, not even bothering to send in a Q School application. Rose plans to spend the upcoming year in his beloved North Carolina, moving his family into a new house, taking in his kids' basketball and soccer games and school plays, and putting on his own pro-am to raise money for junior golf in Wayne County. With more than $2 million in career earnings, he may play in a dozen tournaments, using sponsors' exemptions or his status as a past champion to sneak into the field. He may not play in any.

Rose, at least, was a friend and a mentor. Taking on an unfamiliar journeyman—which was shaping up as one of Duplantis's few remaining options—was an unappetizing prospect. "I was spoiled, I admit it," he says. "Life was too good with Jim. It wasn't until it was over that I really realized what an incredible run we had and how fortunate I was to be a part of it." Duplantis gets a reminder every time he walks out the front door. In the driveway of his expansive house, in the middle of a gated community, next to a gleaming Grand Cherokee, is the beat-up old Chevy Cavalier he used to crisscross the country when he was just starting out as a caddie.

"Something will come up," Duplantis says. "I'm just waiting it out for now. I've got enough money in the bank to buy me some time. Believe me, nobody knows as well as I do that caddie changes are inevitable."

"Steve is at a crossroads," Duplantis's mother, Sandy Chantin, said the week before Thanksgiving. "He needs to make a lot of life decisions, and none of them are fun. Does he need to be stationary? Does he still need that big house of his? Is there another line of work he should pursue? I know how much Steve loves caddying, but I want him to understand how many options there are available to him and I plan on discussing it with him when I go down there for the holiday. He could rep a line of golf equipment—the guy's a born salesman. He could become a golf writer—he was always a good writer in school and he could certainly offer a unique perspective on things. He's really at loose ends about what his future is gonna be. He's feeling a little out of control about his own destiny."

In 1998, when Furyk was third on the money list with $2,054,334, Duplantis earned upward of $150,000. In '99, despite making some $27,000 in the season's first three months with Furyk, Duplantis barely cleared half of his previous year's salary. Even so, Duplantis, with only a high school degree, would be hard pressed to make that kind of money in another line of work. He is dismissive of trying. "I can't just quit caddying and go back to school," he says. "I've got a little girl to take care of. She needs somewhere to live. That means a mortgage. She needs to be driven around. That means car payments. Those are just the big expenses—you got clothes, food, entertainment, and on and on and on. It's hard for me to think about anything besides caddying. That's the only job I've ever known."

By the fall of 2000 Sierra will be a little more than four and a half years old. Duplantis won't be able to put off her schooling any longer. With Sierra anchored to one place geographically, his future will only become more complicated. "He's got another year and then he's got to make a decision," says Cantin. "It's definitely on everyone's mind." Including Duplantis's.

"Of course I'd like to have my family back together," he says. "I don't want my daughter to live like this, where she's dragged around the world and never knows what's coming from week to week. But I can't just go out and buy a mom. I tried that once with Shannon [Pennington], and it didn't work. In a perfect world I'd meet the girl of my dreams, we'd be married in six months, she'd take care of Sierra, I'd get a top bag, and everything would be great. That's not reality, unfortunately."

Duplantis's decision making was further clouded by the life changes of Sierra's surrogate mother, Sollange Lewis. In the new year she was planning to begin working toward a degree in forensic psychology in hopes of landing her dream job at the FBI, à la Clarice Starling. Lewis was also pursuing a singing career, and had already caught her first break, doing backup vocals on *Recollection*, an album by underground reggae star Half Pint, which came out in December 1999. "I care so much for Steve and

Sierra, but I have to do my own thing," says Lewis. "Steve has asked me to move to Florida, but my life is here. It's really a heartbreaking situation." With Lewis no longer available to take on Sierra for months at a time, the question of how Duplantis will care for his daughter, if and when he begins to travel the Tour again, looms large.

"He can't just bring Sierra to Canada to stay with all of us, even though we'd love to provide a home base for her," says Cantin. "Legally, that's a problem, because of the custody situation."

"I don't think Steve would ever just dump Sierra off," says Pennington, who in the fall of '99 went back to school to get a teaching credential, in hopes of one day having her own classroom of elementary schoolkids. "He's fought too hard to get her. Say what you want about Steve, but he does love his daughter very much. Almost too much. Most guys would just leave her with her mother and that would be the end of it. But Steve won't let go."

"You've seen my little girl—she's an angel," Duplantis says. "How anyone could walk out on her is unfathomable. It's happened once, but it won't ever happen again."

Obviously Duplantis's wife—or ex-wife; he calls her both from conversation to conversation—is still on his mind. Robert Tropp, Steve's lawyer, says, "I've been practicing family law for longer than I care to remember. There is one thing I've learned through the years: just because you are legally separated, or divorced, doesn't mean your lives are not still intertwined. Once you make a baby with somebody, that is a bond that will keep you together forever, whether you like it or not." This Duplantis was finding out the hard way.

"Vicki still calls when she's in the mood," he says, "and then she just lays it on Sierra: 'You know Mommy loves you and wants to be with you but Daddy took you away and won't let Mommy see you.' And Sierra believes it. I have to sit there and talk to Sierra like she's an adult. She'll say, 'Daddy, why are you mean to Mommy?' And I'll say, 'I'm not mean to Mommy, I just don't like that Mommy left.' We just go around and around on this."

Here Duplantis's voice rises. "It's un-fucking-believable," he says. "I have to have this conversation with my daughter every time Vicki calls. It's just sick."

Duplantis pauses to catch his breath. "My life is a soap opera," Duplantis says. "Just that I haven't jumped off a bridge yet speaks volumes."

BEEM SPENT MUCH of the so-called off-season reflecting on the lessons of his rookie year. "What did I learn?" he asks. "What didn't I learn? I learned as much about life as golf. I learned about heartache, about great emotional highs and lows. I learned I need to slow things down, not try to be everything to everyone. I learned I can be a pretty good player, but that I still have a long way to go. It was by far the longest year of my life, the hardest, and by far the best."

There were plenty of on-course positives to dwell on. "I'm a better player now than ever, for sure," Beem says, "even if it hasn't always shown up in my scores. I'm driving straighter, hitting irons more consistently, putting better, thinking better." His toughest critic also sees dramatic improvement. "Rich used to be short, crooked, a suspect putter, and he couldn't hit a wedge," says Larry Beem. "Now he's long, straight, and a good putter. He still can't hit a wedge for shit, but three out of four isn't bad."

In a season of inconsistency there were two obvious highlights—victory at the Kemper Open and the near miss at the Texas Open. "There are two kinds of players on tour," says J. P. Hayes. "Those who have won and those who haven't. For Rich to win as a rookie is a heck of an accomplishment. Most guys come out here their first year wondering if they belong. They're not even thinking about winning. It's something that gnaws at you until you do win and the pressure and the doubts just keep growing as the years go on. Then to almost win again, like he did in San Antonio, that was big, too. It shows he's not afraid to keep throwing himself in those situations."

Says Beem, "At the start of the year, it was like, 'Gosh, I hope I'll be able to keep my card.' That was the goal. Win a golf tournament? Never in a million years. If you would have offered me a season where I made every cut, had a handful of Top Tens, and made the exact same amount of money, I would take my year every time. To win, and win the way I did, it was the thrill of a lifetime."

Despite a few minor high jinks, Beem managed to stay grounded even after his heady victory, and the importance of this can't be understated. In July, less than two months after the Kemper, he went back to his old stomping grounds, Westward Ho Country Club, honoring a previous commitment to play in a charity outing. According to Ted Thie, the uncle of his ex-fiancée and the club's general manager, Beem's presence raised an additional $6,000 for a group of local foster homes, a third of that coming in one swing, when he earned a bonus for the charities by acing one of the par-3s. After the round Beem and Thie got to talking. Back when Beem had been a lowly shop hand playing the Dakotas Tour, he would occasionally crash in the home of a gent named Duane Harmes. At one point during the conversation, Beem asked Thie, apropos of nothing, "So how's Duane?" Says Thie, "I told him, 'That's what's special about you, Rich. You'll never forget who you are or where you came from.' "

Adds El Paso Country Club's Bill Eschenbrenner, "Rich was behind the counter, okay? Once you've handled Ladies Day and Seniors Day and had to clean the deer shit off Mr. Smith's golf shoes it humbles you. Forever."

That Beem managed to keep his perspective is admirable, considering how dramatically everything around him was changing. A handy example comes by way of Cameron Doan, who gave Beem his job at EPCC, and who became an important mentor and inspiration. By the early fall it was Doan who had Beem to thank for the marked improvement in his own career. On November 1, Doan reported for work at Preston Trail Golf Club in Dallas, where he was the new head golf professional, as good a job as any young club pro could ever dream of landing. Preston Trail is golf's Mt. Olympus, where the gods play—Arnold Palmer, Byron Nelson, Tom Watson, Lee Trevino, and Lanny Wadkins are all part of the membership. The place is golf, no chaser. There's no tennis courts at Preston Trail, no pool, no women's tees, no women members. Preston Trail is so hypermasculine they ought to dispense Viagra next to the witch hazel in the locker room. Throughout the interview process, "There's no question my association with Rich helped," says Doan. "It brought a credibility, to have taught a Tour winner."

Of course, the geographic separation between student and teacher was one of the many issues facing Beem as he settled into his comfortable new life in Scottsdale. "I'll still see Cameron and we'll still talk regularly," Beem says. "Cameron has been using videotape as a teaching tool for years, and that's an option, too, for me to send images of my swing to him to look at. Plus, Esch has a place out here in the Phoenix area and he can also keep an eye on me."

Duplantis, for one, doesn't think this is enough. "What Rich really needs is an experienced, respected teacher who can very simply explain his golf swing to him, because he has no fucking clue," he says. "It's okay to call yourself a feel player, but that doesn't excuse you from having a basic understanding of your swing. As it is now he knows so little about himself that when his swing breaks down, he can't fix it. Then he's screwed."

Larry Beem has other, somewhat related concerns. "Rich needs someone on his ass all the time, because he doesn't know how to practice," he says. "He thinks the driving range is a social gathering. I'll never get over the last practice session we had. He hits a ball, looks down the range to the left, looks down the range to the right, looks down to the left again, looks down to the right, says something to his caddie, says something to me, looks around some more, then maybe hits another ball. Christ, who or what is he looking for? That's what I don't understand. In forty-five minutes he hit maybe thirty shots. That's not gonna get it done."

Rich Beem is nonplussed by the discussion. "There were a lot of things that cut into my practice time last year, cut into my focus," he says. "Most of those distractions are over and done with. Plus, I'll be in the Wednesday pro-am next year [by virtue of his finish on the money list], so that will only make it easier to prepare for the tournaments."

Nevertheless, Beem will have to adjust to not being around El Paso Country Club, where the bustling money games and personal rivalries always sustained his interest. "I've noticed a difference since I left," Beem says. "Being here in Scottsdale it's been hard to find a foursome." It will be that way at least until he is made by the Scottsdale golf mafia, whose members include

Phil Mickelson, Tom Lehman, Billy Mayfair, Gary McCord, Lumpy Herron, Andrew Magee, Kirk Triplett, and Tom Purtzer. If Beem can get in with that crowd, he'll have plenty of outstanding playing partners and access to the best private clubs. For now he's on his own at TPC of Scottsdale. There is a special section of driving range—the so-called West End—reserved just for touring pros, with balata balls and a series of practice bunkers and greens. But if Beem wants to play the course, he has to get in line with the other two or three hundred players who flock daily to this high-profile public facility. "It's terrible," Beem says. "It's a five-hour round, if you're lucky. Last time R.C. and I went out we quit after seven holes. Too slow."

Then again, maybe what Beem needs is less golf, not more. "The last few years I played every chance I got because I couldn't wait to get the hell out of the golf shop," he says. "Now that I have unlimited time and access it's different. I have to run away from golf because it's always there, and when I do play I have to make sure my focus is there. It's finding that balance that is so difficult and I'm still working on it."

To be sure, Beem is not content with his up-and-down play, or so he says. "I want to be a Top-Ten player, a guy like Justin Leonard, who contends consistently. I want to be there every week." There is no doubt he has the talent to scale these heights.

"Rich can be as good as he wants to be," says Duplantis. "It's that simple."

"He's got all the tools," says J. P. Hayes. "There's no reason he can't be a consistent winner out here."

"He told me his immediate goal is to make the next Ryder Cup team," says Larry. "It's pretty ambitious, but I think it's one of the most realistic things he's ever said."

One of the knocks on Beem was that he didn't play enough tournaments as a rookie, that he didn't grind as hard as he could have. (According to Intrepid Sports's Greg Romine, this was why Tommy Hilfiger chose to pass on Beem for an endorsement deal and instead selected David Toms, who played thirty-two events in '99, eight more than Beem.) Some of the most successful players of the past generation kick-started their careers by toughing out an insane number of tournaments as a rookie—Mark O'Meara played thirty-four events, while Davis Love, Fred Couples, and Jim Furyk teed it up in thirty-one tournaments apiece. To his credit, Beem seems to have taken the critique to heart, though in typical fashion he may wind up overcompensating. He has decided to play the entire West Coast swing in the new year, eight tournaments in as many weeks to start the season. On the PGA Tour playing four tournaments in a row is considered exhausting. Playing six in a row is thought to be lunacy. Eight? "I'm not sure I've ever heard of that before," says Hayes.

Clearly Beem is trying to make up for lost time. So often as a rookie when he did show up at a tournament his play was compromised by outside factors—alcohol, the law, breakups, illness, fatigue, caddie issues. "It's almost like golf is the easiest thing," says Beem. "It's life that has been tougher to deal with. I haven't found a balancing point yet."

To that end, says Doan, "We've had a lot of talks, especially lately, about becoming more disciplined on the road, about establishing a routine. That means not getting on the cell phone until after his round, not getting caught up in email. There's nothing wrong with going out and having a good time but do it on Monday night, not Wednesday or Thursday. For six or seven hours a day, every day, Rich has to treat this like a job."

Beem spent most of his rookie year with a ball and chain back in El Paso. With Amy Onick now out of his life, there is some concern among those close to him that his partying may only intensify. "Rich has been trying to chase girls his whole life but he's never been real good at it," says Larry Beem. "He always thought being the class clown, being one of the boys and going out drinking was the way to get girls. He was wrong, of course. It's having money. For a long time Rich has wanted to be a ladies' man but he didn't have the key. Now he does."

This is a recurrent theme around El Paso Country Club, where Beem's love life has long been the source of great interest and endless conversation. "Those guys create so many stories out of sheer nonsense," Beem says. "That's Texas for you. I may stretch the truth a little, give it a little grease, just to make them feel special, like they know some kind of scoop. But the second coming of Hugh Hefner? Puh-leeze."

In fact, throughout the off-season Beem was growing increasingly serious with Sara Waide, the gal he met at the Las

Vegas Invitational. In the days after returning from Mexico he had traveled to Seattle to spend some time with her (as well as visit Wyatt and monitor the sluggish negotiations with Magnolia Hi-Fi), and he was planning to return for a New Year's Eve that also included David and his daughter. Sara, meanwhile, was to visit Beem in Scottsdale following the JCPenney Classic. Beem was heading to Crate & Barrel for the occasion, to obtain some grown-up housewares, which surely was a sign of something. "It's a much healthier relationship than his old one," says Wyatt, always quick to supply a thumbnail psychoanalysis. "Rich relied heavily on Amy to be the center of his life. It was almost a codependence. He's much happier with himself now, so he doesn't have that need to get his self-worth from his girlfriend. Sara's been good for him."

One thing about Amy Onick, she did help keep Beem out of the bars. On this point, too, Beem seems ready to mend his ways. At the Disney Classic, he said, "I might have a beer or two with dinner, but nothing excessive. I've learned my lesson. Four weeks ago I didn't drink that much, and it was like, 'Hey, this feels good.' " Four weeks ago? That was the Texas Open, when he played such inspired golf. Picking up the topic later, Beem says, "It's just not worth it. There's too much money to be made out here to be screwing around during tournament weeks. When I go to tournaments I'm gonna start treating them like business trips. If I want to go out on the town and get after it, well, that's what off weeks are for." Being out of El Paso should only help Beem abstain. "The guys at the club always wanted me to go out and get crazy with them just so they'd have more stories to tell their buddies," he says.

As Beem likes to say, there is no class to prepare you for the PGA Tour, no handbook on how to deal with the many life changes that come with winning your first Tour event. It is a perilous journey, especially for a rookie less than three years removed from hawking cell phones. The number of players who have won one tournament on the PGA Tour and then never been heard from again runs into the triple digits. On the other hand, it took Tom Watson and David Duval three years on tour to get their first victory, Tom Kite and Mark O'Meara four seasons, and Tom Lehman waited a full ten years from the time he turned pro until his first victory. Beem is way, way ahead of the curve, but it doesn't get any easier from here.

"This whole year has been his bar mitzvah," Larry Beem says of his son. "It's as if he's suddenly a man because someone shook a religious instrument at him and said so. He can have a long career and a great living at this game or he can fall into the abyss. It remains to be seen. I will say this: I get the feeling Rich has finally decided what he wants to be when he grows up."

DUPLANTIS HAS REGRETS, of course, but not many. "I've seen the world, met so many famous people, done so many cool things," he says. "I would do it all over again in a second."

Memories come to him at the funniest times, and one round more than any other plays on the movie screen of his imagination: Sunday at the 1998 Masters, destined to go down as one of the wildest days in golf history.

Through three rounds of that tournament the leaderboard was so glittery it could scarcely be believed. A trio of middle-aged warriors led the pack—Couples (with a cumulative score of 210), followed by O'Meara and Paul Azinger (both 212). Then came the young lions—Mickelson, Duval, and Jim Furyk—all at 213, Ernie Els (215), and Justin Leonard (216). Also in the mix were international stalwarts Jose Maria Olazabal (214) and Colin Montgomerie (215). The two most intriguing players were Jack Nicklaus, age fifty-eight, and Tiger Woods, twenty-two, both lurking with scores of 215, bookending some four decades of history-making golf. Woods was defending his epochal victory, during which he broke Nicklaus's thirty-two-year-old scoring record. The Olden Bear, meanwhile, was showing his first signs of life since his preposterous victory at Augusta in 1986. On Sunday Nicklaus and Woods would play in consecutive pairings.

Furyk was in the third to last tee time, playing with Duval, his friend and neighbor. After opening with a deflating 76, Furyk ground out a second-round 70 to make the cut by two strokes. He stormed into contention on Saturday with a 67, earning a crystal vase for the day's low score (the Masters gives out all kinds of goodies to the players during the week). In four of Furyk's previous eight major championships he had finished in the Top 6. He had paid his dues. Duplantis woke up early Sunday morning and couldn't fall back asleep. "I had the very strong feeling that we were going to win the green jacket," he says.

Nicklaus set the tone for the wild final round, birdying four of the first seven holes. When he reached the eighth tee he was tied for third place, a mere two shots back. Pandemonium reigned at Augusta National. There is something about the way a gallery's cheers echo through the pines there. It is not that the roars are necessarily louder; they are simply more expressive, more symphonic. "You could tell exactly where Jack was on the course by the noise," says Duplantis. "We're on number two and it sounded like all these cannons were going off, so we knew he hit if stiff on number six. There was another roar a few minutes later, so that meant he made the putt. It was like that for a while."

Eventually Nicklaus began acting his age (he would wind up finishing tied for sixth) meaning the tournament would be decided by mere mortals (Woods couldn't generate any momentum and would finish eighth). Players began flying up and down the leaderboard at such a relentless pace that the poor kids who operate the manual scoreboards must not have been able to move their arms the next day.

"I was a golf fan that round," says Duplantis. "It was such an incredible tournament and I was glued to the scoreboards. I couldn't help it. It was like, 'Hey Jim, check it out, can you believe Freddie just made double bogey on thirteen?' "

That double was posted as Furyk and Duval were playing the 15th hole, the short, watery, do-or-die par-5 that determines the outcome of so many Masters. Duval was suddenly leading by two strokes and facing an eighteen-footer for eagle. Furyk, meanwhile, was looking like he had just lost the tournament. On his second shot he had had 235 yards to the front, 250 to the pin. On the flat it would have been a perfect yardage for his 3-wood, but on such a steeply downhill approach a full 3 was too much stick. "Jim had to cut it a little to take off the yardage," says Duplantis. "Unfortunately, the ball was on this little mound, above his feet, and he put just a little hook on it." It bounded over green, into the water. Facing a frighteningly fast chip, Furyk ran his ball well past the hole and missed the putt to take a devastating bogey. Duval, meanwhile, lagged his eagle putt to an inch. With the birdie he was now leading the tournament by three strokes, and Furyk by four.

The pin at the par-3 16th was in its traditional Sunday spot, front left, hard by a pond popular with turtles, as well as golf balls. Duval played a defensive shot back right and got unlucky when his ball hung up on the steeply pitched bank, forty feet from the hole. Furyk rifled a 6-iron to fourteen feet. Says Duplantis, "As Duval's first putt was rolling it was obviously hot, and I figured he was looking at a three-putt. I turned to Jim and said, 'When you hole this we're right back in the tournament.' " Furyk nailed his birdie putt dead center and Duval did indeed miss his eight-foot comebacker to take bogey. Furyk was now tied for second, only two back.

Both players drove well on the tricky 17th. Furyk proceeded to cover the flag with his approach, stopping it ten feet from the hole. "The hair on my arm stood straight up," says Duplantis. Furyk banged in the putt. One down.

"As we were walking off the green I couldn't help it, I started thinking about winning," says Duplantis. "I got chills just imagining it." Duval cautiously parred 18. Furyk had an eighteen-foot birdie putt to tie for the lead, but on that dastardly green, under those circumstances, he couldn't hold the line. The putt skidded by the hole, ending his furious comeback. O'Meara wound up birdying the final two holes to win the championship, Furyk finishing fourth, two strokes back of the winner, one in arrears of Duval and Couples.

"There is nothing in the world like that feeling," Duplantis says. "Imagine being the biggest fan in the world, watching the most intense, nerve-racking sporting event you've ever watched, from the best seat in the house. Now multiply that feeling by a hundred. Or a thousand.

"It was the same with the Kemper Open. I wasn't as nervous, because I felt like I had more control over what was going to happen. But the overall emotion was probably just as intense. I don't care what happens from here on in my life, or what has happened. No one can ever take those memories away from me. No one. I've been part of something special. I've been part of history."

•

THE JCPENNEY CLASSIC falls in the middle of the Silly Season, the two months between the end of the official PGA Tour season and the new year. The Silly Season is so-called because it comprises a series of cheesy made-for-TV events played in far-flung places on substandard courses for excessive amounts of Monopoly money. The Penney is an archetype of this kind of event, featuring two-person teams made up of one PGA Tour player and one LPGA player, over seventy-two holes of team best-ball play. Nevertheless, the Penney still held a certain significance for Beem, if only because the Silly Season events are reserved for the upper echelon of players. Sure, the Penney wasn't an institution like the Skins Game or as lucrative as the Sun City Million-Dollar Challenge (so named because that's the size of the first-place check), but it was Beem's first chance to feed at the trough, another little reminder that he had arrived as a player.

Beem's partner for the event was Anna-Jane (A. J.) Eathorne, who was also coming off a promising rookie year. Eathorne, too, had gone to New Mexico State and she and Beem knew each other from around the way. They had often talked about playing together someday in the professional ranks and now it was a happy reality. Nobody took the golf too seriously. In fact, the undisputed highlight of the week was a Jimmy Buffett concert that Beem, Duplantis, and Eathorne attended. The team shot rounds of 68-67-67-70, finishing thirty-fifth, twelve strokes back of the winners, the big-bopping, hard-living duo of John Daly and Laura Davies. Beem and Eathorne split $5,775.00. More than anything, the week was a time of reflection for Beem and Duplantis.

"In a lot of ways I wish Rich and I could've done things over," says Duplantis. "It's weird because we're such good friends off the golf course. We had a blast together—and still do—but we couldn't take that between the ropes. We couldn't talk to each other as a player and a caddie. The tension just built up and built up until it exploded. If we ever worked together again, I think all we'd need is a weekly team meeting, just to clear the air. Sit down, have a beer, speak our mind, make sure everything is okay. That's all we need."

On the possibility of working together again, Beem says, "I

could see it happening, sure. I don't know when or where, but it's certainly a possibility. Especially if Steve can get a handle on some things in other aspects of his life. He's had to deal with so much in his life, and he still does. I worry about that kid, I really do."

Following the final round of the Penney, player and caddie retired to Beem's hotel room to settle accounts. Beem presented Duplantis with the $10,000 end-of-the-year check and then something unexpected happened.

"We got really emotional," says Beem. "I think it finally hit us both, like, 'Wow, this is it. The end.' "

"We just kind of started hugging and crying," says Duplantis. "It was pathetic."

It had been six months since their vastly different trajectories intersected during a magical week at the Kemper Open. Beem and Duplantis will always have that bond, but now it was time for their embrace to end, for good-byes to be said, and for them to go their separate ways. Where they're headed remains to be seen.

"Golf," says Beem, "has a way of taking your life in unexpected directions."

AFTERWORD

Rich Beem started the 2000 season with a bang—eighty-four of them, in fact. That was his score for the first round of the Mercedes Championships, the ultraexclusive tournament reserved for the players who had won Tour events during the previous season. Beem had spent most of the off-season trying to get away from the game, but in the process his game had gotten away from him. The embarrassing opening round only highlighted the crazy dichotomy of his professional life: As a Tour winner he now had entrée to the best tournaments and all their lavish stylings, yet here he was, staying at the idyllic Ritz-Carlton in Maui, rolling a shiny Mercedes courtesy car, and continuing to play like an 8-handicapper. "I can't say I wasn't ready, but I just didn't know what to expect," Beem said of his inauspicious opening round. "I got on the first tee, the wind was blowing forty miles an hour, and I wasn't prepared for it. I honestly didn't play that bad."

The 84 was a rude reminder of the struggles of the latter half of his rookie season, and quite a buzz kill at that. Beem had spent the early parts of the tournament week feeling like he finally knew the secret handshake: On the morning of one of the practice rounds Hal Sutton beckoned Beem over to his table, and the starry-eyed Kemper Open champ shared breakfast and small talk with the guy who only a few months earlier had been the U.S.'s Ryder Cup hero. On another occasion, at lunch, David Duval pulled up a chair, saying casually, "Hey Rich, how you doing?" They had never met before, but still had an easy camaraderie, chit-chatting about snowboarding and the like. "I'm still in awe of these guys," Beem says. "They're the best in the world and I'm just honored to be out there with them." Later in the week Tiger Woods did his usual pretournament press conference, and he told a roomful of sunburned reporters, "There are thirty guys here, and any one of them can win. You can go down the list of names, Rich Beem or whoever, and every single guy here is a great player."

"It was awesome to read that in the paper," said Beem. Of course, in Tiger's example Beem is the guy who doesn't really belong, a notion Beem would not dispute. "Before my first tee shot of the first round I looked around and chuckled," he said. "It was like, *Suckahs.* That's the way I feel."

Determined to erase the embarrassment of his 84, Beem came out firing on Friday, going -4 on his first 6 holes. He faded to a 77, but in the cushy world of the Mercedes Championship, there is no cut. He came back to shoot 76 on Saturday. "I improved every day," Beem says, earnestly. "Sunday I was grinding it out. I didn't want to finish last." Though he hung up a respectable 70, Beem still finished, by three strokes, DFL—caddie parlance for Dead Fucking Last. Then again, a $45,000 payday for getting lapped by the field was not a bad way to start the season.

The following week brought the Sony Open on Oahu, where Beem's improbable journey on the PGA Tour had begun a year earlier. "It was such a different experience this time around," says David Wyatt, who flew in for the week. "Rich was so much more relaxed. He knew where to stay, and he wasn't afraid to spend a little money, so he was at a nice hotel right on the beach. He knew the course; he knew the town; he knew the players. And there wasn't a PGA Tour pro anywhere who didn't know Rich—whether it was at the range, the beach, wherever. He had definitely entered the clique." That wasn't true of everyone. Beem's girlfriend Sara Waide also jetted in from Seattle for the tournament, and she had a funny experience during the first round, when Beem was paired with former British Open champ Tom Lehman. Strolling in the gallery, Sara had on prominent display a round brass pin stamped with the PGA Tour logo, a glittering bauble reserved only for a player's significant other. "It's the grand prize," says Wyatt. "Tom Lehman's wife, Melissa, saw Sara's pin and comes up and says, 'Oh, are you a Mrs.?' Sara said 'No.' When Melissa heard that she just spun around and took off. Apparently girlfriends are a dime a dozen out there. Only the wives get any kind of respect from the other wives."

Steve Duplantis was also making the scene in Waikiki, as he had flown in at the last minute to caddie for Brian Gay. Duplantis's buddy, Chris Hanrattie, was supposed to be on Gay's bag for the season, but four days before the start of the tournament Hanrattie had opted for a saner, more secure life, taking a job with American Express. Desperate, Gay rang up Duplantis, who swallowed his pride and caught the next flight out of Tampa. He crashed with Wyatt, giving him a chance to observe the older, wiser Beem. "Rich went jogging with David a couple of times, and that impressed me," says Duplantis. "If he keeps it up, that will really impress me."

Following Hawaii, the Tour traveled to a place called Hope, and Beem finally found a little of it in his golf game. He opened the 90-hole Bob Hope Chrysler Classic with a promising 67 at Bermuda Dunes Country Club, and that evening he repaired to Morton's steakhouse, on Country Club Drive in Palm Desert. During the week of the Hope, Morton's is one of the axes on which Palm Springs spins. Midway through Beem's salad course his old Kemper Open foil, Tommy Armour III, rolled in, looking like Shaft in a knee-length black leather coat. Beem had been venting about having fired his agents at Intrepid Sports earlier in the day, but seeing Armour got him reminiscing about the Kemper. He detailed all the ways he was memorializing the victory. "I'm getting the clubs I used that week framed, having collages made of all the press clippings, and putting aside tapes of the telecasts for future generations," he said. "I may never win again. I may not even have another chance. You never know with this game. It's so fickle."

The next day Beem went out and shot a 63, the low round of his career, to storm into the lead, along with Greg Kraft.

The Hope is the worst logistical nightmare in golf, played simultaneously on four courses that are dotted around the Coachella Valley. The host site, Bermuda Dunes, is well appointed, but at the other three venues there are virtually no on-course scoreboards or TV towers. Playing at the remote Arnold Palmer Private Course at PGA West, Beem knew he was in the midst of a hot round, but his only inkling that he was leading the tournament came when a camera crew huffed out to pick him up in the middle of his back nine. Following his ten-birdie-one-bogey effort Beem was warm and relaxed in an interview on national TV with Judy Rankin. How does a guy go from self-immolation in Hawaii to suddenly burning up the desert? "You hit a good shot, make a putt, hit a good shot, make a putt, and all of a sudden the game is easy again," Beem says. "If I could explain it any better than that I'd have a best-seller."

On Friday Beem dropped a 65 on La Quinta Country Club to charge into the lead. With a cumulative score of 195 (-20) he now owned a piece of the three-round tournament scoring record, and he hadn't even gotten his fangs into the Hope's easiest course. At a flat 6,478 yards, Indian Wells Country Club is laughably short to be hosting a Tour event. Though par is officially 72, anything worse than a 68 is considered a missed opportunity, and Beem knew it. "I was antsy all day," he says. "Indian Wells was supposed to be the course where I could go really low, and I was trying to force things a little." Never more so than on the 3rd hole, an innocuous 382-yard par-4, when Beem hit what he calls "the ol' hookerooni" out-of-bounds, taking a momentum-killing double bogey. Beem, however, would fight back valiantly, making five more birdies to get to three under on the day by the time he arrived at Indian Wells's closing hole, a narrow 501-yard par-5 that is framed on the right side by dramatic desert landscape. In the group ahead of Beem was another contender, Rory Sabbatini, a little guy who packs a big wallop, and from the tee Beem could see him idling in the fairway, waiting to go for the green. "He knocked it stiff, so that got me going a little bit," Beem says. After a pretty good drive Beem had 230 yards to the stick. In the absence of any scoreboards, Beem incorrectly assumed his middling play had cost him the lead, and he decided to go for it. In fact, at that moment he was still one stroke in front of the field. "I had no idea I was leading the tournament," he says. "If I had, there's no way I go for the green. There's no need." Alas, he sliced his 5-wood up into the mountainside, into the heart of a scrubby bush. The terrain was so extreme there was nowhere for Beem to drop, even if he had wanted to take an unplayable lie. He was forced to play a left-handed recovery shot, which he barely bunted forward. Still in the gunch, he slashed his fourth shot into a greenside bunker. He would make 7 on a birdie hole. The confidence-rattling double bogey dropped Beem into a four-way tie for third at -21, two back of Sabbatini, one in arrears of Matt Gogel.

That night an unemployed Duplantis was hanging around Dallas with Hanrattie. At dinner he reached Beem on his cell phone. "Steve gave him a great pep talk," says Hanrattie. "He was like, 'You don't have an experienced caddie, but you don't need one. You're not some clueless kid, you're a veteran now. You've been through it all. Don't be in awe of anyone or anything. Just play balls-out, and you can win. You're good enough, and everyone knows it.'"

Beem would get plenty more encouragement on Sunday, but it didn't come without a price. "It was a big melee," he says. "Twenty or thirty people flew in for the final round, and I had to deal with tickets, hotels, meals, rides, phone calls, everything. I should have shut off my cell phone. It's not in my nature, unfortunately. I promise, I'll know for next time."

For the final round Beem was in the second to last pairing, alongside Jesper Parnevik, who a few months earlier had solidified his standing as one of the world's best players with a sizzling performance at the Ryder Cup. On the 1st hole Beem hooked his drive into the first cut of rough, and then misjudged the wind on his approach, coming up fifteen yards short. He played an indifferent chip to ten feet and then missed the putt. Bogey. Parnevik, meanwhile, made an insane up-and-down from the left bunker to save par. Beem again missed the green on the 2nd hole, a 418-yard par-4. Though he would produce a par, Beem's swing looked loose, his nerves unsteady. Parnevik, meanwhile, clanged his approach off the flagstick and tapped in for birdie. On the short par-4 3rd hole Beem blew his drive into the right rough, from where his path to the green was blocked by a towering tamarisk tree. He punched short of the green, then stubbed a weak chip eighteen feet short of the hole, a putt he missed to make another bogey. Parnevik pured another flawless iron to six feet for his second straight birdie, which gave him the outright lead in the tournament, and then on the par-3 4th hole the Swede hit it stiff for yet another tweeter. Just like that Beem was 5 strokes back of Parnevik, and the tournament was all but over.

The disappointment showed in Beem's gallery. All the usual suspects had turned out. Wyatt was wearing a familiar get-up, Beem's Cubs hat and blue polo shirt, but at one point he lamented, "I'm afraid the lucky hat is losing some of its mojo." Among the other mourners was Wyatt's daughter Cady, with her Goth Lite look, strolling along with Beem's girlfriend, Sara, who was desperately trying to maintain a brave smile. Max and Dina Schroeder were also in the crowd, pushing in a stroller their cooing baby boy, Evan Richard.

By the time Beem limped to the 18th tee he was in fifteenth place, having made only one birdie all day. Parnevik was still clinging to a narrow lead, which meant a huge crowd was lining the home hole, and numerous network cameramen and reporters were scurrying around. Duly inspired by the spectacle, Beem finished off his round in style with a stellar birdie, and after his fifteen-footer dropped he raised both arms over his head in triumph. That closed the books on a disappointing 72, which left him in twelfth place (good for $60,750), seven back of Parnevik. The closing birdie gave Beem a much-needed boost, and after the round he retreated to the comfort of cliché. "That's golf," he said, standing outside the scorer's tent. "You can't win 'em all." Later—much later—he would admit, "What happened at the Hope really took the wind out of my sails. It affected me for a long time, but I didn't know that right away."

Actually, the fallout was rather immediate. Beem would miss his next four cuts, failing to break 70 in any round.

Duplantis returned to action in the season's fifth week at the Pebble Beach National Pro-Am, his first job since working the Sony Open in Hawaii, where Gay had shot a second round 76 to miss the cut. Duplantis still wasn't sold on Gay's potential, but lacking any other viable options he headed out to the Pro-Am, committing to pack for Gay over the final four tournaments of the West Coast swing. "Nothing much is going on here, so I'm gonna get off my ass and go get in the mix," Duplantis said from Tampa, a few days before flying into Pebble Beach. "I gotta make something happen."

With the season now in full swing, Duplantis's frustration at not being able to land a steady bag was mounting. "There's so much bullshit out there, and it's costing me jobs," he said. "All I ever hear is, 'Oh yeah, Duplantis, he's drunk all day and in strip joints all night.' Nothing could be further from the truth. I haven't been to a strip joint in ages. Sure, I'll have a couple of beers like anyone else, but it's no big deal. Problem is people think they can get ahead by stabbing me in the back, so the shit never ends."

Gay's slow start hardly brightened Duplantis's outlook. They missed the cut at Pebble Beach, finished sixty-eighth the next week in San Diego, and then missed another cut at the L.A. Open. By the time Duplantis arrived in Tucson he was in need of some cheering up.

Hooking up with a MasterCard girl? Priceless. At every PGA Tour event there is a little booth where fans are beseeched to sign up for their very own PGA Tour MasterCard. Filling out the paperwork is always a crew of toothsome young women. At Tucson Duplantis made the acquaintance of one of them, Jennifer, and spent much of the week pursuing the burgeoning romance. He did, however, make time to hang out with Beem, who rang him up on the eve of the tournament. Beem had set up shop at Dirtbags, a happening bar near the University of Arizona campus. Duplantis met him there, and finally, after so many awkward silences and unspoken grievances, "We had the talk," says Duplantis. Over a heartfelt forty-five minutes, "Everything we should have said six months ago just came pouring out," Duplantis says, "What we did wrong, what we should've done, what we would need to do in the future. It was great to finally clear the air like that."

They went to a strip joint to celebrate.

Alas, even such a momentous night couldn't stop Beem's freefall. He played his worst golf since Maui, shooting 75-76 to miss his fifth straight cut. Gay, meanwhile, was heading in the opposite direction, thanks in no small part to Beem's ex-caddie. After opening with an uneventful 70 at Tucson, Gay was playing some electric golf on Friday, despite a series of lightning delays. As the day grew later his two playing partners began literally running around the golf course. Both were going to miss the cut by a mile, and did not want to have to return to the course early Saturday morning to finish their rounds. Amidst all the hustle and bustle Duplantis made Gay walk slowly next to him, continually whispering in his ear to remain calm and composed, and to make every shot count. "Steve did an unbelievable job of keeping Brian in the moment, of keeping him focused on the shot at hand and not all the other craziness going on around them," says Gay's wife, Kimberly. Gay putted out his 65 under a vivid sunset, and continued to play well on the weekend, shooting 69-70 to finish thirteenth, by far the best showing of his career. Duplantis took his usual 5 percent of the $56,250. "It's about time I get a decent check," he said. "I haven't made shit all year." Of Gay, he added, "He's getting it. Slowly but surely."

"On the weekend, when I was playing good Steve was really into it," says Gay. "I could tell that's what he lives for."

Two weeks after Tucson, Gay and Duplantis traveled to the Honda Classic, in Ft. Lauderdale, and Gay produced the best golf of his career. He opened with a 65 to snare a share of the lead, then followed with rounds of 70-67 to head into the final round in second place, two back of Beem's old El Paso mentor, J. P. Hayes. The final-round action was hot and heavy, with a bevy of contenders all making runs at the lead. Gay, soothed by Duplantis's constant pep talks, played bravely, and was among the last standing; at the 17th hole he faced a thirty-foot birdie putt to tie for the lead with Dudley Hart, who was already in the clubhouse, having fired a final round 65 to finish at -19. Gay's putt inched toward the cup, and then hung perilously on the lip, as if afraid of the dark. Gay walked gingerly toward the ball, peering at it from a safe distance. Finally, dramatically, it tumbled into the cup, setting off an explosion of cheers. Gay was tied for the lead. Or was he?

Gay had stepped into one of the biggest gray areas in the oft-murky rules of golf. As Gay was awaiting the results of his gravity experiment, NBC's Roger Maltbie, following the action on foot, was the first to pipe up: "He's got ten seconds to wait, is all he can wait." Maltbie was correct. Rule 16-2, "Ball Overhanging Hole," reads, "When any part of the ball overhangs the lip of the hole, the player is allowed enough time to reach the hole without unreasonable delay and an additional ten seconds to determine whether the ball is at rest." After ten seconds, a player must brush his ball in, even if he thinks it is still moving. It is the only time in golf you are allowed to play a ball in motion.

After Maltbie's comment, Johnny Miller speculated that

Gay had taken more than ten seconds, at which point Gary Koch spoke up. "He has a few seconds to wait to determine if the ball is still in motion," Koch said. "He walked up, took a look, thought it was still in motion, waited, and it went in. It counts." Koch's confidence—however misplaced—stemmed in part from having been told by the official scorer in the group that the putt counted.

When Duplantis reached the 18th tee he took a moment to gather his thoughts. "I was like, wait a minute, what just happened there?" he says. "It all happened so fast." Duplantis knew of the ten-second rule but was sure Gay had not waited anywhere near that long (then again, time slows down between the ropes on Sunday afternoon). Gay and his caddie played the 18th believing they were tied for the lead. Two cautious shots brought him to the final green at the TPC of Heron Bay, but Gay nervously 3-putted, to finish a stroke back of Hart (along with J. P. Hayes and Kevin Wentworth). When a disconsolate Gay stepped into the scoring tent he was met by Slugger White, the hard-ass PGA Tour rules official. White informed Gay that he had waited at least thirteen seconds for his ball to drop back at 17, thus violating Rule 16-2. The one-stroke penalty dropped Gay into a tie for fourth, costing him $88,933. Duplantis was part of the discussion with White, and he says, "Here's what happened. Some slapdick USGA official was sitting on his couch in New Jersey, saw the TV replay from the blimp, and called Slugger White, who went along with penalty, even though Brian's playing partners called the putt good, and so did the official scorer in the group. The whole thing was a joke. Does David Stern call NBC to point out a shot-clock violation?"

Lost in the controversy was the fact that Duplantis almost got another young nobody in the barn with his first victory. "It could have been very sweet," he says.

Beem would find Florida no less hospitable, as his slump changed time zones, too. He shot 75-72 to miss the cut at the Bay Hill Invitational, then went to the "fifth major," the Players Championship, and hung up an abysmal 77-79 for his seventh missed cut in a row. "He's taking bullets out there," Wyatt said. "He's just getting killed. The guy's confidence is so low right now. It's hard to play golf like that." The end of March did bring a modicum of good news. Around the time of the Players Championship Beem signed with Gaylord Sports (formerly known as Cornerstone), the second biggest agency in the golf world. His agent, Tim McNulty, sees Beem as a potentially valuable property. "We're waiting for the right brand fit," McNulty says. "It's no secret Rich likes to have fun, and we're looking for companies that service that lifestyle—electronics and outdoors equipment would be a couple of examples. There is certainly a niche out there for a guy like Rich."

Beem finally stopped his downward spiral at the BellSouth Classic, shooting 71-73 to squeak under the cut line. "It was the best feeling you could ever imagine," Beem says. Did he celebrate? "Are you kidding? I was too worn out." His next time out, at Hilton Head, Beem opened with a 69, the first time he had broken 70 since the third round of the Hope, a span of three months and twenty-one rounds. It looked like he might be ready to turn his season around, but then on Sunday he was upended in the kind of freak accident that could only happen to Rich Beem.

He was walking from the 8th green to the 9th tee at Harbour Town Golf Links when a golf cart came barreling toward him. A volunteer dropped the gallery rope to let the cart pass, but not in time. The rope became entangled on the cart's steering wheel, uprooting a series of stakes and whipping the rope at Beem with enough force to catch him by the ankle and flip him upside down. Beem landed with a thud on his back and neck. "There was a nurse and an EMT around and they said I was unconscious for a few seconds," he says. "I was in shock. They put my neck in a brace, strapped me to a gurney, put me in an ambulance, and took me to the ER. It was wild." Beem was forced to withdraw, obviously, but red-faced officials of the MCI Classic still paid him last-place money, though it didn't count toward the official money list. Save some scrapes and bruises, Beem's person was okay, though he was deeply shaken by the incident. He returned to action two weeks later at the Houston Open and shot a jittery 79 in the opening round. "I have never felt so uncomfortable on a golf course," he says. "It was a feeling of complete uneasiness, just looking around and seeing all the potential pitfalls." Beem took a couple of weeks off after Houston, and in mid-May, before heading to the Colonial Invitational, he made a little pit stop in Potomac, Maryland. The Kemper Open was two weeks away and the defending champion's presence was needed for the traditional media day.

On a sunny Monday afternoon Beem sat in the dining room of the TPC of Avenel, about to dive into a towering ham sandwich, a stem of grapes, two pickles, and a tall glass of lemonade. Before he could enjoy his first bite, however, the local reporters descended on his table. First it was Len Shapiro, the veteran scribe for *The Washington Post.* Beem and Shapiro had bonded during the tournament a year ago and have stayed friendly. Beem greeted Shapiro with a friendly "Leeeennnnyyyy," and a half-hug. Soon Barker Davis of *The Washington Times* and Don Markus of *The Baltimore Sun* arrived, and the questions came fast and furious. All three writers were working on big one-year-later pieces to run the week of the Kemper. Few, if any, no-name winners produce this kind of interest, but Beem's victory was so captivating that, even now, readers and editors simply can't get enough.

It took Beem an hour to finish his sandwich, by which time the dining room was packed with reporters (though, it must be said, many were on hand for the free round of golf at Avenel that would follow). Beem stepped to a dais at the front of the room, and, looking out at the assembled crowd, said, "I didn't think I'd be this nervous. I'll tell ya, it's good to be back at the site of my biggest accomplishment in golf." He fielded questions from the group with grace and candor. Asked if he would be reuniting with Duplantis for the week, Beem said, "We'll get back together someday, I just don't know when it will be." Later, Beem said, "I certainly haven't had a spectacular year to this point, but being here gives me nothing but positive memories. Hopefully I can get jump-started these next two weeks and by the Kemper the stars will be in alignment once again."

Immediately after the press conference Beem flew to the Colonial, where he missed the cut. The week before the Kemper he traveled to the Memorial, and on one of the Tour's most daunting golf courses he seemed to find his game, opening 71-69 to go into the weekend in eighth place. He faded to a 75-75 finish, to place fifty-first. "It was just dumb fucking golf," Beem said. "I had a hot putter the first two rounds. I was making everything I looked at. On the weekend, I just figured if I could stuff it next to the flag a little more, I'd have a chance to win. So, of course I hit a bunch of stupid shots and they cost me. Instead of playing safe and letting my putter do the work, I got carried away. It's just like what happened to Saturday at the Hope. Going for the green in two on the eighteenth hole was ridiculous. It's not about hitting hero shots out here. It's about minimizing mistakes and using your head. Someday I'm going to figure that out for good."

Though Duplantis wasn't invited to media day, the Kemper was on his mind as well in the weeks leading up to the tournament. The same reporters who had been hounding Beem were calling the ex-caddie for comment. One person who wasn't calling was Beem, at least not to arrange the details of their working together at the Kemper. "I kept putting it on Rich to call Stevie," says Wyatt, "because we all knew that would've been a wonderful thing for them to work together again at the Kemper. Rich just kept blowing it off, saying he'd do it later. Sometimes Rich is generous to a fault. He felt like it wouldn't be fair to R.C. to dump him like that." Eventually Beem offered Duplantis his old bag, but, says Steve, "By the time he asked me it was too late. I didn't want to screw Brian like that. It's too bad the way it worked out."

Duplantis's allegiance to Gay was born of improved play. Of the near-miss at the Honda, Duplantis says, "Brian played well enough to win, and that was a huge thing for his development." Since then Gay was playing steadily better. He followed a solid thirtieth at the BellSouth with an opening 66 at Houston. At the Byron Nelson Classic, in early May, Gay shot a 75 in the first round but came back with rounds of 67-69-68 to grind out another thirtieth place finish. The next week, at the exacting Colonial Country Club, he hung up three straight 70s to finish forty-first. If Gay wasn't tearing up the Tour, he had at least found the kind of consistency Beem could only dream of, and Gay was showing a far steeper learning curve. Duplantis had backed into a pretty good bag, and he wasn't willing to strain the relationship just for old time's sake.

It wasn't just Duplantis's professional situation that had stabilized. In the months since Tucson he had grown increasingly serious with Jennifer, the MasterCard girl. Though she wasn't hawking credit cards that week, she traveled with Duplantis to Atlanta for the BellSouth, serving as a de facto nanny for Sierra, and by the week of New Orleans, in early May, she had moved in with Duplantis and gotten a job in the Tampa area, so she could stay home with Sierra when Duplantis was on the road. Of course, there is never an absence of drama when it comes to Duplantis's love life: It turned out that Jennifer had recently dumped her boyfriend, a Tour player of some note. In the incestuous world of pro golf, he quickly got wind that Jen was shacking up with a caddie, and he was so distraught at the news that he began blaming his poor play on the golf course on the heartache she had inflicted. When she returned her wife's pin to her ex the week before the Kemper, that made the situation that much more volatile. "It's just typical," Duplantis says. "I wanted to go to Kemper and enjoy the week, even if I wasn't caddying for Beemer. Then all this comes up."

In an effort to duplicate his success in Potomac, Beem toyed with the idea of staying in the same fleabag hotel that had been his home a year earlier. In the end he decided to go uptown, but he did request a courtesy car with the same number—007—as he had had in '99. Early in the Kemper week it didn't seem as if Beem would need this kind of voodoo, as he was tearing it up in his practice rounds. On Tuesday he teed it up with John Daly and Hank Kuehne, and in a series of escalating bets Beem took this trash-talking, titanium-denting duo for winnings that ran into four digits, according to Beem's sister, Tina. Once again Beem was also basking in all the extra attention that came with being a media darling. All the big preview stories dropped that week, most notably Shapiro's in *The Washington Post,* at the top of the front page of a special pullout guide to the tournament. Under the headline "The Triumph of Team Beem," Shapiro recounted the wild year Beem had experienced since his victory, focusing on "a hastily assembled amalgam of the player, his new caddie, his girlfriend, and his best friend . . . an unlikely cast in a story that seemed more fantasy than nonfiction." Shapiro quoted Duplantis and Wyatt extensively, though Amy Onick was considerably more terse. "It was a great weekend," she told Shapiro in the quote he used to end the story. "I was very happy for him, and I still am. It's very special to see someone's dream come true."

A big crowd turned out for Beem's opening round, and he began his defense with a rousing birdie at the first hole. "That opening tee shot was the most comfortable I've felt all year," Beem said after the round. "Being back here was an incredible feeling." Beem struck the ball with authority throughout the round, but he was betrayed by his putter and could do no better than a one-under 70—all things considered, not a bad opening salvo. On Friday Beem eagled the par-5 second hole, loosing a Tigeresque fist pump when the putt dropped. This big bird may have actually hurt him: Straining to put together a big charge, he began playing with reckless abandon, and after three-putting the 15th hole he was back to even par on his round. On the tough par-4 16th Beem smoked a drive and hit what he calls a "perfect" 8-iron dead on the flag. His ball landed only a couple of feet beyond the hole, which was tucked in the back of the green. Unfortunately, by this time in the late afternoon the greens had firmed up considerably, and his ball took a big hop over the green into a nasty patch of rough. With the putting surface plunging away from him, Beem had little chance to save par, and he didn't. Now +1 on the day and even for the tournament, he had pushed himself to precipice of a devastating missed cut.

Back at his hotel Duplantis was monitoring the scores on pgatour.com. Earlier in the day Gay had shot a 69 to easily make yet another cut. "I was sick watching the numbers change," Duplantis says.

Beem never missed Duplantis more than when he arrived at the 17th hole, that nasty downhill par-3 over water. Standing on the tee, shaking his head and cursing under his breath, Beem was obviously still rattled from the back-to-back bogies. His caddie, R. C. Ordish—former college drinking buddy, burned-out club pro, rookie bagman—stood by mutely, overwhelmed by the pathos of it all. "R.C. wasn't experienced enough to stop me before I hit that shot at 17," Beem says. "I needed someone to get in my face and get me refocused, but R.C. wasn't that guy." Beem slashed a screaming hook way left of the green. He was now swinging with one hand on his club, the other on his throat. A weak chip left him a thirty-footer for par. Up on the hillside overlooking the green, Beem's usual gallery of friends and family were chewing on their cuticles; watching Beem line up his thirty-footer, Wyatt said to himself, "For fuck's sake, Rich, knock it in. Gawd, do we need this putt." Beem missed it badly, taking his third straight bogey. He was now +1, which was the projected cut line. He needed a par on the exacting par-4 18th.

Beem somehow managed to hit the fairway, but he dumped a sickly approach into the right front bunker. Not only had the spin left him a fried-egg lie, but his ball buried hard against the back of the bunker, leaving him an awkward stance to a tight, downhill pin. Beem's explosion skittered eighteen feet past the pin. While his playing partners were tidying up, Beem veered over the scorer's tent to ask about the cut line. Standing over his putt, then, he knew he had to bury it. A year earlier Beem made a bogey on the 18th hole, on Sunday, to clinch his life-altering victory. This time around he made another bogey, to miss the cut.

After signing his scorecard Beem stumbled toward the clubhouse, looking punch-drunk. Slumped in front of his locker, head buried in his hands, it was all he could do to mumble, "I can't even express the disappointment."

That evening Beem dined with Duplantis. It was a bittersweet gathering. "I still feel a little guilty about not having packed for Rich at Kemper," Duplantis says. "No way he makes four straight bogeys to miss the cut. I wouldn't let him."

A month later, near the end of June, Beem and Duplantis met again for dinner, at a steakhouse in Memphis, where they had journeyed to for the FedEx St. Jude Classic. Beem picked up the check, as he often does, but what really impressed Duplantis was that Beem refrained from drinking during the meal. "Rich has been a lot more responsible this year," Duplantis says. "I know what he's up to. We talk on the phone at least a couple of times a week. He's been more committed to treating this like a job, and I'm proud of him for that."

Pause.

"Of course, he still turns it loose once in awhile, especially after he's missed a cut. We had a big night on Friday in Houston, at Papa's Icehouse. Beemer put a big bottle of Jack on the bar and we talked the night away."

In Memphis the conversation was a little more sobering. Beem and Duplantis finalized the details on a plan they had been kicking around for a while—in a couple of weeks Beem was returning to the scene of the crime, Scotland, to attempt to qualify for the British Open, and Duplantis was going to join him in a much-anticipated reunion. Though Gay had continued his solid play—he shot a career low 64 in the final round at Kemper to move up to twentieth—Duplantis still missed the freewheeling fun of traveling with his old boss. "Brian's really quiet," Duplantis says. "He doesn't say much of anything, and he doesn't do much away from golf. Put it this way, he's not the Beemer. He's not going to drop a grand to have a big night on the town. About the only fun we've had together was going to WWF Smackdown." That also happened the week of Memphis. During a practice round Duplantis answered Gay's cell phone, and someone growled on the other end of the line, "Tell him to keep his head down and swing smooth."

"Who the hell is this?"

"Sgt. Slaughter."

Apparently a friend of a friend of Gay's knew the wrestling icon, who was happy to hook player and caddie up with free tickets. As eventful a week as Memphis was, the most interesting turn of events came on Sunday, when Beem and Gay were paired together. Both were enjoying a pretty good tournament, at -5 through three rounds. (Following the evisceration at Kemper, Beem had found a rare resolve, making the cut the next week at the Buick Classic, despite an opening 75.) On Sunday in Memphis, Beem "was definitely trying to kick Brian's ass," says Duplantis. "It was obvious. He was really grinding. Actually, I think he was trying too hard." Gay, oblivious as ever, shot a carefree 69, to move up to twentieth place. An overwrought Beem chopped his way to a 74, skidding all the way to fifty-fourth. How much did Beem's schoolyard grudge cost him? The difference between twentieth and fifty-fourth was $26,850.

Beem spent nearly $10,000 on traveling to Scotland, but to his way of thinking it was a bargain. "That's a small price to pay for the love of the game," he says. "It's the Millennium Open at St. Andrews, the home of golf. If you are a pro golfer you absolutely gotta go." In the aftermath of his DUI at the '99 Open, Beem had vowed to exact his revenge on the tournament, but he never got the chance, shooting 73-70-143 at Scotscraig Golf Club in Fife to miss qualifying by 5 strokes. "The courses over there are so hard, and I don't just mean difficult," he says. "The ground is so firm, it's a totally different way to play golf, and I'm still learning how. I can promise you this, I'll keep going over there until I've run out of money. I'm not ready to declare defeat yet."

Beem did not have the benefit of Duplantis's linksland experience, as he was a last-minute scratch from the trip. "As usual, it was shit going on at home," Duplantis says. The week before the trip he had a falling out with Jennifer, and she packed her stuff up and went home to Hickory, North Carolina. "I was left holding the bag," Duplantis says. "I didn't want to be out of the country for two weeks and spend all that money with so much uncertainty about my daughter."

In Duplantis's absence Beem took a buddy named Billy Heim over to Scotland to serve as his caddie. Beem had known Heim since his playing days at UTEP; Heim was trying to scratch out an existence playing on various minitours, but caddying on the PGA Tour had long appealed to him. He had actually approached Beem at the end of '99, but it wasn't until the Kemper that Beem decided he was ready for another caddying change. "R.C. and I had a tough year," Beem says. "He was getting depressed out there. It got to the point where I was having to give *him* pep talks. He'll always be a great friend, but I just needed to shake things up."

In the end, Duplantis's decision not to journey to Scotland worked out for all parties. By staying behind he was able to caddie for Gay at the Greater Milwaukee Open and B.C. Open (Duplantis convinced Jennifer to watch Sierra in North Carolina). At Milwaukee Gay shot 69-65-66 to put himself among the leaders; on Sunday he struggled to a 72 to finish fourteenth, but still cashed a check for $43,750, a nice payday for Duplantis. The following week Gay opened 67-68 and went on to finish eighteenth, scoring another $22,666 to crack the top 100 on the money list. Meanwhile, Heim performed well enough overseas that Beem offered him the job for the rest of the season, which was to feature a heavy number of tournaments. Unlike the previous season, when a worn-out Beem tapered off his schedule, he was committed in 2000 to grinding it out until the season's bitter end. "I haven't given up," he said in July, upon his return from Scotland. "Every time I tee it up I still believe I'll be in contention, and sooner or later I will. I can still have a great year. All it takes is one week. I'm proof of that."

Starting with the International, in the first week of August, Beem played nine of the final twelve tournaments on the schedule, and this finishing kick began with a rousing pep talk from Mark O'Meara. Beem had approached O'Meara at the International's range to ask a quick question about some niggling detail. "It was a two-minute conversation that turned into twenty," Beem says. "Mark just kept saying, this isn't a game, it's a business, and you have to treat it that way. If anybody comes up to you and asks why you're not playing better, ask them how their business is doing. Have they ever had a slow quarter or two?

"He was just really positive, really upbeat. He says, 'Rich, no matter what happens, you've already had a great career. There are thousands and thousands of pro golfers out there whose only dream is to make it to the PGA Tour, and not only have you done that, you've won a tournament. Nobody can ever take that away from you.' It was an inspirational deal. It's gotten me super fired up. I'm optimistic as hell."

Beem needed to be, because suddenly he had more to play for than just pride. "The more money I make this fall, the more I can put down on my house, and the smaller my mortgage," he says.

After less than a year Beem had decided that his grand

Scottsdale experiment had been a failure. He was moving home to Las Cruces, to live in a new development called Sonoma Ranch. He had already picked out a house on the eponymous golf course, with sweeping views of the Oregon Mountains. Beem had never found his niche in Scottsdale, either socially or with the other Tour players in the area. This rated as something less than a surprise to Duplantis. "Rich is too nice a guy for that North Scottsdale scene," he says. "That's a sleazy, lying, L.A. kind of crowd. He doesn't belong at a fancy place like Grayhawk. Beemer's kind of golf is shorts, a Hawaiian shirt, a few beers, and a lot of laughs." Beem agrees. "Why am I going home? I miss playing El Paso Country Club, basically," he says. "I'm not a practicer. That's no secret. I don't have the attention span to sit on the range and beat balls 'til my hands bleed. I need to play in a competitive environment, and I wasn't getting that in Scottsdale, at all." Beem also had little use for Scottsdale's bustling singles scene. He was growing increasingly committed to his girlfriend, Sara Waide. "She's a cool, down-to-earth girl who likes to have fun," Duplantis says. "She's a great match for the Beemer. I could easily see them getting married."

Beem was having less success in his other long-distance relationships—with his Texas-based instructors, EPCC's Bill Eschenbrenner and Cameron Doan, who had moved on to Preston Trail Golf Club in Dallas but was still known to hang around the El Paso on occasion. Beem was anxious to be closer to both of them. In the 2000 season's first nine months Beem had seen Doan, his primary teacher, exactly one time. That had come in March, when they decided to straighten up Beem's posture, which would prevent him from dipping on the downswing. It took time for the change to gel, but heading into the fall Beem said, "I'm swinging at it better than I ever have before."

Beem got another important lesson at the Buick Open, which he traveled to following his seventy-second place finish at the International. Over the first two rounds at the Buick Beem was paired with Jim Furyk and Hal Sutton, who are among the very best players in the world at ball control. Both hung up terrific scores. "Furyk doesn't make a bogey for thirty-six holes," Beem says, incredulously. "Sutton just gives himself birdie chance after birdie chance. Me, I'm all over the fucking map. It's either a party or a train wreck on every hole. I'm watching them, and I'm going, You know what, they're not doing anything that special. They're not pulling crazy shots out of their cakehole, they're just playing good, solid golf. If they're content to hit it to the middle of the green every hole, than why am I firing at every flag? Who the fuck do I think I am?" Beem shot 76-76 to miss the cut at the Buick, giving him an extra two days to stew before the start of the Reno-Tahoe Open. When the tournament began he played the most boring brand of golf imaginable, fairway-and-greening the Montreux Golf and Country Club into submission. With rounds if 70-72-68-72 Beem finished a very encouraging seventeenth, his most consistent performance of the season. The next week he went 69-70-70-68 at the Air Canada Championship to finish thirty-first. "What can I say, I'm a slow learner," Beem chortles. The solid finishes in Canada and Reno were part of a late season surge during which Beem made seven of ten cuts, the most sustained, consistent stretch of his career. His improvement was reflected in the PGA Tour's statistics—for the 2000 season Beem was among the top 40 in both driving distance and total driving (which takes into account accuracy), and he had moved up to 90th in greens in regulation, up from 138th a year earlier. Though Beem didn't quite sneak into the top 125 on the money list, he proved to himself that he is finally ready to be a consistent force on Tour. Good thing, too, because Beem's victory at the Kemper makes him exempt in 2001, but not beyond. "Success out here is about so much more than swinging the golf club," says Beem. "It's about thinking right and getting on a roll and not being afraid to fail. It's so hard to reach that point, and this year I never really did. But you know what, I've still got a job next year. I promise you, next year I'll be more prepared."

The close to Duplantis's season was typically eventful. He spent much of August and September talking with his lawyer; his divorce from Vicki was finally being finalized. At a pretrial meeting in mid-September most of the details were ironed out to ensure that Duplantis would keep custody of Sierra, and he was expecting to sign the settlement shortly after the turn of the year.

Though Sierra was nearly five years old in September 2000, Duplantis decided to put off her schooling for another year, buying him time to figure out his next move, whatever that might be. His professional future was again hazy, following yet another screwup, this one at the Buick Challenge at the end of September: On the eve of the tournament Duplantis went on a late-night bender, and was unable to crawl out of bed for Gay's tee time the next day. He was unceremoniously fired as a result.

"It's no big deal," Duplantis says. "I wasn't that into it with Brian." Throughout his tenure with Gay, Duplantis grumbled about his man's limited potential. Of course, even a mediocre bag is better than none at all, but Duplantis is nothing if not an eternal optimist. "Something will come up, I'm sure," he says.

Duplantis's confidence is born of his knowledge of how screwy the golf world can be: His firing came at a perfect time to allow for a reunion between the ropes with Beem. Beem's caddie for the latter part of 2000, Billy Heim, decided to try to play his way through Q School, leaving Beem without a looper for the season's final month. With two of the final three tournaments—the Tampa Bay Classic and Disney—practically in Duplantis's backyard, it was a gimme for these old cohorts to reunite. Over those two Tour weeks in central Florida, Beem and Duplantis attended a Barenaked Ladies concert and a Tampa Bay Lightning hockey game and availed themselves of all the various nightlife possibilities, Beem often crashing at Duplantis's house. They also missed a couple of cuts together, but the on-course vibe was far different from how things had ended a year earlier. During the second round of the Tampa Bay Classic Beem four-putted the eighth hole to go six over par on his round. "Last year he would've packed it in," says Duplantis. "But he has matured a lot as a player. He fought like hell to try to make the cut." Beem birdied five of the last ten holes, missing the cut by a lone stroke. The following week at Disney Beem birdied the 36th hole, which he thought earned him a weekend tee time—but the cut line wound up dipping by one more stroke late in the day. Duplantis was still impressed by Beem's play. "Rich's hitting the ball great," says Duplantis. "He's really close." As for his own performace, Duplantis says, "No doubt about it, I was a better caddie for him than at the end of last season. It was really upbeat out there, really positive. Was it easy working together again? Definitely. It was like slipping right back into the saddle."

It would seem that fate is pulling these two kindred spirits back together again, but Duplantis is reluctant to speculate about the future, with Beem or otherwise. "This business is week to week, day to day, hour to hour," he says. "You never know what's around the next bend." With a chuckle, Duplantis adds, "That's all part of the fun."

EPILOGUE

Rich Beem Media Day at the El Paso Country Club. Ten days have passed since his epic victory at the 2002 PGA Championship. Beem so captured the imagination of the public with his gunslinger style and aw-shucks charm that, in wake of the PGA, David Letterman served up the Top 10 Surprising Facts About Rich Beem, a rare pop culture crossover for a golfer. (Number 2 on the list: *Even he has never heard of him.* Number one: *He doglegs to the left, if you know what I mean.*) To satisfy the cresting demand, today Beem has scheduled a marathon block of media moments, beginning with a 7:00 A.M. photo shoot for *Sports Illustrated* and ending with a live spot for local KTSM-TV at 6:23 P.M.

Over and over Beem emotes for the cameras and offers polished sound bites to the assembled reporters, his professional manner only slightly compromised by a shorts and flip-flops ensemble that recalls 1998, when Beem was making $347.50 every two weeks folding sweaters in the EPCC pro shop. Things have changed a bit since. This morning he screeched up to the club in a gleaming drop-top 500SL, the oversize Wannamaker trophy buckled into the passenger seat. Beem, however, was not toting any superstar airs. Throughout his twelve hours at the club he warmly greeted by name every dishwasher and lawn mower on the property, to say nothing of his fellow members. Two days earlier Beem had plunked down $10,000 to officially join the club, alongside the prominent local citizens whose tee times he used to book.

All the media attention was a bit heady, but it was just a prelude. The following evening EPCC threw a victory bash in honor of Beem, with a guest list running to six hundred names and live coverage on the Golf Channel. Uniformed El Paso cops stood sentry at the gates of the club, trying to maintain order.

All of the important people in Beem's life were on hand: his father, Larry, hanging out in the shadows, cracking wise with his cronies; his mentor, J. P. Hayes, sporting blue jeans and a goatee; his three dozen back-slapping sponsors, making liberal use of the open bar; his swing instructors Cameron Doan and Bill Eschenbrenner, each of whom would get face-time on the Golf Channel; his down-to-earth caddie, Billy Heim, holding hands with his wife, cradling his young daughter, and rebuffing all entreaties to do an interview on national TV; and, not least, his blushing bride, Sara, who was visibly mortified by all the attention. Not so the Beemer, who strolled the grounds of the club like a small-town mayor, dispensing sloppy hugs, mugging for pictures, and signing autographs. Eventually he was called up to a makeshift stage, where a proclamation by Texas governor Rick Perry was read, and Beem narrated highlights of the victory, when he stared down Tiger Woods on the back nine on Sunday.

"How it all worked out this way . . . it's just mind-blowing," Beem said at one point. "So many things could have turned out differently. So many things could have happened along the way."

Steve Duplantis wasn't a million miles away from the excitement, but close. He had spent the summer of '02 in self-imposed exile on the European tour, caddying for an unknown young Englishman named Grant Hamerton. Duplantis very nearly missed his old boss's victory. "You lose touch with reality over there," he says. "I knew Rich was off to a good start, but I wasn't really keeping track of the action until Sunday."

Following the final round at the Northwest of Ireland Open, where Hamerton finished sixty-first, Duplantis had called Beem's cell phone and was stunned to have him answer. Their conversation was brief.

"Dude, how do you feel?"

"I feel great. I'm ready to play."

"Nervous?"

"Not yet, but I expect to be."

"Hey man, I want you to know you belong there. You have already won tournaments, this is just another step. Just go for it out there today."

Upon arriving at the Belfast airport Duplantis monitored the early round action at the PGA by calling friends back in the United States. By the time Duplantis reached baggage claim in London, Beem was leading by four strokes midway through the back nine. "[Scottish Ryder Cupper] Andrew Coltart asked what was going on, and when I told him, he was like, 'Are you going to be okay?' Everyone thought I was going to be upset that Rich was winning. I was nothing but happy for the guy."

Duplantis finally tuned into the telecast at a friend's flat in London as Beem was playing the 71st hole. Reached on his cell phone moments after Beem had done his now-famous victory jig, Duplantis was hoarse with emotion. "I'm so proud of him," he said. "What a great story. It's hard to believe how far the Beemer has come."

Beem's unlikely journey to the PGA began during the final days of 2000. He rang in the new year by proposing to his girlfriend, Sara Waide, in Hawaii. The engagement was the highlight of a period of tremendous personal and professional growth. Between September and the trip to Hawaii, Beem made three sojourns to Dallas to work with Doan, for a long-overdue tightening of his swing and tweaking of his grip. It was a big commitment for a feel player who had always been dismissive of swing mechanics. Beem had also done a lot of soul-searching, stewing on his disastrous results in the preceding year and a half, and all that he was letting slip away. "At the end of '99 and most of 2000, I had gotten pretty satisfied," Beem says. "I was kind of living high off of my win, just because everybody was coming up and congratulating me and telling me: 'Oh, I saw you won the Kemper, that's a great story,' and I bought into it a little bit too much. Finally I decided I can't live off of that. Even if I don't win another tournament ever again, even though it's my one moment of glory, I still have to make a living. If not, I'm going to end up who knows where." By the time Beem arrived at his first tournament of 2001, the Tucson Open, he was, he says, "More relaxed and rested than I've been since I made the Tour." And it showed—he broke par all four rounds, tying for ninth place.

That strong finish was hardly a fluke. Early in the year it was apparent Beem had matured as a player, and no wonder. The exemption that came with winning the Kemper was now up; Beem was fighting for his livelihood, and every stroke counted. He opened the Phoenix Open with a 74, but instead of packing it in as he had so often in the past, he came back with a 67, just missing the cut by one shot. At the Bob Hope Classic he opened with a pair of middling 72s, but he ground out a 65 on Friday to make an important cut. At his next tournament, the Buick Invitational, Beem shot a final round 67 to move up two dozen spots. A twentieth-place finish at the L.A. Open was followed by a twelfth at the Greater Greensboro Open, and Beem continued his strong play during May's Texas swing. He spent much of the early week of the Byron Nelson Classic at Preston Trail Golf Club, refining his strengthened grip with Doan. "I was hitting it so good I just wanted to go out and try to get the ball in the hole real quick," Beem says. In both the Nelson's second and fourth round he didn't record a bogey, a far cry from his typical 18—"eight jagillion birdies, and just as many bogeys." With rounds of 71-65-70-71, Beem finished a very solid eleventh. Though the Nelson was Beem's fifth straight week on the road, he received a sponsor's exemption to the ensuing Colonial Invitational, and away he went: With four consistent rounds he finished twenty-sixth, and through the season's first four months Beem was hovering around the Top 40 on the money list.

"It took two tough years [following the '99 Kemper Open] for Rich to learn how to be a pro, and that entailed a lot more than swinging the golf club," says Doan. "He learned how to travel, and how to take care of himself on the road. After changing equipment a lot he finally got a perfect bag. He got a great caddie who brought a lot of stability. And he found the right woman, who was supportive, and who understood life on the road. Bottom line, it took a little while for Rich to grow up as a player."

•

Without a decent bag early in 2001, Duplantis latched on to Sean Murphy, a Buy.com lifer who had finally earned a shot in the big leagues. In six tournaments together Duplantis saw the weekend only once—in L.A., where Murphy went 74-79 to finish second from last. At the Houston Open, in late April, Duplantis overheard Gabe Hjertstedt talking on the putting green about needing a caddie. Duplantis caught him after the round, and it was decided that he would caddie for Hjertstedt over the next three weeks.

Hjertstedt was a much better fit for Duplantis than a straight arrow like Murphy. A stylish, rakish fellow, Hjertstedt is sponsored by one of Sweden's leading pornographers, though he only flies the company's logo when playing overseas. After taking the 1999 Tucson Open—thus becoming the first Swede to win two tour events—the talented but enigmatic Hjertstedt had fallen into the abyss, and he had started 2001 by missing seven of nine cuts.

In their first week together, at Greensboro, Duplantis poked and prodded and cajoled Hjertstedt to opening rounds of 70-69-67. Idling in the fairway of the par-5 15th hole on Sunday, they were just two strokes off the lead. Hjertstedt proceeded to rip a 3-wood that faded just right of the 15th green, where it hit a cart path and took a freakish hop O.B. He saved bogey, but victory was no longer a possibility. Now he was playing for money. Hjertstedt got up-and-down for pars on 16 and 17, and made a good-size putt for a birdie at the last.

"It was a different kind of feeling," Duplantis says. "If Jim Furyk makes a putt on the seventy-second hole to finish tied for fourth, instead of tied for ninth, it was like, Big deal, whatever. This was big. I was three months behind on my mortgage."

Hjertstedt and Duplantis continued to ride the good vibes of Greensboro. In their next two tournaments—New Orleans and the Nelson—they broke 70 in six of eight rounds. Of course, if there is one constant in Duplantis's caddie career, it's that his off-course conduct always complicates what could be a good partnership. In Memphis, following the Nelson, he decided to share a room with a veteran caddie known far and wide as "the Punk." "He's a good guy, fun to hang out with, but you should never, ever stay with the Punk," says Duplantis. "I have a couple times in the past, and I always get in trouble. Anyway, one night in Memphis I went out, got back to the room at like four A.M., and I tell Punk to wake me up the next morning. Of course he doesn't. At 7:05 A.M. my phone rings. It's Gabe. We're on the tee in forty minutes. I'm like, Oh, I'm in the car right now, I'll be there in a couple minutes. I jump up, don't shower, don't even look in the mirror. I get to the course twenty minutes later. He double bogies the first hole, and it's just a death march the rest of the way.

"After the round he's just steaming. He's like, "You stink like a fucking brewery. I want to fire you right now. I want to fire you so much right now.' He didn't, though. It must mean I'm a pretty good caddie."

Beem's strong play early in 2001 season was dangerously seductive. Afraid of losing his mojo, he kept playing during what were supposed to be off weeks, and by the time he looked up he had soldiered through a staggering eleven consecutive tournaments, on a tour where four in a row is considered overdoing it. After taking one week off at the end of June, Beem went back to work at the Western Open, and for the rest of the summer he played like a tired man, which he was. Beem had also become increasingly obsessed with perfecting the changes in his action. "I wasn't scoring worth a damn," he says. "I got so into my swing, I forgot to get the ball in the hole." From the Western to the Texas Open at the end of September, a span of eight events, Beem missed four cuts and never finished better than sixtieth, pushing him to the precipice of the Top 125. Beem had so little confidence in his ability to retain his card that, near the end of the slide, he sent in his Q School application.

After a dispiriting 73-74 weekend at the Texas Open, Beem had planned to withdraw from the ensuing Michelob Championship in Williamsburg, Virginia, but he decided to go at the last minute, blowing in on Wednesday afternoon. Instead of cramming in a practice round, he leisurely strolled Kingsmill Golf Club without his clubs, charting yardages with a laser guide and trying to envision the shots he would need to play. "It was the most relaxed I had felt on a golf course in a long time," he says.

Beem started the first round birdie-birdie and went on to

shoot a 66, putting himself near the lead. Friday he came back with a solid 70. All he needed was a Top 10 finish to secure his card, but it wouldn't be a gimme. Saturday morning it hailed sideways, and the round was played in some of the coldest, most extreme conditions of the year. "I thought seventy-five would be a great score," he says. He fought his way to a 72.

Heading into the final round, "I was sweating it, big time," Beem says. "I knew what an important round it was." Throughout the season Beem had displayed tremendous patience and resolve—he would finish the year 117th in overall scoring average, but forty-fifth on Sunday—and during the final round he was finally rewarded. He birdied the first hole and brawled with the course on every ensuing shot. On the 16th hole he drained a fifteen-foot birdie putt, cracking the Top 10 on the leaderboard. "Now I'm really nervous," he says. "I've come this far and I really don't want to screw up."

On 17 Beem "puked it onto the green" and two-putted for par. The long par-4 18th at Kingsmill is an exceedingly difficult driving hole, with water up the left side and its rolling fairway pinched by trees on the right, and when Beem arrived on the tee, two groups were waiting to hit, so he had to stew on the shot for some twenty minutes. "I was just getting more and more nervous," he says. "I've been in this position before, and have usually hit a quick hook, because I'm too jacked up. This time I did everything I could to relax." When it was finally his turn to hit, Beem ripped a 3-wood down the middle, followed by "the best six-iron of my life." He two-putted for par, tying for seventh and earning $101,850, shooting to 109th on the season-ending money list and securing his card for 2002. The close call had a galvanizing effect on Beem.

"After almost losing my job," he says, "I decided I would never put myself in that situation again."

Duplantis also got some closure at Kingsmill, as he was fired by Hjertstedt. The Michelob was their eighth missed cut in nine events, and Hjertstedt said he wanted to try to shake things up. (It didn't work—he would miss four more cuts to close the year.) Duplantis played out the string caddying for David Morland (fifty-eighth at Las Vegas) and Doug Dunakey (missed cut at Disney, fifty-fourth at the Southern Farm Bureau Classic). One thing about Duplantis: For all of the mistakes he makes, none of his former employers stay mad for very long. In addition to an enduring friendship with Beem, he sometimes plays golf with Brian Gay in Florida, and Hjertstedt invited Duplantis to caddie for him at Q School, in December of 2001. They finished a distant ninety-fourth, which meant Hjertstedt would be playing primarily in Europe in 2002. Once again Duplantis was at loose ends heading into a new season.

After a cameo with Hjertstedt at the '02 Pebble Beach National Pro-Am, where they finished seventy-second, Duplantis spent most of the early season hanging out at home, playing golf, attending Tampa Bay Lightning games, and visiting his daughter, Sierra, in Hickory, North Carolina, where she was now living full-time with ex-girlfriend Jennifer (the MasterCard salesgirl) and her sprawling family.

He did make time to catch a couple of Warrant concerts; somehow Duplantis had befriended members of the seminal eighties hair-metal band, to the point that he is pictured on their website (http://warrantweb.net/rockfestpage.htm), adorned by the caption, "Our bro Steve Duplantis, the rock star trapped in a PGA caddie's body." "I've been backstage with a lot of big-name bands, and it's boring," Duplantis says. "These new bands, all they do is sit around checking their e-mail and sipping mineral water. The boys in Warrant, they don't know the eighties are over. It's wild—drugs, half-naked chicks everywhere, just a non-stop party. Anything goes."

Duplantis professed to being unconcerned about missing the start of the golf season, as he was buried in the paperwork of trying to sell his house, which required doing business with his estranged and unpredictable wife, Vicki. The house—too big and too expensive for just Duplantis and his daughter—finally sold in late April. Duplantis, without a bag, headed back to the Tour.

For a player not known for his practice habits, it seems odd that Beem chose to get married on a driving range, but the December 2001 ceremony at El Paso Country Club was a rollicking good time. Under an elegant white tent, amidst a forest of flowers, Rich and Sara affirmed their lifelong commitment to each other in "a real traditional wedding, except for the bar in the tent," says Beem's friend Rick Hillbrecht, who caught the garter and still displays it in his bedroom. "Everybody had a cocktail in their hand for the ceremony, which is how Rich wanted it."

The newlyweds enjoyed a dreamy honeymoon in Pebble Beach, but after the New Year they were quickly thrust back into the real world. A refreshingly no-nonsense gal, Sara insisted on keeping her job in pharmaceutical sales, to take some of the financial burden off her hubby, as well as to keep one foot planted in the real world. However, Beem has always found the road a lonely place, and it was even more so without his wife. He missed the cut at four of his first six events in 2002, but had a breakthrough at the seventh, Doral, where he finally found monogamy with a putter.

In 2001 Beem had developed into one of the Tour's premiere ball strikers, finishing seventeenth in the total driving stats, which combines accuracy and distance. Only twenty-eight players made more eagles. But he was a desultory 125th in putting, in part because he could never find a putter he fancied. In the six months leading up to Doral he had fiddled with, he says, "Three or four dozen different putters. No joke."

At Doral, Beem took a shine to an unorthodox NXT putter, with a head that looked like it was inspired by the Stealth Bomber. With some superlative work on the greens he surged to a fourth-place finish, and the $225,600 payday finally convinced Sara to quit her job and travel full-time with Rich.

"It made such a huge difference immediately," he says. "She had it all figured out—where we were going for dinner, where the dry-cleaners was, the gym, the movie theater. Life suddenly became so much easier, and so much more fun."

Beem continued to build on his good play throughout the spring. At the Players Championship he shot a final round 66 on the Tour's toughest golf course, and that was followed by a strong fourteenth at New Orleans. In early June Beem traveled to what will always be his favorite tournament, the Kemper Open, and he damn near pulled off another victory, going 68-68-69-69 to finish second, one lone stroke back of Bob Estes. It was

Beem's best finish in three years. He was not disappointed to have come up short but, rather, elated to have finally sniffed victory again. "I grinded my butt off all day and just fell one short," he said in a Sunday evening press conference. "So be it. I played well, and I kept my head together, which was probably the biggest thing I'm going to take away from this. I walked off the eighteenth green and I was getting a little emotional just because I actually grinded it out hard for seventy-two holes. And it was just well worth the satisfaction. I didn't let down. I didn't let myself down at all."

Beem continued to play solid golf through the summer, including a 64 on Sunday at the Greater Milwaukee Open, his low round of the year. He got a little jolt the following week when his El Paso Country Club mentor, J. P. Hayes, stormed to victory at the John Deere Classic, shooting 22 under and blowing away the field by four strokes. That Sunday night Beem was reached on his cell phone outside Denver, where he was preparing for the International; in between bursts of yelling at a telecast of his beloved Atlanta Braves, Beem said, "Watching J. P. win today has got me super-fired up. I've been feeling for a while like my game is on the verge of exploding, and I can't wait to get out there."

Duplantis resurfaced in New Orleans, in the first week of May, trolling the parking lot for a job at the Compaq Classic. He wound up with Fred Wadsworth, thirty-nine, who has barely made a ripple since winning the 1986 Southern Open. Wadsworth opened with a 76 and missed the cut. At the Byron Nelson Classic Duplantis missed the cut with John (Rambo) Riegger, who is widely regarded as the Tour's most accomplished hunter. Riegger, a thirty-nine-year-old who has never finished better than 162nd on the tour money list, offered his caddie the job for the rest of the season, and it is a measure of Duplantis's desperation that he accepted. However, Riegger wasn't playing again until the Greater Hartford Open, six weeks later, so in the meantime Duplantis journeyed to the Kemper, where he was again reduced to parking lot duty. Wadsworth tapped him on the shoulder one more time, and they shot 75-80 to miss the cut by a mile.

After a sixty-third at Hartford and a fifty-fourth at Memphis, Riegger and Duplantis went 66-69 on the weekend at the Western, tying for fifteenth place and earning an automatic spot in the British Open field. Duplantis was more than ready for an overseas adventure. "The European caddies, those are my boys," he says. "You go out with caddies here and everyone is all uptight, like, Hey, man, isn't it your turn to buy a round? The Euros, they don't give a shit. You've got two full glasses of beer at all times."

Which explains why Riegger canned Duplantis after they shot 78-74 to miss the cut at the Open Championship. "I did a good job for John," Duplantis says, "but he was a little pissed because I came home late a couple of times and woke him up."

With the likes of Fred Wadsworth beckoning, Duplantis decided he wasn't ready to head back home. "I figured if I wasn't going to make any money I might as well have some fun and see the world," he says. Hello, Euro tour.

Duplantis quickly latched onto Grant Hamerton, a twenty-nine-year-old who had earned his spot on the circuit thanks to some fine play on the Challenge tour, the European minor leagues. Their first tournament together was the Scandinavian Masters in Stockholm, where Hamerton finished forty-third, earning 10,260 Euros, and Duplantis availed himself of the local culture. "I met a nice girl in Sweden. . . ."

Here we refer to an e-mail from Australian reporter Bernie McGuire, the most dogged chronicler of the Euro tour's comings and goings. "Steve turned up at the Swiss event with this Swedish glamour," Bernie writes. "White-blonde hair, fishnet stockings, thigh-length black boots . . . say no more."

"Okay, maybe she wasn't so nice," Duplantis allows. "She was exactly what you'd expect. Very . . . uh . . . very . . . aggressive. She didn't speak much English, but that was fine."

Over the next five weeks Duplantis journeyed to the Wales Open at Celtic Manor (where Hamerton missed the cut), the Northwest of Ireland Open (sixty-first, worth 875 Euros), the Scottish PGA at Gleneagles (M/C), the BMW International Open in Munich (M/C), and, finally, the European Masters in Crans-su-Sierre, Switzerland (M/C). For Duplantis this jag across Europe was a fresh start, and he impressed Hamerton with his dedication.

"I had read the book, so I knew his reputation, but he was quite a good caddie," says Hamerton. "He turned up on time, no problems like that. He did everything well on the course. You could rely on what he said. He gave me a little shot of confidence when I needed it."

Hamerton also noted how easily Duplantis was welcomed into the tour's tight-knit community. "He seemed to know all the lads by the second week," Hamerton says. "But then he's not one to sit back in the hotel room reading a book, is he?"

For Duplantis it was a chance to see how the other half lives. "I've been to Europe plenty of times in the past," he says, "but this time I got to do it like they do. It's not easy over there. You look at a map, and it's like, How the hell are we supposed to get from here to there? Everything is a struggle. To get to the course you take a cab to the train station, a train to the player's hotel, then a bus to the course." In Sweden the bus was so full that Barry Lane—a Ryder Cupper who has twice finished in the Top 10 on the Order of Merit—was barred from boarding and had to find his own way to the course.

The flipside is that the endless hassles of European travel, the unfamiliar tongues, and the smaller, more intimate trappings of the tour make for an unrivaled camaraderie among the players and caddies, which Duplantis spooned up. (Also, the purses are so small that only the top players can afford to have their families travel with them.) The sightseeing could also be thrilling. "It's pretty cool to be driving on the Autobahn, doing a hundred forty miles an hour and get high-beamed by a Porsche that just blows by you. In the Alps, you're on these twisty little rounds zigzagging around glaciers." And then there was Amsterdam—"all the fun you can have for thirty-five Euros," Duplantis says. His Swedish paramour also popped in for the occasional visit. By the last week of the journey, in Switzerland, Duplantis was out of clean clothes. "There is absolutely nowhere to do laundry over there," he says. "I had to clean up my act, because I was looking forward to this visit—she had been sending me dirty e-mails. So I filled up the bathtub with hot, soapy water and grabbed a broomstick and did my own laundry in the hotel room."

Eventually the fun had to end, and getting home provided its own adventures. Riegger had paid for a round-trip ticket with Chicago and Edinburgh as the ports of call. So Duplantis took an $80 cab to the train station in Crans, caught a ride to Geneva, flew to London, then Edinburgh, then Chicago, then on to North Carolina. "At this point I was really ready to get back to the comforts of the PGA Tour," he says.

On a weekly stipend of £500, plus Hamerton's meager earnings, Duplantis somehow managed to break even for the summer fling. "It's not something to make a career out of," he says of the Euro tour, "but for two months it was an absolute blast."

The International, at Castle Pines Golf Club outside Denver, is played under the modified Stableford system, where players accrue points, not strokes: 8 for a double eagle (which almost never happens), 5 for eagle, two for birdie, -1 for bogey, -3 for double or worse. Par is worth nothing, which made the format perfect for Beem's gunslinger style. During the first round he rang up ten points, surging into second place. However, because of a weather delay, Beem finished just before dark, attracting scant attention; seven players journeyed into the media room but he wasn't one of them. During the second round Beem got bageled, slipping to ninth place and further off the radar. On Saturday he piled up fifteen points, moving into fourth place, but most of the attention was trained on players behind him: Sergio Garcia was in fifth place, and Ernie Els and Greg Norman were tied for sixth.

There would be no ignoring Beem on Sunday. He roared to seven birdies in the first eleven holes to take a commanding nine-point lead, setting the stage for one of the wildest finishes in PGA Tour history.

After parring the 16th hole Beem's lead was eight points, and the CBS commentators had all but conceded the tournament to him. The finish looked so devoid of drama that conversation turned to Beem's hair; months earlier he had had the tips frosted blond, as if he were a thirty-one-year-old Backstreet Boy. As Beem removed his cap to run his fingers through his mane, Gary McCord hooted, "That looks like a spotted owl's nest. That's horrendous."

"It's not a hairdo," David Feherty added. "It's a hair *don't.*"

The yukking didn't last long. Behind Beem, Steve Lowery, the 1994 International champ, was beginning to go berserk. He made birdie on the 14th hole by splashing a shot out of a greenside pond onto the green, then jarred an approach shot on the par-4 15th hole for eagle. Suddenly Beem's lead had been cut to three points, which he discovered moments after bashing his second shot pin-high on the par-5 17th hole. With an awesome focus he then stepped up and rolled in a curling twenty-footer for an eagle and five more points. Beem repeatedly pumped his fist, loosing the frustration of three-plus winless years. He, like everybody else, was sure that the eagle iced the tournament. But not so fast.

After a three-putt bogey on 16, Lowery proceeded to hole a 204-yard 6-iron on the par-5 17th, an albatross worth a whopping eight points. Suddenly Beem's lead was down to one lone point.

"I have never seen anything like this," Jim Nantz intoned on the broadcast.

Beem got the bad news while walking to the 18th green, and it seemed as if all the blood drained from his body. It was all he could do to wiggle in two putts for par, ceding the stage to Lowery, who could steal the tournament with a birdie at the last. Beem had torn up one of the Tour's best golf courses to the tune of nineteen points, one shy of the single-day tournament record (in stroke play he shot 63), yet he was on the verge of losing to one of the flukiest finishing kicks the game has ever known. The cruelty of the situation caused Beem to have a mini-nervous breakdown on national TV. Standing behind the 18th green, watching Lowery attack the hole, Beem alternately ran his fingers through his hair, rubbed his temples, exhaled huge gusts of air, and occasionally stared to the heavens, apparently looking for intervention.

"Good thing there's no chance for a playoff," CBS's Lanny Wadkins said, while watching Beem's torment, "because I don't think he would be able to handle it."

Lowery played a brilliant approach to twelve feet, but he missed the putt on the high side by maybe a quarter of an inch.

Behind the green Beem wrapped Sara in a long bear hug, and his eyes flooded with tears as he did a breathless interview with Feherty. "I can't even talk right now," Beem said, but he quickly rallied. "El Paso Country Club, the guys in the men's grill, run up the tab."

Two days later the club hosted a joint party for Beem and Hayes, with all the usual trimmings. The evening was notable for an exchange between Beem and Doan. "Rich told me he never thought he could win on that good a course, against that strong a field," says Doan. "He said to me at the party, 'This off-season I want us to figure out what I have to do to contend for major championships.' I was thrilled to hear that kind of focus, but I said, 'Shoot, you may not have noticed, but you're already there. Just go to the PGA next week and let it rip. Who knows, you might beat 'em all again.' "

Beem opened the eighty-fourth PGA Championship with a 72 at Hazeltine National Golf Club, in Chaska, Minnesota, attracting little notice on a day when there were half a dozen sub-70 scores. On Friday he shot a dazzling 66, moving into a five-way tie for the lead, along with Retief Goosen, Mark Calcavecchia, Justin Leonard, and Fred Funk. Tiger Woods was tied for sixth, two back. Though Beem's ball striking had not been crisp over the opening thirty-six holes, he made up for it with deadeye work on the greens. "If he keeps putting like that he'll win for sure," Beem's playing partner Robert Allenby said on Friday. "I've never seen anybody roll the ball like that for two days in a row."

Following the second round Beem was led into the vast media center, his first real exposure to the full national press corps that turns out for the majors. Never one to be shy around a microphone, he went through the details of his round but spent most of the time waxing on his unlikely life story and belated maturation as a player. He was by turns funny—asked why he still imbibes Pepto-Bismol before every round, a habit that began at the '99 Kemper, Beem said, "So I don't go number two on the golf course"—and self-deprecating, saying, "I'm just as surprised as you all that I'm sitting here."

Picking up on Beem's mirth, the Saturday morning papers treated him as an amusing sidelight, a fun story for a day but not a serious contender, what with Woods lurking and three other major championship winners—Calcavecchia, Goosen, and Leonard—also atop the leaderboard. But during the third round, with the course all the more fraught thanks to forty-mile-per-hour gusts and brutal pin placements, Beem shot a scrappy 72, leaving him in solo second place, three behind Leonard, whose flawless 69 had the look of a career-defining performance. (Fred Funk was in third place, four strokes behind Leonard, while Woods and Calcavecchia were tied for fourth, five back.) By the time Beem ambled into the press center Saturday night the tone had changed. Suddenly he was a threat to win the season's final Grand Slam event, and he was asked thoughtful questions about how he would handle his emotions during the final round, whether he would monitor the scoreboards, and how the swirling winds affected his club selection.

Beem may have earned the respect of this discerning audience, but he was still playing possum. "I don't feel like I have anything to lose tomorrow," he said. "I don't have any expectations of winning, I guess that's the easiest way to put it. I know I can play with these guys, but to win a major you have to have something special, and I don't know if I have it. . . . It's so huge that I'm having a hard time comprehending it. It's a major, and guys like me are not supposed to contend in majors. Yet here I am."

Beem sounded like an awestruck fan in discussing Leonard's 69. "I think he's going to be really tough to catch," he said of the 1997 British Open champ, who had spent the previous year and a half rebuilding his swing under the watchful eye of Butch Harmon. "Not saying it's impossible. But if he keeps hitting the ball like he did today and has his usual touch around the greens, he's going to be pretty unbeatable. So I'm looking forward to watching it firsthand."

Near the end of the press conference Beem was asked another question about *Bud, Sweat, & Tees*. The book had come up the day before during the press conference, as the nation's newspapermen were scrambling to figure out who in the world is Rich Beem. This time he was asked, "Now that you're becoming more known for your golf, do you wish some of the stuff that was in the book wasn't printed?"

"No, because that was who I was at the time," Beem said. "The only thing I regret about the book was the use of profanity in it. The written word is certainly different than the spoken word. That's the only thing I didn't really enjoy about it. That was me at the time. That's probably me every so often now. But it's not the same. I mean, I'm a totally different person than I was then. I'm a better player. I have a much more stable life off the golf course. When I get to the golf tournaments, I don't go out anymore. I go to dinner and I go home. I'm a lot more focused and the golf is a lot more fun. I get a lot more sleep on the road."

Saturday night at the PGA Beem slept like a baby, according to his wife. He had done such a good job downplaying his chances that maybe he really did believe he had nothing to lose. (When it was all over, Leonard would say, "I've played dumb before. It's a pretty good place to be. After this week, he won't be able to do that anymore.")

Beem was playing in the final twosome with Leonard, the flinty Texan who has HOGAN on his cap and Hogan in his heart. Early in the round it seemed as if the players had gotten their roles reversed. While Leonard's swing and psyche completely unraveled, Beem methodically took apart the golf course. He coolly birdied two of the first four holes, then drew more blood at the par-5 7th. Idling in the fairway, 260 yards from the pin, Heim said, "What do you think?"

"We haven't backed off all week," Beem said. "Why start now?"

He ripped a 3-wood to the front of the green and two-putted for another birdie. By the time Beem reached the 10th tee he was leading the tournament, and his only serious challenger was Woods, who was one stroke back playing two holes ahead.

The back nine was one for the ages. Beem landed an uppercut with a stunning eagle on the 11th hole, set up by a 267-yard 7-wood that nestled to within six feet of the hole. That big bird pushed Beem's lead to three strokes; Woods saw the scoreboard change as he was idling on the 13th green, and for the first time in his already legendary career his knees seemed to buckle. He promptly three-putted from twelve feet for a bogey, then hit a screaming hook into the cabbage off the 14th tee. The ensuing bogey pushed Beem's lead to a whopping five strokes, but he gave one back on 14, as his drive settled in a fairway divot, and, after a wayward approach shot, he was unable to get up-and-down from a plugged lie in the greenside bunker.

Despite the bogey, it seemed as if Beem had landed a knockout punch, but there's no quit in Tiger Woods, which he proved yet again with an electric finish. "When I was on fifteen," he said following the final round, "I told [my caddie Steve Williams], 'If we birdie in, we'll win the tournament. Let's just suck it up and get it done.' That is exactly what I did. I didn't miss a shot coming in."

Woods was four strokes behind Beem at the time of his prognostication. Do the math, and he expected Beem to close in at least one over par. What Woods never expected was that Beem would play two textbook shots into Hazeltine National's signature hole, the watery par-4 16th, then drain a curling thirty-five-footer that was arguably the putt of the year in professional golf.

"He just went out there and played great today," Tiger said following the final round. "That's awfully impressive, to go out there and shoot a round like that, when he absolutely had to do it."

Leading by two strokes on the 72nd hole, Beem needed only a bogey to hand Woods his first ever runner-up finish in a major. Beem's description of the final hole: "I just thinned an eight-iron onto the front edge and managed to three-jiggle it down there." The three-putt was his first of the week—Beem led the PGA with only 107 putts—and after tapping in for his 68 he did an unforgettable white-man's boogie, a spontaneous showing of euphoria that has come to symbolize his unlikely victory. When Woods wins majors he displays more relief than joy; it's as if this most relentless of competitors is crossing one more item off his to-do list. Not so with Beem.

"What I like about Rich is that he plays to his personality," says J. P. Hayes. "I'm a pretty boring guy, and when I win, no one really gets excited, and I don't blame them. Rich is just the opposite. He's got the smile, the fist pump, the dancing, that blue-collar humility. No wonder people love him."

For Beem the magnitude of the success was new, but he shared it with an old friend. "Rich arrived about twelve-thirty the night of the final round at Boeing Field, and I was the only one there to pick him up," David Wyatt says of the small general aviation airport outside Seattle, the site of the ensuing NEC Invitational, one of four so-called World Golf Championship events that Beem could only dream of playing in just three weeks before. "He walked into the terminal and he had the biggest shit-eating grin I've ever seen. We didn't say a word, we just started hugging and crying. We stayed up till four that morning, just giggling. I mean, are you kidding me? It was only a few years earlier that we were working at Magnolia Hi-Fi and he had quit the game. Now he's the PGA Championship winner, with a big ol' shiny trophy and a check for a million bucks in his pocket? Who's writing this stuff?"

The script would only get more outlandish. Beem returned to Seattle as conquering hero, and the symmetry of his journey from cell phone salesman to the PGA Championship was so tidy even Beem couldn't resist revisiting his past. On his first day in Seattle he skipped Sahalee Country Club in favor of a visit to Magnolia Hi-Fi. "My wife needed a digital camera, and I couldn't think of anywhere else to go," he said, unconvincingly.

While Beem was in the store a couple of reporters happened to call, hoping to get a comment from a current employee about the new PGA champ. Beem shocked them by answering the phone himself and chatting away. He spent the rest of the day getting a haircut and shopping for a Porsche. "My wife said I could go buy whatever I felt like," Beem said, but he left the showroom without new wheels. "Nobody wanted to help me because I was wearing shorts and sneakers and a baseball cap. Nobody recognized me, which was totally fine."

The carefree day bopping around town was an anomaly. Beem had become an overnight folk hero, equal parts Tin Cup, Walter Mitty, and the boy next door, with a playful on-course manner, self-deprecating sense of humor, and the clean-cut good looks of a J. Crew model to boot. Beem's star turn at the PGA had created a tremendous amount of media interest, and beginning Tuesday it was time to feed the machine. After an early practice round at Sahalee Country Club he held a packed press conference, which was followed by remote interviews with Jim Rome and Connie Chung. The next morning Beem awakened at 3:45 A.M. to appear live on the *Today* show. By the time the first round of the NEC rolled around Beem was worn out, and it showed. His opening drive clanged off a 150-foot tall Douglas fir tree, and he finished with a three-over 74, missing ten putts inside of fifteen feet. "I wasn't prepared mentally or physically," he said afterward.

Beem's unfocused play rekindled memories of the swoon that followed his victory at the Kemper Open. Now that he was on top of the golf world, was Beem going to party like it's 1999? He provided an emphatic answer at the NEC, posting three consecutive 67s to climb into a tie for 6th place. Beem's resolve in some small way validated his overnight superstardom. "I didn't come here to lay down and take my check and go home," Beem said following the final round. Even his harshest critic was bowled over: "That was the most impressive thing he's done lately," said Larry Beem. "That showed a hell of a lot of pride and professionalism. I think the kid has finally figured it all out."

Beem earned $150,000 at the NEC, bringing his total haul for the month of August to $1.95 million. He didn't earn another trophy but he still had a hand in the victory. Following his win at the NEC, his first in 235 starts on the PGA Tour, well-traveled Australian Craig Parry was asked to explain his long overdue breakthrough. "Well, to be honest, I haven't changed anything in my game," Parry said. "I watched Rich Beem win last week at the PGA and I thought, Why can't I do that? The shot he tried to play, he played without hesitation. For me lately, I haven't been focused a hundred percent on the shot I wanted to play. I saw in Rich and in his mannerisms a confidence in the way he was playing. And thinking about him gave me a bit of belief that I could go out and do it."

Beem calls Parry's praise "one of the nicest compliments I've ever gotten," but it wasn't the highlight of his week. That came Thursday night, when Beem celebrated his thirty-second birthday by taking twenty friends and family members to the swank Metropolitan Grill in downtown Seattle. "Rich shows up in nice slacks, a nice shirt . . . and flip-flops," says Wyatt. "It was perfect. Anyway, midway through the meal this lady sneaks up to Rich and does the whole song and dance about how she's sorry to bother him, but. . . . Turns out it's her dad's birthday, he's a huge golf fan, a huge Rich Beem fan, and would Rich mind saying hello. So he just pops up, goes out, and spends like fifteen minutes talking to the guy, signing autographs, taking pictures, just working the whole room. He lit up the entire place. On the way out, the owners wanted a photo with Rich, so he jumps behind the bar. Then he starts tending bar. He's back there mixing drinks, chatting up customers. I finally had to drag him out of there. He would have been making Jack 'n' Cokes all night." Wyatt stops to catch his breath. "I guarantee Tiger Woods has never enjoyed any of his majors like Rich is going to enjoy the PGA."

During the week of the International, Beem took the time to change the course of his old caddie's career. Beem buttonholed tour bad boy Garrett Willis and encouraged him to offer his vacant caddie job to Duplantis. "I thought they would be perfect for each other," Beem says with a knowing laugh.

Willis burst onto the scene at the 2001 Tucson Open, becoming only the third player to win his first PGA Tour start, along with Ben Crenshaw (1973) and Robert Gamez ('90). His talent was matched only by his petulance; in its March 4, 2002, edition, *Sports Illustrated* released the results of an anonymous survey of seventy Tour players, in which Willis's colleagues named him their least favorite playing partner, quite an accomplishment for a player only in his second year.

Willis's reputation among the caddies was even worse. By the International he had gone through eight or nine loopers in 2002 alone, and he lost another one during the second round, when after nine holes Ken McCluskey simply walked off the course, tired of being abused (Willis's wife, Jennifer, was called in from the gallery to carry the bag over the final nine holes). With all this tumult Willis's play has suffered dramatically. In his first twenty-six tournaments in 2002 he missed eleven cuts and withdrew four times following the first round, including a quick getaway after an 84 to open the Buick Classic.

And yet for all of his troubles, Willis was a tantalizing bag for Duplantis, the kind of talented reclamation project at which he excels. During their first week together, at the Tampa Bay Classic in September, Willis shot 71-72-74-76 to finish seventy-fourth, yet he kept his composure, no small feat. "I'm just looking for somebody who will help me on the golf course, help me make the right decisions and not make mistakes. That's where Duplantis comes in," Willis said afterward. "The guy is so solid as a caddie and makes so few mistakes. The asset that he is on the bag is immeasurable, and saves me one or two shots a round."

If Duplantis could turn Willis around it would be his most stunning accomplishment yet, but, as always, he was his own worst enemy. Four days after the Tampa Bay Classic, in its September 28, 2002, issue, *Golf Week* carried an item in its well-read gossip column "The Forecaddie":

> *Leave it to veteran looper Steve Duplantis to make things interesting around the caddyshack. Duplantis, working for Garrett Willis at the Tampa Bay Classic, showed up at the caddie trailer Sunday morning after an all-night party wearing only a T-shirt and a towel wrapped around him. He had no pants, no shoes, no socks, no underwear, no money, no car keys [hence no car], no yardage book, no cap, no sunglasses. Nothing, except the T-shirt, towel, and a hangover. Duplantis, whose former bosses include Jim Furyk and Rich Beem, somehow . . .*

Duplantis has a slightly different version of what happened. "I had socks on, they were just different colors," he says. "I didn't misplace my rental car, my keys were stolen. I knew exactly where the car was. And I didn't have a bad hangover, I just felt a little weird, which is why I think I was drugged."

It seems that on the night in question he had gone to a Tampa Bay Lightning game, setting up shop in his usual spot, Ron Campbell's luxury suite (Duplantis is nothing if not well connected). Here he picks up the narrative: "This little kinky bitch kept coming up to me, asking for my number, telling me to meet her after the game. I finally said okay just to get rid of her. I had had three or four Bud Lights at the hockey game, no big deal. I was fine. I met her at a bar near the stadium. She offered to get me a drink, and next I know it's three-thirty in the morning and a security guard is nudging me awake on the sidewalk. My shorts were gone and everything in them—cell phone, wallet, everything. My ass didn't hurt. I wasn't violated in any way. But I was definitely robbed."

The story spread like the flu. "You can't imagine how many calls I got," Duplantis says. "The whole tour saw it. One of the other caddies ratted me out to *Golf Week*, and it's just another example of how guys are always trying to fuck you over out here. No one contacted me to get my side of the story, and that stupid little article is only going to make it harder for me to get a good bag."

Duplantis still puts his usual spin on the tale. "Bottom line, I had a little incident, but I still arrived at the course early and did a good job for Garrett."

Willis, no stranger to turmoil, was understanding. "I didn't even know about it until people started calling me," he says. "Steve may have some problems off the course, but he did a fine job for me that day."

Duplantis would get a more tangible vote of confidence. Following Tampa Bay, Willis went to the Texas Open, where he had long since promised his bag to an old college roommate. Willis opened with a 74, but maybe Duplantis's preaching about patience from the week before was still ringing in his head: He closed the tournament 61-66-66 to finish second and cash a check for $261,333.33. With other caddies suddenly whispering sweet nothings in his ear, Willis still wanted Duplantis to pack for him at the season-ending Southern Farm Bureau Classic. At the start of the week he even affirmed their partnership into 2003.

"I asked Garrett if we were on for next year, like we had talked about," says Duplantis. "He said, 'If I can stand the sight of you after next week.' That's Garrett-speak for yes."

At the rain-shortened Southern Farm Bureau Classic, Willis shot 68-71-70 to finish twenty-fifth, his third-best showing of the year. He talked about Duplantis following the second round. "The guy's such an excellent caddie. He's one of the best

I've ever had. He's great with yardage and helping me keep my cool. Everybody's got their own personal problems. As long as he shows up and does a good job at work, that's all I'm concerned with. What he does with his spare time is his own business. He's done a great job. He's shown up."

Willis is a little less flowery between the ropes. "He's the most difficult guy to work for out here, by far," says Duplantis. "He beats you down. He pretty much makes you eat shit at least once a round. Guaranteed at least once a day he'll say 'Just shut up and give me yardages.' I can take it. I know I'm good at what I do. As long as we're making money it doesn't bother me in the least."

In addition to fame and fabulous riches, the PGA victory brought Beem a five-year PGA Tour exemption, during which he is automatically in the field of all four majors, as well as every other important tournament. "I'm now freed up to play without a care in the world," he says. "I can play for trophies, and not have to worry about job security and paying the bills. My whole life I've been scratching and clawing to get out here. Now I've finally arrived, and I'm getting greedy—not for money, but other stuff: world ranking points, spots on the money list, big, shiny trophies. I'm already thinking about the Ryder Cup in two years. That's my real goal. That's the mack daddy of them all."

That Beem already has a objective for 2004 is a promising sign. Staying hungry will be the key for a player who was previously known only for his thirst. As he continues to grow into the role of leading man, he will increasingly need to lean on the solid support group he has assembled, Sara in particular. "I've matured so much outside of golf," Beem says, "and a lot of it has to do with my beautiful bride. She grounds me on the days I need to be grounded and she lets me be a free spirit on the days when it's okay."

Sara even gets a stamp of approval from Wyatt, her biggest rival for Beem's affections. "She's a classy lady who brings out the best in Rich," says Wyatt, who has continued to move up the ladder at Microsoft and will be married sometime in late 2003, pending the ever-fluctuating schedule of his best man. "If I had to say one bad thing about her, it would be her taste in jewelry. She likes a lot of it."

Beem has also benefited from the stability that Billy Heim has brought to the bag. A solid family man with a strong playing résumé, Heim was once the number-two-ranked junior in the land, behind Phil Mickelson. As recently as 2000 Heim tried to play his way through Q School. He brings an air of authority to Beem's bag, but more importantly, he is mellow to the point of catatonia, a perfect complement to his boss's passionate style.

Beem is also lucky to have the resources of El Paso Country Club at his disposal. He recently sat down with three members—an accountant, an attorney, and a financial planner—to form what he calls "the committee" to help him navigate the brave new world of superstardom. Says John Butterworth, Beem's accountant and the man who, in the fall of '98, helped organize the syndicate of EPCC members that ponied up $75,000 to send Beem out on tour, "Rich can buy all the baubles he wants for Sara"—Beem's big splurge following PGA wasn't an exotic car but rather a five-carat diamond necklace for his wife—"but we're here to make sure he doesn't get exploited, whether it's a bad real estate investment or any number of other ways he can get in over his head. Rich is going to meet a lot of people who are only looking out for themselves. Here we're all looking out for Rich."

Then there's the steadying influence of the understated Doan. Unlike most swing gurus, he's not a tireless self-promoter looking to turn himself into a multinational corporation. Beem is Doan's only tour client, and he's not looking to add to the stable. Under Doan's tutelage the five-foot-eight, one-hundred-sixty-pound Beem has blossomed into pound for pound one of the longest hitters in the game. In 2002 he averaged 292.1 yards a pop, tenth in the driving distance stats, and he uncorked the third-longest recorded drive of the year, a 393-yard missile. Beem remains a devout feel player, and Doan explains his charge's remarkable power in the simplest terms—balance. "Over the last year or so it has become perfect," says Doan, "so now he's able to use everything he's got. A lot of guys are protecting against a miss when they swing, Rich feels so good over the ball he just lets go; the club releases, and it's like he's stepping on the gas."

Beem breaks it down on an even more basic level. "The harder I swing, the farther and straighter it goes," he says, echoing the grip-it-and-rip-it philosophy of another PGA Championship winner, John Daly ('91), who has become a good friend and frequent practice round playing partner. "I like to attack. I don't like the golf course to dictate anything to me. I want to hit driver pretty much everywhere and pile up as many birdies as possible."

Beem's basher's mentality is part of his tremendous popularity. The PGA Tour has lacked a lovable, long-hitting iconoclast ever since Daly's talent and country charm was swallowed by his destructive alcoholism in the early nineties, but Beem's fearless victory—and his hardscrabble story—instantly resonated with Joe Six-Pack, for whom Woods is too corporate, Phil Mickelson too slick, David Duval too tortured, and Davis Love too preppy. Beem is well positioned to be the game's next big star, not only in the corporate world—in November he signed the inevitable sponsorship deal with Pepto-Bismol—but, more importantly, to a nation of golf fans that has turned its lonely eyes to him. No one expects Beem to supplant Woods atop the world ranking, but what the game has long needed is someone to play the Trevino to Woods's Nicklaus, pushing, inspiring, and even occasionally beating the great man. Ray Sanchez, an El Paso resident and one of the doyens of Texas golf writers, sees parallels in Beem's emergence with that of Trevino, a one-time El Paso resident. "It's Lee all over again," says Sanchez, who was golf editor of the (now defunct) *El Paso Herald-Post* in 1968, when Trevino made the U.S. Open his first tour victory at the age of twenty-eight. "They're both little guys who play big—Trevino's five foot seven, Beem is five foot eight, but they attack the ball. They act the same, jokesters, real happy-go-lucky, but they get that game face on in the crunch. Both reached the tour in their late twenties, meaning they were pretty battle-tested. And, of course, both set El Paso on fire."

What it all comes down to with Beem is this: What's next? Is the PGA destined to be the highlight of an otherwise unfulfilled career, or is that victory merely a prelude to future heroics? Beem already has his answer. "I truly believe," he says, "this is the start of something big."

•

Heading into the 2003 season Duplantis has his first decent job prospects in years, if he is able to forge a manageable partnership with the combustible Willis. The real question surrounding Duplantis is a familiar one: Will he ever get a handle on his life away from the golf course, the key to Beem's renaissance? "I'm the first to admit my personal life and professional life go hand in hand," Duplantis says.

He took a big first step toward normality in October 2002. "I finally got divorced last week," he said. "After six years and seventy thousand dollars in legal fees and other bullshit, it finally dawned on Vicki I don't have any money, so she signed the agreement."

Steve will retain custody of Sierra, with Vicki compelled to pay a dollar a month in child support. He recently received his first payment. "She spent two dollars and seventy-one cents on certified mail to send me a dollar bill," he says. "She's a beauty."

Despite the tumult that has surrounded her first six years, Sierra remains, by all accounts, a happy and well-adjusted child. She has settled into a full life with Duplantis's ex-girlfriend and her extended family in the small town of Hickory, in North Carolina's lovely Piedmont region. She has even developed a little Southern twang, and a taste for sweet tea. Says Duplantis, "It's a great environment for her. Every day she's got something different going on—cheerleading, tap, ballet, church every Sunday with family and friends." Sierra has her own room, where Duplantis crashes when he's in town. "I don't need a place of my own because I'm on the road so much," he says. "Plus I don't have the money."

Relations between Duplantis and his ex remain cordial. "Jen and I are friends," he says. "I took her grandma and sister shopping yesterday."

Duplantis had planned to spend the off-season working the various stages of Q School and earning spare change by looping for the weekend golfers at Tampa's Old Memorial Country Club, but in mid-November he had an epiphany.

"I'm done drinking," he said, calling from Hickory. "I just got off a plane to North Carolina, because I knew leaving Tampa was the only way I could make this work. I never thought I had a problem. I don't drink alone; I don't keep alcohol in the house. But when I go out with the boys I always overdo it. I've tried to have just a couple, but it never works.

"I've known for a while that if I was ever going to get a decent bag again I would have to stop drinking. But it's more about life than golf. I've had too many incidents lately where I was scaring myself, and not all of them wound up in 'The Forecaddie.' If I kept going like I was, I was going to end up dead, or in jail."

Duplantis is candid in admitting that his drinking has escalated as his professional situation has grown more depressing. "When I was with Furyk and even Beem I really didn't drink that much," he says. "I might overdo it occasionally, but it wasn't taking over my life. But when things are going bad out here on tour it feels like no one gives a shit about you. You sit in the hotel and it feels like the walls are closing in around you. You sit there thinking, God, my life sucks. All you want is a couple of beers to make all that go away. It's especially bad when you know your guy is going to shoot seventy-five the next day. If I had a nickel for every time [in] the last few years I was in a bar on Friday or Saturday night and I was thinking, I gotta get up at seven, I should shut it down. But then it's like, Who cares, it's not gonna make a difference what kind of shape I'm in, because this guy can't break seventy anyway. There's been whole weeks where I was drunk every day. That happened in Mississippi [at the Southern Farm Bureau Classic with Willis]. I was drunk when I got to the course a couple of those days."

The timing of Duplantis's confessional couldn't have been more striking. Earlier in the day Beem had swept to victory at the Hyundai Matches, a made-for-TV event during golf's November-December "Silly Season," where the checks are big and the pressure nonexistent. "It was fun to watch," says Duplantis, who monitored the telecast from Hickory. "The guy is playing with an unbelievable amount of confidence. At this point you can't say he's still riding a hot streak. He's just that good."

Clearly Duplantis still pines for the bright lights of the PGA Tour, but for now he is resisting the siren song of the road. "I need to learn some new habits," he says. "North Carolina is going to be great for me. I'm just going to be a dad for a while. To spend a couple of months with Sierra, that hasn't happened in probably two years. It's gonna be great for both of us. Last night I went to a little fair at her school—we played all the games and had a real nice time. We've been seeing a lot of movies. It's been good."

The 2003 season is shaping up as make-or-break year in Duplantis's career. Despite his endless misadventures, his talents as a caddie are undiminished. He need look no further than his former boss to see the great things a reformed wild child can accomplish. In fact, Duplantis recently referred to Beem as "my new idol."